ABUL A'LA MAUDUDI
Al Jihad fil Islam *and Other Writings*

Abul A'la Maududi (1903–79) was arguably one of the most influential and controversial thinkers of the twentieth century, and a foundational Islamist thinker. This volume brings together a broad range of his important works for the first time, covering concerns such as anti-colonialism, permissibility of violence, capitalism and gender roles, principles for an Islamic economy, and innovation in legal frameworks, as well as the limits of nationalist politics. Showcasing his writings across different genres, this volume includes influential early works such as his seminal *Al Jihad fil Islam*, Quranic exegesis and essays, as well as later works on Islamic law. An extensive introduction situates Maududi's ideas within global anti-colonial conversations, as well as Islamic and South Asian debates on urgent contemporary political questions, and highlights the conceptual innovations he carried out. Fresh translations allow readers to critically engage with Maududi's writings, capturing nuances and shifts in his ideas with greater clarity.

Humeira Iqtidar is a professor of politics at King's College London. Her research focuses on modern Islamic and South Asian thought, with an emphasis on questions of justice and tolerance, and the legacies of colonialism, as well as the place of religion in contemporary politics. She is the author of *Secularizing Islamists?* (2011) and has published widely in leading journals such as *American Political Science Review*, *Journal of Politics* and *Political Theory*.

CAMBRIDGE TEXTS IN THE HISTORY OF POLITICAL THOUGHT

General editor
QUENTIN SKINNER
Queen Mary University of London

Editorial board
MICHAEL COOK
Princeton University

HANNAH DAWSON
King's College London

ADOM GETACHEW
University of Chicago

EMMA HUNTER
University of Edinburgh

GABRIEL PAQUETTE
University of Maine

ANDREW SARTORI
New York University

HILDE DE WEERDT
Leiden University

Cambridge Texts in the History of Political Thought is firmly established as the major student series of texts in political theory. It aims to make available all the most important texts in the history of political thought, from Ancient Greece to the twentieth century, from throughout the world and from every political tradition. All the familiar classic texts are included, but the series seeks at the same time to enlarge the conventional canon through a global scope and by incorporating an extensive range of less well-known works and previously marginalized voices, many of them never before available in a modern English edition. Where possible, the texts are published in complete and unabridged form, and translations are specially commissioned for the series. However, where appropriate, abridged or tightly focused and thematic collections are offered instead. Each volume contains a critical introduction together with chronologies, biographical sketches, a guide to further reading and any necessary glossaries and textual apparatus. Overall, the series aims to provide the reader with an outline of the entire evolution of political thinking on a global scale.

For a list of titles published in the series, please see end of book

ABUL A'LA MAUDUDI

Al Jihad fil Islam *and* *Other Writings*

EDITED AND TRANSLATED BY
HUMEIRA IQTIDAR
King's College London

CAMBRIDGE
UNIVERSITY PRESS

Shaftesbury Road, Cambridge CB2 8EA, United Kingdom

One Liberty Plaza, 20th Floor, New York, NY 10006, USA

477 Williamstown Road, Port Melbourne, VIC 3207, Australia

314–321, 3rd Floor, Plot 3, Splendor Forum, Jasola District Centre,
New Delhi – 110025, India

Cambridge University Press is part of Cambridge University Press & Assessment,
a department of the University of Cambridge.

We share the University's mission to contribute to society through the pursuit of
education, learning and research at the highest international levels of excellence.

www.cambridge.org
Information on this title: www.cambridge.org/9781009230452

DOI: 10.1017/9781009230438

First published 2026

A catalogue record for this publication is available from the British Library

A Cataloging-in-Publication data record for this book is available from the Library of Congress

ISBN 978-1-009-23045-2 Hardback
ISBN 978-1-009-23044-5 Paperback

Contents

Acknowledgments

Mr Tariq Mahmood Hashmi undertook meticulous translations of many of the excerpts from *Al Jihad fil Islam* and *Tehrīk-e-Azādi Hind aur Musalmān* included in this volume. I am grateful to him for the care and thoughtfulness with which he approached this complicated task. I would also like to thank Mudabir Wani for his scrupulous record of the differences between various published versions of some of the essays included here.

Professor Andrew Sartori's invitation served as a catalyst for me to take concrete action regarding frustrations I had long expressed about the limited availability of sound translations to facilitate teaching and scholarship on South Asian Islamic thought. I am grateful to him for galvanizing the project. Liz Friend-Smith has been immensely patient through the rather long process of putting this volume together, and I thank her for her support. I owe Christopher Jackson an immense debt of gratitude for his careful and painstaking attention to detail in copy-editing this collection of different texts. Thanks to him this is a much more accessible volume for a range of readers. I would also like to thank Lisa Carter, who has always been there with sound advice and helpful responses throughout the production process.

The Department of Political Economy at King's College London, my intellectual and institutional home for the last eleven years, has generously provided funding for translations and archival research for this project. This manuscript was finalized as I completed a year of fruitful scholarly conversations with colleagues and students at Columbia University, and I am grateful for the inspiration these provided.

Salim Mansur Khalid sahib was outspoken in his criticism of my selection of material included here and immensely kind in his guidance. I am grateful to him for all his questions and criticisms, as well as his help in getting permissions from Islamic Publications and *Idara Tarjuman-ul-Quran* for including and translating sections from *Al Jihad fil Islam, Tehrīk-e-Azādi Hind aur Musalmān, Pardah, Islamic Law and Constitution* and *Tafhīm-ul-Quran*. I would also like to thank to Mr Farooq Murad of Islamic Foundation and Kube Publishing for allowing me to republish segments from the translated essays included in *First Principles of Islamic Economics*. I have relied primarily upon the following editions: *Al Jihad fil Islam* (2007), *Tehrīk-e-Azādi Hind aur Musalmān* (1999), *Pardah* (2003), *Islamic Law and Constitution* (1960), *Tafhīm-ul-Quran* (2005) and *First Principles of Islamic Economics* (2011).

I am grateful to Shohini Ghosh for generative conversations regarding the relationship between the history of political thought and contemporary South Asian politics, to Sanjay Seth for his thoughtful comments, and to Muhammad Qasim Zaman and Leigh Jenco for their suggestions regarding working with 'complicated' thinkers. The limitations in translations, selection and interpretations presented here remain mine alone.

Abul A'la Maududi: Conservative Anti-colonialism and the State

Towards the end of a globally turbulent decade, in the late 1920s, the twenty-six-year-old Abul A'la Maududi (1903–79) observed that:

> it is a natural consequence of human weakness that once people fail to stand on the battlefield against their opponent, they lose ground intellectually as well. When they succumb to the force of the sword, they fail to contest the same enemy through the pen. Hence, the ideas and opinions that tend to dominate an age are generally those expressed by the people implementing their agenda through hands that hold the pen and the sword together.[1]

Potentially one of the most controversial yet consequential thinkers of the twentieth century, in terms of both the following and the opposition he generated, Maududi set out to contest the terms of colonial political control, its normative frameworks and conceptual architecture in a systematic manner.[2] In the process he played a leading role in setting the terms of debate for twentieth-century Islamic thought. His critique of colonialism was not premised on Enlightenment principles, and, unlike many other anti-colonials, he did not call upon imperial states to fulfil the promise of freedom and equality that they claimed to uphold. Instead, he relied upon his reading of norms and ethics in the Islamic tradition to articulate a critique of colonialism and an alternative vision of modernity.

---

[1] *Al Jihad fil Islam*, page 9 this volume.
[2] For some he is 'the most systematic thinker of modern Islam': Wilfred Cantwell Smith, *Islam in Modern History* (Princeton: Princeton University Press, 1957), 233.

A prolific public intellectual and combative political activist, Maududi was associated in much Euro-American scholarship, somewhat reductively, with fundamentalism, and, largely inaccurately, with violent militancy. There have also been more thoughtful analyses of the reasons for his influence and substantive critical engagement with his ideas.[3] Among Islamic scholars (*ulama*) Maududi's ideas have long generated debate, and many have disagreed profoundly with his ideas, methodology and proposals.[4] Yet, in charting out their differences from him they have engaged with the distinctions he set up and the questions he raised. Maududi's critique of colonialism and its impact on Muslims was linked to his deep concern for the eradication of a way of life that privileged ethical formation. Unlike many other anti-colonial thinkers and activists around him, he was not invested in the concept of progress, or in privileging equality above other values. As I will discuss below, we can think of him as a 'conservative anti-colonial', as his vision of social change was not predicated on the principle of equality, but on the question of balance.[5]

Conservative anti-colonialism might seem an oxymoron, given the ready association of anti-colonialism with 'progressive' politics. The canon of anti-colonial thought focuses on Frantz Fanon, Aimé Césaire, Kwame Nkrumah, Amilcar Cabral, Jawaharlal Nehru, Nguyen An Ninh and C. L. R. James. These thinkers were indeed profoundly influential and important. However, it remains pertinent to note that they accepted

---

[3] Charles J. Adam, 'Mawdudi and the Islamic State', in *Voices of Resurgent Islam*, ed. John L. Esposito (New York: Oxford University Press, 1983), 99–133; S. V. R. Nasr, *Mawdudi and the Making of Islamic Revivalism* (Oxford: Oxford University Press, 1996); Jan-Peter Hartung, *A System of Life: Mawdudi and the Ideologisation of Islam* (Delhi: Oxford University Press, 2014); Irfan Ahmed, 'Genealogy of the Islamic State: Reflections on Maududi's Political Thought and Islamism', *Journal of Royal Anthropological Institute* 15:1 (2009), 145–62.

[4] For a largely positive assessment, see Khurshid Ahmed and Zafar Ishaq Ansari, eds., *Islamic Perspectives: Studies in Honour of Sayyid Abul A'la Mawdudi* (Leicester: Islamic Foundation, 1979); Salim Mansur Khalid and Jamil Ahmad Rana, eds., *Tadhkirah'i Sayyid Mawdudī* (Lahore: Idārah-'i Ma'ārif-i Islāmī, 1998); Masudul Hasan, *Sayyid Abul A'la Maududi and His Thought*, 2 vols. (Lahore: Islamic Publications, 1984). For more critical assessments, see: Fazlur Rahman, *Islam and Modernity: Transformation of an Intellectual Tradition* (Chicago: University of Chicago Press, 1984). For an overview of some ulama concerns, see: Maulānā Mufti Mohammed Yusuf, *Maulānā Maududi par aitrazāt ka ilmī jaiza* (Lahore: Islamic Publications, 1971); Maulānā Waheedudin Khan, *Ta'abīr kī ghaltī* (Delhi: Al Risala Books, 1963).

[5] For more details, see: Humeira Iqtidar, 'Conservative Anticolonialism: Maududi, Marx and Social Equality', *Journal of the Royal Asiatic Society* 32:2 (2022), 295–310.

the idea of progress as a historical imperative and normative ideal. Most self-identified as Marxists or socialists, even as they 'stretched Marxism', in Fanon's famous phrase, to articulate an internal critique of European Marxism. However, generative as it was, Marxist and socialist anti-colonialism, despite significant internal variation and debate, did not exhaust reasons for and modes of opposition to colonialism. In fact, in philosophical terms, anti-colonialism remains underconceptualized. It is clearly an opposition to colonialism, but on what terms, and to what purposes?

Even a casual survey of anti-colonial thinkers from South Asia would indicate huge variation among those recognized as anti-colonial political actors and thinkers. There was, to take a prominent example, a profound gulf between M. K. Gandhi and Jawaharlal Nehru in their reasons for opposing colonialism even as they collaborated politically over many decades. Gandhi was concerned primarily with the impact of European civilization on human life, while Nehru's opposition to colonialism was premised on the question of foreign control of Indian resources.[6] In his perceptive assessment of anti-colonial thought as a genre, Julian Go identifies two characteristics of anti-colonial thinkers. First, they are mostly born in the colonies and draw upon their experience there. Second, they were often educated in imperial centres.[7] This is certainly true of the canonical thinkers mentioned above, and Go is correct to identify exposure to imperial metropoles as a characteristic of these anti-colonials. However, there were many who did not visit the metropole or write in the languages of imperial power.[8] Some, like Bhagat Singh, Maulānā Bhashani and Abdul Ghaffar Khan, had never travelled much beyond South Asia; nor did they write or speak primarily in English. Notwithstanding one's own political inclinations, it remains historically

---

[6] For Gandhi, see: Mohandas Karamchand Gandhi, *'Hind Swaraj' and Other Writings*, ed. Anthony J. Parel (Cambridge: Cambridge University Press, 1997); Uday Singh Mehta, 'Gandhi on Democracy, Politics and the Ethics of Everyday Life', *Modern Intellectual History* 7:2 (2010), 355–71. For Nehru, see: Sanjay Seth, "Nehruvian Socialism", 1927–1937: Nationalism, Marxism, and the Pursuit of Modernity', *Alternatives: Global, Local, Political* 18:4 (1993), 453–73; Sandeep Bhardwaj, 'Three Meanings of Colonialism: Nehru, Sukarno, and Kotelawala Debate the Future of the Third World Movement (1954–61)', *Journal of Global History* 19:1 (2024), 118–34.

[7] Julian Go, 'Thinking against Empire: Anticolonial Thought as Social Theory', *British Journal of Sociology* 74 (2023), 279–93, at 282.

[8] This would include those who travelled widely in Asia or South America without making their way to European metropoles.

accurate and intellectually fecund to note that the diversity of views among anti-colonial thinkers and activists was manifested not just in the different proposals for eradicating colonial and imperial control, but more importantly in their assessment of its harm. Flattening the range of reasons for opposing imperialism and modes of resistance practised historically affects our understanding of the complexity of imperialism today. The context and influence of Maududi's ideas cannot be understood fully without engaging with the centrality of anti-colonialism to his endeavour.

Paradoxically, given the ready association of Maududi's thought with conservatism, that category is more slippery than it might seem at first glance. Heavily indebted to the politics of the French Revolution, it is associated with reaction against progress, resistance to change and support for the status quo. Parking for now questions about specific visions of progress and the role that some of these have played in sustaining colonial legacies, we can ask if Maududi really is a clear candidate for being called a conservative.[9] Given the conceptual innovations that he carried out, his proclaimed goal of bringing about a revolution in social life, and the alleged radicalism of his positions, is it still feasible to think of him as a conservative?[10] Similarly, while he and other conservatives draw upon a distant past, so do many progressives, be it the Athenian democracy or the French Revolution. What then constitutes the substantive core of conservatism more generally? Few South Asian thinkers self-identify as conservatives, although many will claim the mantle of traditionalists. In European debates, many contemporary proponents of conservatism have been reluctant to elaborate core concepts, precisely because they have 'disdained theoretical reflection on political life, implying that political knowledge is ... best left inarticulate'.[11] Oakeshott famously argued that conservatism is not a creed or a doctrine, but a disposition.[12] In contrast, Michael Freeden argues that it is very

---

[9] On progress and coloniality, see: Amy Allen, *The End of Progress: Decolonizing the Normative Foundations of Critical Theory* (New York: Columbia University Press, 2016).

[10] For an example of his conceptual innovations, see: Humeira Iqtidar, '*Jizya* against Nationalism: Abul A'la Maududi's Attempt at Decolonizing Political Theory', *Journal of Politics* 83:3 (2021), 1145–57.

[11] John Gray, *Enlightenment's Wake: Politics and Culture at the Close of the Modern Age* (London: Routledge, 1995) 78–9.

[12] Michael Oakeshott, 'On Being Conservative', in *Rationalism in Politics and Other Essays* (Indianapolis: Liberty Press, 1991 [1962]), 407–37.

much an ideology, but to 'ransack conservatism for the substantive core concepts and ideas located in rival progressive ideologies, such as liberty, reason, sociability, or welfare, is to look in the wrong place'.[13] Foremost among conservatism's central concepts, argues Freeden, is the idea of organic change.[14] The emphasis on organic change may indicate a hesitation towards radical change. However, that hesitation is rejected by some who were also classified as conservatives by their opponents. Friedrich Hayek, associated with conservatism because of Margaret Thatcher's adoption of his ideas, was scathing about the 'timid mind' that sought to reduce the speed of change.[15] Interestingly, Thatcher too was anything but timid in the transformations she wrought as the leader of the Conservative Party.

Richard Bourke opens a generative space for reconsidering the viability of 'a unified tradition that has transmitted conservative principles down the generations intact'.[16] In reassessing the place of Burke as a founding father of European conservative thought, Bourke highlights the fluidity of 1789 to argue that 'competing visions of the future collided in 1789, each of them claiming in their different ways to be committed to the advancement of society', that is, to progress.[17] Later packaging of different groups into conservative, radical or liberal camps obscured Burke's support for reform in France. Similarly, Uday Mehta has argued that Burke's profound questioning of the East India Company's operations in India and his respect for the differences among peoples allowed a more critical approach to empire than that of the more 'progressive' Mill.[18] These re-evaluations allow insights not just into the complexity of placing Burke but of the necessity for attending more carefully to how we define conservative thought.

---

[13] Michael Freeden, 'Theorizing about Conservative Ideology', in *Ideologies and Political Theory: A Conceptual Approach* (Oxford Online, 1998), 317–47, at 334. See also Noel O'Sullivan, 'Conservatism', in *Twentieth-Century Political Thought*, ed. Terence Ball and Richard Bellamy (Cambridge: Cambridge University Press, 2010), 151–64, at 151.

[14] Freeden, 'Theorizing about Conservative Ideology', 333.

[15] Hayek rejected the association with conservatism. See: Friedrich Hayek, 'Why I Am Not a Conservative', in *The Constitution of Liberty* (Chicago: University of Chicago Press, 1960), 400.

[16] Richard Bourke, 'What Is Conservatism: History, Ideology and Party', *European Journal of Political Theory* 17:4 (2018), 449–75, at 452.

[17] Ibid., 460.

[18] Uday Mehta, *Liberalism and Empire: A Study in Nineteenth-Century Liberal Thought* (Chicago: University of Chicago Press, 1999).

In pointing to the complication of placing Maududi's thought, my interest does not lie in recuperating him as a progressive thinker, but in delineating more sharply the contours of his resistance to a particular vision of progress. In the process, I indicate an important element of the substantive core to conservatism that sits alongside the vision of organic society: conservatives do not privilege equality. This is not to say that they are against equality *tout court*. Conservative thinkers have made arguments in support of justice, harmony and, in particular, freedom. For instance, many twentieth-century North Atlantic conservatives, from Allan Bloom to Roger Scruton, expressed a deep commitment to freedom. In fact, many are also not explicitly against equality, but they refuse to accord it centrality. Maududi's questioning of colonialism was not predicated on the principle of equality. This is not to say that equality was unimportant to him, but that it was not fundamental. He supported equality in some cases, for instance across races, but not in others. The paradigmatic case was his opposition to women's political and social equality. Instead, he advocated balance, by which he meant equity rather than equality. This was tied intimately to his vision of society as an organic whole. Such an organic whole could only function if members accepted differentiation. He saw demands for social equality for women as calls for homogenization, that is, for men and women to be interchangeable in their roles in society. Such substitutability was ultimately impossible, because it went against the natural biological differences between men and women, a claim that Maududi substantiated through heavy reliance on American medical textbooks of the time.[19] More critically for him, by attempting to make possible that impossibility, society would be torn apart.

A foundational concern for Maududi was moving beyond colonial intellectual and political impositions. Closer to home, Gandhi provided inspiration as another thinker who did not privilege legal equality but sought to bring about profound internal change, a revolution, by moving away from liberal framings.[20] As part of his larger project of considering political modernity without being beholden to European normative commitments and conceptual conflations, Maududi undertook a serious

---

[19] Iqtidar, 'Conservative Anticolonialism'.
[20] Aishwary Kumar, 'The Ellipsis of Touch: Gandhi's Unequals', *Public Culture* 23:2 (2011), 449–69; Arundhati Roy, *The Doctor and the Saint: Caste, Race and the Annihilation of Caste* (Chicago: Haymarket Books, 2017).

consideration of the state as an institution for facilitating ethical social development, as well as of the relationship between popular sovereignty and majoritarianism, and the long-term effects of nationalism on democracy. These are issues that continue to engage political and intellectual energies today. In the process Maududi created one of the more systematic, albeit intensely contested, bridges between sharia, Islamic normative principles and European political theory. To build it, he reworked existing ideas within the Islamic repertoire and popularized conceptual innovations by imbuing existing terms with new meanings. This is the case, for instance, with his immensely influential articulation of the concepts of *hakimiyyat* and *jahiliyyah*.[21] These terms and their new meanings have become commonplace within public discourse in many predominantly Muslim polities.

Even as he boldly reconfigured long-held Islamic ideas in creative conversation with contemporary political problems and other traditions of thought, Maududi did not present these ideas as innovations. He did, however, argue that many ulama, as well as Muslim political leaders, such as Muhammed Ali Jinnah, did not correctly understand either Islam or the reality of contemporary political challenges, or both. He was particularly scathing in the early part of his career about the ulama, when he argued that they remained mired in details of everyday practices of piety without recognizing that the political context had changed dramatically and the now dominant political institution, the state, had developed immense powers to regulate and transform social life in profound ways. In generating a response to European imperialism (*jehangiriyyat*) and colonialism (*nau-abādi nizām*) he was, however, concerned to move beyond critique to provide what he saw as implementable alternatives to the Islamic tradition which the existing norms of Islamic education and ulama debates had failed to provide.[22] Over the course of more than half a century of activism and writing, Maududi refined, modified and sometimes repudiated earlier ideas, but the overriding concern remained the same: the use of Islamic ideational resources to address contemporary political problems.

---

[21] Muhammad Qasim Zaman, 'The Sovereignty of God in Modern Islamic Thought', *Journal of the Royal Asiatic Society* 25:3 (2015), 389–418, at 405; Humeira Iqtidar and Oliver Scharbrodt, 'Divine Sovereignty, Morality and the State: Maududi and His Influence', *Journal of the Royal Asiatic Society* 32:2 (2022), 277–93.

[22] For his investment in reworking existing concepts, see: Iqtidar, '*Jizya* against Nationalism'.

With some formal training in a madrasa, though not enough to be recognized as an *'alim*, Maududi was largely an autodidact who brought together a wide reading of Islamic history, philosophy and jurisprudence with a broad, albeit uneven, engagement with European history and philosophy. Having to earn a living from his late teens owing to the early demise of his father, he worked as a journalist, becoming the editor of the Urdu journal *Taj* at the age of seventeen. The fact that he made his ideas available to a wide reading public in accessible Urdu must go some way towards explaining their reach. Moreover, once they were translated into Arabic, as well as other Asian languages, many of his key ideas found wide circulation in the broader Muslim world through forceful advocates and commentators. The best-known of these was the Egyptian scholar and public intellectual Syed Qutb, who built upon Maududi's ideas and also propagated them extensively to an Arabic-speaking audience. A number of ideas that were at one point attributed to Syed Qutb, such as the reworking of the term *jahiliyyah*, were first developed by Maududi.[23] Finally, Maududi's political ideas also travelled widely through the institutional mechanism of the party, Jama'at-e-Islami (JI), that he founded in Lahore in 1941, and which has chapters and associates around the world, notably in India, Pakistan and Bangladesh, but also South Africa, the UK and the US.

It is, then, somewhat surprising that despite translation into several Asian and African languages, large parts of such important works as *Al Jihad fil Islam* are not available in English. Some abridged and truncated versions are available, but they often lack the depth and nuance of the Urdu originals. One reason for this lack of attention might be that for much of the last half-century, Euro-American scholarship has tended to view the Middle East, rather than South Asia, as the locus of Islamic thought. This volume includes a more faithful rendition in English of some of these key writings.

The Cosmopolitanism of Islamic Thought

An oft-stated aim for Maududi was to free Muslims from colonial intellectual slavery or *zehni ghulami*. To do so, he brought together

---

[23] This is recognized by such scholars as Yvonne Y. Haddad, 'Sayyid Qutb: Ideologue of Islamic Revival', in *Voices of Resurgent Islam*, ed. John Esposito (New York: Oxford University Press, 1983), 67–98, at 67, and Roxanne L. Euben, 'Killing (for) Politics: Jihad, Martyrdom, and Political Action', *Political Theory* 30:1 (2002), 4–35.

different traditions of thought, a cosmopolitanism that was not unique to him and is an underappreciated hallmark of much political thought from the global south, particularly Islamic thought. In the South Asian context, the influence of Partha Chatterjee's thoughtful argument regarding 'derivative discourses' of Indian anti-colonial nationalists has tended to obscure the creativity with which thinkers and activists approached the question of imagining different futures, as well as histories.[24] However, there is significant variation in how deeply different anti-colonial ideas were anchored in Enlightenment universals. In any case, there is a clear case for moving beyond diffusionist histories of political ideas.[25] Maududi went further than many contemporary anti-colonial thinkers by questioning the colonial hierarchy of knowledge that placed European political ideas and normative values at the apex, and he sought to do so through his reading of the Islamic tradition. In so doing he raised important questions for ongoing conversations about the legacies of colonialism in knowledge production, and their implications for political practice and norms of governance. Even if his answers were not persuasive to all, including many Muslims, the questions he raised about the possibility of imagining modernity beyond European experiences were prescient and generative.

Much scholarship has tended to place Maududi's ideas primarily within the Islamic or the South Asian context.[26] This is important and valuable. Maududi operated in the highly complex, vibrant and diverse South Asian political and intellectual context. His early appreciation, as well as later contestation, of M. K. Gandhi's ideas and political decisions

---

[24] Partha Chatterjee, *Nationalist Thought and the Colonial World: A Derivative Discourse?* (Minneapolis: University of Minnesota Press, 1993).

[25] Stefanie Ganger and Su Lin Lewis, 'Forum: A World of Ideas: New Pathways in Global Intellectual History, c. 1880–1930', *Modern Intellectual History* 10:2 (2013), 347–51; Andrew Sartori, 'Beyond Culture-Contact and Colonial Discourse: "Germanism" in Colonial Bengal', *Modern Intellectual History* 4:1 (2007), 77–93; Andrew Sartori and Samuel Moyn, eds., *Global Intellectual History* (New York: Columbia University Press, 2013). Regarding cosmopolitanism specifically, see: Humeira Iqtidar, 'Anticolonialism without Nationalism: Cosmopolitan Imaginaries for a Deglobalizing World', in *Handbook of Cosmopolitanism*, ed. Prathma Bannerjee, Dipesh Chakrabarty, Sanjay Seth and Lisa Wedeen (New York: Oxford University Press, forthcoming; published online, Oxford Academic, 22 July 2025).

[26] Zaman, 'Sovereignty of God'; Nasr, *Islamic Revivalism*; Omar Khalidi, 'Maulānā Mawdūdī and Hyderabad', *Islamic Studies* 41:1 (2002), 35–67; Ahmed, 'Genealogy of the Islamic State', 145–62; Hartung, *A System of Life*. Hartung recognizes Maududi's engagement with debates about fascism and communism in Europe and Asia.

manifests itself in his attempt at inverting the colonial matrix of knowledge and values, like Gandhi, tempered with a sharp focus on the Islamic tradition in opposition to Gandhi's emphasis on the Vedic one. Gandhi, however, developed his suspicion of the state and democracy in a more robust manner than Maududi. Maududi also sought to carve out a space between Muslim Nationalists, such as Jinnah, who wanted a separate national state for Muslims, and Nationalist Muslims, who wanted an Indian nation-state, by opposing both and rejecting the idea of a nation-state. However, despite vehement opposition to Muhammed Ali Jinnah's demand for a separate country for Muslims, Maududi chose to move to Pakistan when India was divided. In Pakistan he formed alliances with a range of political parties, including the communists in the early 1950s, to combat the monopolistic hold of the Muslim League, but his party's increasingly violent competition with leftist groups on college campuses from the 1970s onwards indicates the tensions in his approach. In a similar vein, his decision to hold in abeyance a previously expressed opposition to women as leaders of an ideal Islamic state, to support Fatima Jinnah as a presidential candidate against the military dictator Ayub Khan, gives some indication of the hierarchy of his commitments, as well as the difficulty that many figures faced as political actors and thinkers.

Embedding Maududi's arguments within wider Islamic debates also allows us much insight. It is interesting to note that while he referred primarily to the early days of Islam, focusing on the life of the Prophet and his Companions, he was well versed in modern and more regional history, having published two books specifically on the history of the Deccan during his time in Hyderabad: *Dakkan kī siyasī tarīkh* in 1931 and *Daulat-e-Āsifiyyah aur hakumat-e-Bartaniyyah* in 1928.[27] The influence of philosophical questions raised by Muhammed Iqbal, the poet and philosopher, on Maududi's thought, even as the two proposed different answers, is also an important element of his context and contribution.[28] While Maududi's thought belies a modernist architecture, with an interest in ironing out contradictions and rationalizing inconsistencies, his deep investment in a strand of sufism pushed against

---

[27] Khalidi, 'Maulānā Mawdūdī and Hyderabad', 42–5.
[28] For a generative comparison between Iqbal and Maududi, see: Terenjit Sevea, 'Islamist Questioning and [C]olonialism: Towards an Understanding of the Islamist Oeuvre', *Third World Quarterly* 28:7 (2007), 1375–400.

the constraints of modern visions of religiosity. Islamic sources of inspiration also went beyond the South Asian context, and Maududi sought exchanges and conversations with the Arab world throughout his life, starting with his translation of the Egyptian modernist Qasim Amin's book against the veiling of women, *The Liberation of Women* (1899), from Arabic into Urdu at the age of ten or eleven, to the establishment of international scholarly networks with the support of the Saudi government.

However, placing Maududi only within an Islamic intellectual lineage, or within the immediate political context of British India and, later, postcolonial Pakistan, imposes limits that Maududi sought actively to transcend. Moreover, such an approach ignores the rich and varied hinterland of ideas that he drew upon, including Pan-Asian and European debates. These added to both the structure and substance of his ideas. Given the later acrimonious competition between his party, the JI, and leftist groups in Pakistan in the 1960s and 70s, a surprising and relatively understudied source of inspiration for Maududi and for viewing Islamic ideas as vehicles for anti-colonial movements was the Bolshevik government in Russia. The Bolsheviks supported various regional movements that used Islamic ideas and practices as expressions of anti-tsarism and anti-colonialism from 1917 until the mid 1920s. Muslims constituted about 10 per cent of the Russian empire at the time of the Revolution, and the Bolsheviks needed their support in particular regions.[29] The support for anti-colonialism more generally also formed part of Lenin's pivot away from Europe to the colonized world in the 1920s. The coming together of communist support for subnational anti-imperial groups and the dismemberment of the Ottoman empire created intellectual ripples in direct, as well as subtle and non-linear, ways.

As an example of the more circuitous intellectual influences, consider the paradox that despite the association of communism with atheism, many of the first Muslim communists in India were deeply religious men[30] who had left British India declaring it a *Dār ul Harb* (Land of War against Islam) as a result of British complicity in dismantling the Ottoman Caliphate. These migrants decided to move to Afghanistan to

---

[29] Ben Fowkes and Bulent Gökay, 'Unholy Alliance: Muslims and Communists', *Journal of Communist Studies and Transition Politics* 25:1 (2009), 1–31.
[30] K. H. Ansari, 'Pan-Islam and the Making of the Early Indian Muslim Socialists', *Modern Asian Studies* 20:3 (1986), 509–37.

be able to live their lives in close accordance with Islamic principles. However, the Afghan government was suspicious of them and concerned about their influence on domestic politics. The Afghan government's treatment led some to return and a large contingent to move to Tashkent. Welcomed by the Soviet Union, some of these migrants enrolled in the University of Eastern Toilers and went on to become prominent Indian communist leaders. Maududi too was involved in the earlier stages of this movement, called the *Hijrat* (migration) movement, but moved away from it after disputes with its leaders, apparently because of his insistence that the strategies and goals be planned and realistic.[31]

Pan-Asian anti-colonialism also brought together Marxists, pan-Islamists, liberal nationalists and socialists in interesting conversations.[32] Maududi is known to have attended meetings organized by the socialist Khairi brothers in Delhi,[33] who had, in their appearance before the Central Committee of the Soviets in Russia in 1918, proclaimed, 'The time had come for India to free herself, following what had been done in Russia.'[34] Maududi incorporated questions raised by communists about the place of imperialism in capitalism and assumptions regarding the role of the state in modern politics, as well as communist organizational practices, into his project of thinking through alternatives to European modernity from the Islamic tradition. This led to generative tensions: from his insistence on organizing the JI as a cadre-based Leninist party, though one led by men steeped in pious humility regarding divine sovereignty, to his commitment to establishing the rationality of Islam even as he rejected European definitions of religion as reductive, and his rhetoric of revolutionary takeover of the state even as he remained suspicious of it.[35]

Maududi's direct engagement with Marx's writings seems limited. He did, however, read at least some of Marx's work, although it is not

---

[31] Ahmed and Ansari, *Islamic Perspectives*, 361.

[32] Cemil Aydin, *The Politics of Anti-Westernism in Asia: Visions of World Order in Pan-Islamic and Pan-Asian Thought* (New York: Columbia University Press, 2007).

[33] K. K. Aziz, *The Idea of Pakistan* (Lahore: Vanguard Books, 1987), 88–92.

[34] Quoted in Ansari, 'Pan-Islam', 518.

[35] For more details, see: Humeira Iqtidar, *Secularizing Islamists? Jamaat-e-Islami and Jamaat-ud-Dawa in Urban Pakistan* (Chicago: University of Chicago Press, 2011), 61–4, and Humeira Iqtidar, 'Theorizing Popular Sovereignty in the Colony: Abul A'la Maududi's "Theodemocracy"', *Review of Politics* 82 (2020), 595–617.

clear what exactly, and in 1939 he wrote an essay evaluating the philosophical approach of Hegel and Marx.[36] While admitting that there was much to appreciate in their thought and that they elaborated 'one aspect/element (*juz'*) of reality',[37] Maududi was sceptical about their understanding of the world beyond Europe. He had two major critiques. The first related to the lack of human agency in the thought of Hegel and Marx. Maududi thought that Hegel in particular presented the idea that a human being has no 'independent consciousness, control, and will';[38] this is not something he thought an Islamic view of the self could condone. Moreover, he found Hegel's view of history to rest on speculation rather than historical detail; instead of detailed analysis of the process through which the dialectical process (*jadli 'amal*) takes place, Hegel 'looks at it as a bird flying in the air looks over the whole city'.[39] Marx, he thought, intensified the lack of individual autonomy (*khud ikhtiyari*) that Hegel proposed by relying heavily on the idea of material reality, reducing human beings to biological, rather than spiritual, beings.

Like Marx, Maududi also saw human history as manifesting a profound struggle. But in contrast to Marx, for him this struggle was between the different aspects of human nature, the base elements and the spiritual self. Drawing upon the long-standing idea that Islam presents the most natural (*fitri*) vision of human life,[40] Maududi thought that the Islamic tradition had already recognized both sides of human nature and catered for them by recognizing that while each individual was responsible for the struggle with her own *nafs* (self/soul),[41] society could be so structured as to support this goal. This led, for him, to a profound difference with Marxian understandings of society. Drawing upon a well-established and dominant thrust in Islamic thought,[42]

---

[36] Maududi, 'Hegel aur Marks ka Falsafa-e-Tarikh', *Tarjuman ul Quran*, August 1939, reprinted in *Tafhimat* (Lahore: Idara Ma'arfat-e-Islami, 2001).

[37] Maududi, 'Hegel aur Marks', 255.   [38] Ibid., 256.

[39] Ibid. [This seems to be a translation of the term 'bird's-eye view'. Maududi often employed such translations in his writing.]

[40] For a discussion of this, see: Andrew March, 'Taking People as They Are: Islam as a "Realistic Utopia" in the Political Theory of Sayyid Qutb', *The American Political Science Review* 104:1 (2010), 189–207.

[41] See *Nafs*, Encyclopedia of Islam: https://referenceworks.brillonline.com/entries/encyclopaedia-of-islam-2/nafs-COM_0833.

[42] Wael Hallaq, *The Impossible State: Islam, Politics and Modernity's Moral Predicament* (New York: Columbia University Press, 2013), 118–38.

Maududi saw social harmony as always within reach. The individual was not in tension with the community, nor were the different segments in zero-sum competition with each other. There was, then, a fundamental difference between the Marxist conception of society as comprised of classes with irreconcilable differences, and Maududi's vision of society as the means to individual ethical perfection. Society was not perfect, and needed periodic reforms to respond to historical needs, hence his own efforts, but, for him, pitting different classes and groups against each other could not help resolve the problems that Marxists identified.

Critically, Maududi saw his intellectual project as one that elaborated a balanced point of view not just for Muslims, although they remained the primary audience, but for all humans. Just as liberalism could claim universality despite carrying a deep imprint of European historical experiences and Christian theological debates, he thought Islam could appeal to non-Muslims as a framework for supporting justice in the world. To this end he often presented Islam as the middle path between the 'extremist' philosophies of communism and liberalism, the philosophy of capitalism. These were incapable of providing the point of perfect balance and justice, *nuqta-e-'adl,* where the rights of the individual can be guaranteed alongside those of the community.[43] However, he used different approaches for his critique of communism and liberalism. In questioning communism, Maududi relied essentially on a philosophical critique to argue that it denied the individual agency that was central to the Islamic conception of the self. This changed after the 1950s, when information about life in the communist countries became more readily available and Maududi became even more invested in contesting the irreligiosity that communism supported. However, in his critique of capitalism, which he saw as synonymous with European civilization, Maududi drew upon Euro-American sociological, legal and historical scholarship, as well as philosophical principles. In *Al Jihad fil Islam,* for instance, he drew upon the scholarship of the German jurist Ottfried Nippold regarding international law and historical research by Gibbon on the Roman empire. To engage with alternatives closer to home, such as Hinduism, Maududi drew upon Orientalist scholars such as William Jones, excusing this move on account of his lack of knowledge of Sanskrit. This is in equal measure a reflection of the disruption in local

---

[43] Abul A'la Maududi, *Pardah* (Lahore: Islamic Publications, 2003 [1939]), 43, 173, 233–5.

intellectual traditions brought about by the 'colonial encounter' and the inventive ways in which global-south thinkers brought different traditions of thought together.[44] Whether Maududi did full justice to his reading of other traditions is a different question: he often read the Islamic tradition with more attention to its idealized principles but other traditions with an emphasis on their actual, and inevitably flawed, practices.

Realizing the ideal Islamic state in the newly formed Muslim-majority postcolonial state of Pakistan eluded Maududi's party. There were many challenges: in a system structured around patronage, the electorate remained indifferent to the JI as a political party, the rulers remained staunchly committed to managing Muslims rather than being constrained by Islamic ethics, and imperial power became less visible and harder to dislodge. Most worryingly for Maududi, who had imagined the JI as a vanguard party of educated Muslims that relied heavily on colleges and universities as recruiting grounds, these spaces became hotbeds of leftist ideas in the 1960s. At the same time, Pakistan's ruling elite became increasingly allied with the United States during the Cold War.[45] From the 1960s on, as the new imperial power poured resources, weapons and political support into Islamist parties against communist parties in Indonesia, Iran, Egypt and elsewhere in the Muslim world, Maududi struggled to keep his party independent. In 1971, as Pakistan fragmented and Bangladesh seceded as an independent state, JI-affiliated groups turned violent, and some allied with the Pakistani military in its attempts to silence dissent. Throughout the 1970s the JI-allied student union, Islamī Jamiyyat-e-Tulabā (IJT), increasingly resorted to violence on campuses to combat left-wing influences, and in the process many of its leaders formed close relationships with the military establishment.

Maududi died in 1979, soon after General Zia ul Haq imposed another military dictatorship on the country in 1977. The JI became closely associated with the dictatorship in the early years as the general supported a version of Islamic laws. The JI's leadership was initially enthusiastic about the focus on Islamic governance, but it became

---

[44] Talal Asad, 'Anthropology and the Colonial Encounter', in *The Politics of Anthropology: From Colonialism and Sexism toward a View from Below*, ed. Gerrit Huizer and Bruce Mannheim (Berlin and New York: De Gruyter Mouton, 1979), 85–94.

[45] Ayesha Jalal, *State of Martial Rule: The Origins of Pakistan's Political Economy of Defence* (Cambridge: Cambridge University Press), 1990.

increasingly clear that the laws discriminated against women, minorities and the poor, and they received criticism from many ulama. Zia's dictatorship was maintained by the United States through military, political and economic aid, and Pakistan became a link with the *mujahideen* in Afghanistan fighting against the Soviets. Important JI leaders became involved in the negotiations between American as well as Pakistani intelligence agencies, and the 'freedom fighters', as the mujahideen were called by the American political leadership of the time. After the Soviets left and the 'freedom fighters' supported, trained and armed by the United States were rebranded as terrorists, the JI too had various internal debates to contend with regarding its role and purpose going forward. In the early 2000s, under the leadership of Qazi Hussain Ahmed, the party sought a wider political role in Pakistan by opposing corporate globalization and the new US war in Afghanistan, now against the Taliban. In 2002 the JI was able to form a coalition government in one province of the country, but it has not been able to return to power since then. Its core voters remain the urban, educated, socially conservative lower-middle classes – not a large electoral segment.

The party's career in Pakistan exposes tensions in Maududi's thought while also not exhausting all the possibilities contained within it. The different trajectory of the JI in India and Bangladesh suggests alternative paths, given varied conditions. Despite Maududi's reservations regarding the state, his acceptance of the state as an efficient instrument of social transformation led him to privilege access to it. However, the attempt at making sharia, a broad set of principles rather than codified laws, compatible with the state, was to render it sharply reduced, and to favour statist changes was to shift attention away from slower but potentially more durable social transformations.[46] Critically, truncated in this manner, sharia would lose its resilience and sustainability, denuded of the capaciousness and social embeddedness that had allowed it vibrancy over the preceding centuries.[47]

That millions of people found Maududi's specific vision of the world without colonialism compelling is an important reason, but not the only one, for engaging with and interrogating his thought. The inspiration he provided to many around the world merits critical but serious assessment if we are to move beyond simplistic ideas about the inherent

[46] Iqtidar, 'Theorizing Popular Sovereignty', 615–17.   [47] Hallaq, *The Impossible State*.

conservativism of Muslims or conceptions of false consciousness that privilege the observer over the observed. Given the signal creativity of his approach and the experimentation with new combinations of ideas and concepts, it is worth thinking in substantive detail about what a vision of organic social change offers its audiences. Working through the valences of Maududi's systematic questioning of the civilizational hierarchy set up by colonial regimes alerts us to the similarities between progressive and conservative anti-colonialism. Some of the intellectual and political challenges faced by proponents of conservative anti-colonialism were similar to the ones progressive anti-colonial political actors also struggled with, particularly in the immediate aftermath of decolonization. These included the difficulty of forming nations out of disparate groups bounded into hastily drawn territories, shifting economic structures away from colonial and imperial patterns and dislodging local hierarchies. At the core of all versions of anti-colonialism was a sense of experimentation. No one really knew what the world would look like once colonialism ended. If we are to truly realize the promise of anti-colonial thought to work through contemporary legacies of colonialism and imperialism, we will need to broaden our assessment of anti-colonial thought to include those who raised uncomfortable questions and experimented with awkward alternatives.

Texts Included

Maududi was a prolific writer. He wrote essays, books, pamphlets, newspaper articles, speeches and letters covering a range of areas, including history, politics, economics, law, culture and theology, on topics as diverse as gender norms, nationalism, sovereignty, democracy and legal reform, as well as rates of interest and profit. He even wrote a practical guide for examining Islamic knowledge.[48] Moreover, he completed a major work of Quranic exegesis, *Tafhim ul Quran*. However, he made some of his most original and influential contributions between 1925 and 1955. The selection here goes across this broad range of writings and focuses on some of his most influential works.

---

[48] The exam guide was entitled *Risalah-e-Diniyyat* for matriculation exams in Hyderabad. Written in 1932, it was later translated into English as *Towards Understanding Islam* and became one of his most widely read works (Khalidi, Maulānā 'Mawdudi and Hyderabad', 49).

Maududi used English words in his Urdu works, and I have retained those in the texts where possible. This gives readers a better sense of the arguments he sought to construct. I have included Urdu terms and phrases, particularly those that are associated with a range of different meanings. The hope is that this will aid scholars in assessing the breadth of associations Maududi drew upon. It is also important to note that in remaining faithful to the original, the translations included here contain terms as well as ideas that will be offensive to some. They have been left unchanged in the text, not to endorse such ideas or terms but to render them available for scholarly analysis. Readers familiar with some of the Euro–American texts Maududi cites in his writings might note the variation in his practices: at times he paraphrased and at others provided whole pages of translations, sometimes with clear acknowledgement including page numbers, and at others without. Finally, the tables of contents for the first five books are included to give readers a sense of where the excerpts selected fit within the arc of Maududi's arguments on the topic. There is some variation in the pattern of these tables of contents across the different books included here, and I have not tried to impose an artificial standardization upon them. Sections included in this volume are indicated by an asterisk in the table of contents for each book. Sections that do not follow continuously have also been indicated by a line of asterisks. Footnotes and references in the collection are as they were in the original texts, except when noted otherwise ['Editor's note']. This also introduces a level of variation in referencing styles across the volume. I hope readers will be willing to forgive this lack of standardization, done in the interests of remaining faithful to the texts included.

Al Jihad fil Islam *(Jihad in Islam)*

Originally begun as a series of articles and published as a book in 1930, this hefty volume (600-plus pages) was written when Maududi was still in his twenties and formed the basis of his early reputation as a serious thinker. Several abridged English translations exist but are highly selective in foregrounding parts that press the necessity of violence in particular contexts. Many were published by activists who were attracted by the unapologetic tone of Maududi's justifications of violence as part of a political struggle. However, Maududi had constructed a much more complicated argument, with comparisons across religious traditions (Buddhist, Hindu, Judaic, Christian), as well as empires in different times and regions (Roman, Sassanid, Islamic and modern European) to frame his reading of the ethics and norms of war in the Islamic tradition. This text also contains the first articulation of some key ideas and concepts that Maududi continued to develop over the course of his career. Methodologically too it signposts his use of broad historical generalizations, as well as the systematic breakdown of arguments that remained central to his thinking. Reproducing the whole book is not possible. Therefore, I have selected sections that allow readers an overview of his arguments, as well as some depth in particular strands.

Tehrīk-e-Azādi Hind aur Musalmān *(Freedom Movement in India and Muslims)*

Written between the 1930s and the mid 1940s, the essays selected here detail Maududi's critique of nationalism. In the highly charged context of declining but violent colonial power and increasing enthusiasm for anti-colonial nationalism, Maududi made his arguments against Muslim nationalists who supported the formation of a separate nation-state for Muslims, as well as nationalist Muslims, those who supported the formation of an Indian nation-state after independence from British rule. Many essays included in this volume were first published as articles in the journal *Tarjuman ul Quran* (hereafter *TQ* in editorial notes). I have noted some variations in the text.

Pardah *(Separation; Veiling)*

Published in 1940, this book was immediately controversial and remains so to date. Here, Maududi made an argument for the segregation of the sexes, which included, but was not limited to, the requirement of veiling by women. Refuting progressive arguments explicitly and drawing upon mostly American scholarship in the fields of medicine and biology, Maududi linked the end of gender segregation to capitalism, the commodification of women's labour and a wider civilizational decline. A relatively detailed and accurate translation was carried out by Al Ash'ari and published by the JI-affiliated Islamic Publications (Lahore) in 1979. However, there are several points of variance from the text in Urdu, also published by Islamic Publications (first edition 1959, my edition 2003). I have drawn upon Al Ash'ari's translation but modified the text and added to it, to correspond to the Urdu version.

M'ashiyyat-e-Islam *(First Principles of Islamic Economics)*

Maududi's ideas on Islamic economics have also been very influential across the Muslim world, and some argue that he should be recognized as the father of the contemporary Islamic finance sector, valued at roughly $3.5 trillion today. Arshad Zaman has rightly argued that Maududi's insistence on using the term *m'ashiyyat*, which carries the meaning 'provision of livelihood', rather than *iqtisādiyyat*, which is more readily translated as 'economics', is significant.[49] Maududi was making an explicit statement against the centrality of wealth acquisition and generation associated with the term *iqtisādiyyat*. This collection of essays was first published in 1969, and the writings included range over the thirty years preceding its publication. I have reproduced sections from the edition published by the Islamic Foundation (Leicester) in 2011.

Islamic Law and Constitution

This is a collection of essays and speeches that was published in English by Maududi's associate Khurshid Ahmed. The volume is particularly useful in laying out Maududi's overall vision of the place of sharia in a modern state. I have included an influential essay based on his 1948 speech that sought to demonstrate the possibility of approaching sharia as a body of laws compatible with modern governance.

Tafhīm ul Quran

Maududi also wrote an immensely popular six-volume commentary on the Quran. This genre of writing is often excluded from an assessment of Maududi's political thought. However, for Maududi, all his endeavours were connected. His commentary and translation of Surah Al Fatiha indicate some abiding concerns.

---

[49] Arshad Zaman, 'Sayyid Abū'l A'lā Maudūdī on Islamic Economics', *Islamic Studies* 50:3–4 (2011), 303–23, at 305.

Note on Transliterations

In Sections 1, 2 and 3, IJMES transliteration guidelines have been followed. In these sections I have also sought to remain close to Maududi's writing style by indicating when he used English in essays written in Urdu. At times he provided Urdu translations. I have noted these instances too, because they provide important clues as to how he interpreted specific English terms. Occasionally he transliterated English words into Urdu. In such cases, there is no Urdu term noted.

Translations and transliterations in Sections 4, 5 and 6 reflect the published versions noted in the Introduction. They have been slightly modified to aid readers, for instance by standardizing the transliterations of some terms.

Certain terms that occur repeatedly, such as Quran and sharia, have not been italicized and are written with limited diacritical marks, as is common in contemporary English-language writing.

Selected
Political
Writings

Al Jihad fil Islam

Contents

3

Chapter 3 Reformed War

The Ethical Concept of Universal Obligation
Instructions of Islam concerning the Collective Duty
The Truth about Establishing Virtue and Prohibiting Evil
The Status of the Concept of 'Establishing Virtue and Prohibiting Evil' in Collective Life
The Difference between Establishing Virtue and Prohibiting Evil
The Methodology of Prohibiting Evil
*War against *Fitnah* and *Fasād*
*Research on *Fitnah*
*Research on *Fasād*
*The Need for Divine Sovereignty to Eradicate *Fitnah* and *Fasād*
Directives regarding *Qatal*
Causes and Objectives of War
Reality of *Jizya*
Islam and Imperialism
Reasons for Islamic Conquests

Chapter 4 The Spread of Islam and the Sword

No Coercion in Religion
The True Concept of Invitation to Islam
The Secret of Guidance or Transgression
Role of the Sword in the Spread of Islam

Chapter 5 Islamic Laws of War and Peace

1) Pre-Islamic, Arab Methods of Warfare
    The Arab Concept of War
    Effect of the Frequency of Armed Conflict on Arabs
    Causes of War – Love of Wealth
       Pride
       Vengeance
    Savagery of Wars
    Oppression of the Non-combatants
    Ravages of Fire
    Condition of Prisoners of War
    Surprise Attack
    Sacrilege of the Dead
    Breaking Pacts
2) Roman and Persian Methods of War
    Religious Oppression

7

Author's Preface to the First Edition

The vilest of all the accusations modern Europe has fabricated against Islam, in the service of their political objectives, is that Islam is a bloodthirsty religion that inculcates bloodshed in its followers. Had this fabrication held any weight, it would have been formulated and presented at a time when the sharp swords of the believers in Islam had caused a great upheaval around the globe. It was a time when the world could have suspected that perhaps the victorious Muslim campaigns resulted from the blood-espousing teachings of the religion. However, strangely, this allegation appeared long after the sun of Islam had set from its zenith. They breathed life into the empty effigy of this fabrication at a moment when the sword of Islam had rusted while the sword of Europe, the originators of this allegation, was soaked in innocent blood and when Europe was gulping down weaker nations of the world like a dragon biting and swallowing smaller animals. Had the world followed reason, it would have questioned how the worst enemies of peace and harmony, those who had shed vast amounts of blood to colour the face of the earth and those who were robbing other nations, could have any right to blame Islam of a crime that they themselves are guilty of? Was their historical investigation, and scholarly debate and discovery, meant to divert the universal flood of hatred and anger and direct it towards Islam? Did they fabricate this blame out of their worry that this anger of the victimized nations would overflow and become a threat to the European agenda of bloodshed? However, it is a natural consequence of human weakness that once people fail to stand on the battlefield against their opponent, they lose ground intellectually as well. When they succumb to the force of the sword, they fail to contest the same enemy through the pen. Hence, the ideas and opinions that tend to dominate an age are generally those expressed by the people implementing their agenda through hands that hold the pen and the sword together. Therefore, Europe thoroughly succeeded in hiding the real issue from the world in this regard as well. Nations mired in intellectual slavery adopted the European ideology about Islamic jihad without investigation, specification and deliberation, giving it more importance than divine revelation.

Muslims have responded to the objection that Islam is a bloodthirsty religion several times during the previous and present century. They penned so many books and research studies on this topic that it seems more analysis has become prosaic and redundant. However, a common

9

flaw in such apologetic writings is that those advocating for Islam feel so intimidated by their opponents that they end up standing in the dock themselves and offering explanations like criminals. Some scholars have gone so far as to compromise Islam's fundamental teachings and laws with a view to strengthening their argument. It is a sign of their sense of intimidation that they removed from the record every element of Islamic teachings that they considered dangerous, so that the eyes of their contenders do not fall on such evidence. However, even those who did not take such a weak position have not fully explained the Islamic teachings and have left so many aspects uncovered that doubt and questions remain valid. The primary requirement to eradicate relevant misconceptions is to clearly explain, without reduction or addition, the Islamic teachings and laws regarding jihad in the way of Allah and for the sake of promoting the word of Allah, just as they are enshrined in the Holy Quran, the prophetic hadith and the juridical literature. Nothing should be added or removed nor should there be an attempt at changing the essence and true intention of the message of Islam and its teachings.

I disagree, in principle, with the idea of presenting our beliefs in such a way as to bring them into accord with the views of others. No single issue exists in this world about which all agree on the same position. Every group follows a specific view, considering it the most perfect. 'Each group is content with what it has before it' (Q 30:32). No matter how much we taint our ideologies and principles to make them acceptable to others, it is impossible to make differently inclined people embrace them and adopt the artificial painting of the doctrine. A much better approach is to present the true face of the religion, beliefs, teachings and laws and explain our arguments with complete sincerity. Then we must leave it to others to accept or reject our ideas. If they accept, we welcome them; if they don't, that is not our problem. This is the correct principle of preaching adopted by determined preachers. Even the divine messengers have adopted the same approach.

I had felt the need for this for a while but beyond this was not able to take any practical steps because this work requires some time and time is the one thing a journalist never has.

However, in the last days of December 1926 an event took place that forced me to undertake this project despite the many difficulties. The event was the murder of the founder of the Shuddhi movement, Swami Sharadanad. It provided an impetus to the uneducated and mean-spirited to propagate incorrect ideas about Islamic jihad because, unfortunately, a Muslim was arrested for carrying out this act. Newspapers assigned incorrect ideas to him, that he had thought the swami an enemy of his religion and killed him to secure a place in paradise for himself. Only God knows the truth, but what was available in the public sphere was all this. Due to these developments the enemies of Islam were galvanized. Ignoring the condemnation of various ulama of Islam, Islamic journals and other leaders, these elements attributed responsibility not just to the whole Muslim community [*'ummah*] but to Islamic teachings. They openly alleged that Quranic teachings make Muslims violent and murderous, that these teachings are against the peace and safety of all, and that they render Muslims so prejudiced that they see every non-believer as legitimate to murder and aim to do so to secure a place in heaven. Some went so far as to say that as long as Quranic teachings are available, there can be no peace and that all of humanity should try to eradicate these teachings. These incorrect ideas were allowed such wide and constant publicity that even right-minded people lost their footing. Even somebody like Gandhi, who is a deeply thoughtful person among the Hindus, has been influenced by these ideas to say that 'Islam was born in a context where the decisive power was the sword then and remains so today.'

Although these ideas are not based on any research or scholarly reflection, they are being parroted widely. The unusual event of the murder added some colour of reality to these speculations, such that uninformed people could easily be confused. Such misconceptions place obstacles in the path of Islamic preaching and these are the very moments when it is critical to present Islamic teachings with clarity so that confusion is dispelled and the light of reality can be fully revealed. Therefore, rather than waiting to get some free time to undertake this project, I embarked on this in the little time I had after organizing the newspaper. At the same time I started printing these essays in the newspaper *Al Jamiyyah*. The initial idea was only to write a brief article. However, once the conversation started, so many aspects to the debate came to the fore that it became difficult to contain them all in newspaper columns. Therefore, somewhat reluctantly after publishing issue number 23–4, I stopped its publication in the newspaper. Now I am presenting these all in the form of a complete book. Although this is an improvement on some debates, I am sorry that due to paucity of time I have not been able to fully address all aspects. Some issues needed whole chapters, and I have had to contain them in a sentence or two. A special effort has been made to not let my own or other people's personal opinions influence this book. All overarching and partial concerns have been derived from the Quran, and wherever further explanation was needed we have drawn upon hadith, authoritative books of *fiqh* and established books of *tafsir*. This is so that everybody can see that there is no new creation here following current fashions. Rather, everything is based on the guidance provided by Allah, the Prophet (peace be upon him) and elders of Islam.

I request all those non-Muslims who are not prejudiced against Islam to study the real teachings of Islam regarding war. They should then specify what they object to in these teachings. If there are any remaining doubts, I shall attempt to address them as fully as possible.

Abul A'la
Delhi, 15 June 1927

The Reality of Islamic Jihad

Respect for Human Life

The first clause of the law upon which stands the foundation of human civilization is that human life and blood are sacred. The first civil [*tamadduni*] right of mankind is the right to live, while the first and foremost civil duty is to allow others to live. The moral principle of honour of self has definitely existed in all the sharias and civilized laws in the world. A religion or a law that does not recognize this right can neither be declared the law or religion of civilized people nor enable any human population to live a peaceful life under it, and thus it cannot flourish. Every person's intellect is aware that if human life does not carry any value, lacks respect and has no arrangement for its security, then how can people live together, engage in mutual trade, attain a sense of peace and security, or attain the state of collectivity devoid of fear which is necessary for trade, manufacturing, agriculture, money-making, building homes, travelling and living a civilized life? In addition, if we disregard needs and consider this from a purely humanist [*insāniyyat*] perspective, killing another human life, even if it is for personal gains or enmity, symbolizes the worst form of tyranny and hard-heartedness, the existence of which not only fail to support moral development but also make it impossible for an individual to retain the status of a human being.

The political laws of this world establish this sanctity of human life by using force and invoking fear of punishment. However, a true religion's job is to create real respect in people's hearts for human life so that people avoid violating the sanctity of life even in situations where they need not fear human punishment and are unlikely to be arrested by police officials. From this perspective, the proper and effective education regarding the sanctity of life given by Islam is unlikely to be found in any other religion. The Holy Quran has tried to inscribe this on people's hearts on multiple occasions in various styles. Discussing the story of Adam's two sons, of whom one had killed the other unfairly (*zulman*), in chapter 6 (Surah Mā'idah) of the Quran, Allah Almighty says:

> On that account We ordained for the Children of Israel that if anyone slew a person unless it be in response to murder or for spreading mischief [*fasād*] in the land, it would be as if he slew all humans. And if anyone saved a life, it would be as if he saved the life of all humans. Then, although there came to them Our apostles with clear signs, many of them continue to exceed the limits [*hadd*] set for them.
>
> (Q 6:32)

On another occasion, the Almighty defines the attributes of His pious people in this way:

> They do not slay life that Allah has made sacred, except for just cause (*haqq*), or commit fornication; and any that does this meets punishment.
>
> (Q 25:68)

The Almighty says on another occasion:

> Say oh Mohammed, (peace be upon him), 'Come, I will rehearse what God has (really) prohibited you from. Join not any as equal with Him, be good to your parents, and kill not your children on a plea of want and poverty. We provide sustenance for you and will do for them too; come not close to shameful deeds whether open or secret; take not life which God has made sacred except through the demands of justice and truth [*haqq*]. Thus does He command you that ye may learn wisdom.'
>
> (Q 6:151)

The first addressees of these teachings [*t'alīm*] were those who did not value human life and even killed their own offspring for personal gains. Therefore, the Preacher of Islam, may thousands of blessings and bounties shower upon him, would personally advise his followers to respect the sanctity of human life for the well-being of their behaviour and would impart this advice very effectively. The hadith literature contains many narrations that declare killing the innocent the worst possible sin. For example, we will mention a few hadith for our readers.

Ans b. Mālik has been reported to have said that the Prophet once stated: 'Included among the biggest sins are associating partners to Allah, killing a human being, disobeying parents, and telling lies.'

Ibn 'Umar says that the Holy Prophet has said:

> A believer remains steady in the expansion of his faith as long as he does not shed the blood of a human being unjustly.

A reliable [*mutawātir*] hadith in the Sunan of al -Nisā'ī reads: 'The first thing to be inquired of humans on the day of judgment is prayer. The first cases to be decided among humans are the claims of bloodshed.'

Once a person came to the Prophet and asked: 'What is the biggest sin?' The Prophet replied: 'That is, you declare someone similar to God despite the fact that He created you.' The person asked: 'What is the second biggest sin?' The Prophet replied: 'That you kill a child thinking that he will share your food.' He asked: 'What is the next biggest sin?' The Prophet replied: 'That you commit adultery with the wife of your neighbour.'

Moral Impact of Islamic Teachings on the World

The education about the sanctity of human life did not solely result from the thoughts of a philosopher or a moral teacher for its influence to remain restricted to books and educational institutions. Instead, in reality, it was an education from God and His messenger, every word of which was a part of Muslims' faith (*imān*). Every follower of the religion of Islam was bound to follow, promote and implement it. Consequently, in the short span of a quarter of a century, a bloodthirsty nation (*qawm*) like that of the Arabs had developed such a respect for human life and peace that, according to the prediction of the Prophet, a woman could travel alone from Qādisiyah to San'ā without facing an attack on her life or wealth. This was the same country where many large caravans could not cross safely and fearlessly only twenty-five years previously. Later on, when more than half of the civilized world was under Islamic rule, and the moral education of Islam had spread to all parts of the world, Islamic education also removed the disrespect for human life, like many other sins and forms of ignorance. The status attained by the sanctity of human life in modern civilized laws today is among the many magnificent results of the revolution caused by Islamic education in the moral norms of this world. Otherwise, human life had in reality little value in the dark ages when this knowledge was revealed. The world has heard much about the bloodthirstiness of Arabs. However, the nations that were at that time the centres of knowledge, wisdom, civility and politeness were also not better off regarding their respect for the sanctity of human life. The stories of the Roman Colosseum [English name in text] still exist in the records of history in which thousands of people lost their lives, falling prey to the gladiatory [English word in text] skills and entertainment of Roman elites. Having slaves shredded by beasts, getting them slaughtered like animals, and burnt alive to entertain guests and friends were practices not frowned upon in most of the countries of Europe and Asia. Killing slaves and prisoners in different ways was a routine matter in that era. Not just ignorant and bloodthirsty elites, but even well-known scholars and philosophers of Greece and Rome declared [*ijtihadat*] it permissible to use different means and brutal techniques to kill innocent people. Prominent moral philosophers just like Aristotle and Socrates did not see any harm in allowing a mother to remove her womb. Thus, abortion was not considered illegal or unethical in Rome and Greece. Fathers had a complete right to kill their children, and Roman legislators were particularly proud of their laws, as they gave fathers unlimited powers over their children. The Stoics [the English term is used alongside the Urdu translation, *rawaqayyan*] did not consider suicide a condemnable act. Instead, killing oneself was considered such an honourable act that people gathered audiences to commit suicide. Even a philosopher like Aristotle did not consider suicide an immoral act. For a husband, killing his wife was just like slaughtering a pet. Hence, the laws of Ancient Greece did not ascribe any punishment to killing wives. India, the home of *Jeve Rakhsha*, outdid all others. Here, it was permissible and religiously prescribed to burn a living widow to death in the crematory fire of her deceased husband.[1] The life of a Shudra had no value, and just because the poor Shudra was [believed to be] born from the feet of Brahmanas, shedding their blood was permissible for Brahmanas. For Shudra, listening to Vedas was such a big sin that it was not only permissible but obligatory to kill the listener by pouring molten lead in his ears. *Jal Parva* was a tradition following which parents sacrificed their first child to the River Ganges. They considered such hard-heartedness a sign of great blessing.

---

[1] People may argue that widows were not burnt by force but killed themselves willingly. But the truth is that societal pressure in different forms forced them to do so.

In such dark ages, Islam ordained that 'Allah has made taking human life impermissible [*haram*] unless required by justice [*haqq*]'. This command had a power which, unlike 'Ahimsa Parmo Dharma', did not lack rationality and harmony with nature. Therefore, it reached all corners of the world and enabled human beings to recognize the value of their lives. It does not matter whether a nation or a country embraced Islam or not, their moral life could not avoid submitting to the influence of the divine command. Any just scholar of our collective history cannot deny a pride of place for this voice in establishing the sanctity of human life in the world's ethical laws, more so than the 'Sermon on the Mount' or 'Ahimsa Parma Dharma'.

Rightful Killing [*Qatl bil haqq*]

Now deliberate on the divine command [*lā taqtulū al nafs allatī ḥarrama Allāhū*]. It did not simply say, 'Do not kill anyone.' It also added: unless for just cause [*illā bi al ḥaq*]. Allah did not just say that killing a person in any circumstances is synonymous with killing the entirety of humanity [*man qatala nafan faka'annamā qatala al nāsa jamī'ā*]. Instead, the exception was added: *bi ghayri nafsin aw fasādin fī al arḍ*. Allah did not forbid killing anyone under any circumstances. Saying so would have made the message faulty. It would have been an act of cruelty rather than justice. The world did not require freeing man of all legal restrictions and allowing him to make mischief, spoil peace and commit tyranny and injustice to any extent while still enjoying the protection of his life. The actual requirement was to establish peace in the world, abolish the seeds of mischief and introduce laws to ensure that everyone is free within his own boundaries but should not transgress beyond those of others to disrupt the mental and physical peace of others. For this purpose, saying 'Do not kill anyone' was not enough. Instead, it required the protective authority of *illā bi al ḥaq* [except for just cause]. Otherwise, the only possible outcome would have been anarchy replacing peace.

Any worldly law that remains devoid of the principle of dialectical action and reaction can never succeed. Human nature is not so obedient as to be able to happily accept every command or happily stop doing things that are prohibited. Had that been the case, persecution and anarchy would never have surfaced. Human nature carries an inclination towards the good as well as the bad, and obedience as well as disobedience. Hence, to force the disobedient nature of man into submission, there must be a law that commands something while also prescribing punishment for its violation and clarifying implications of carrying out the proscribed act. Only prohibiting 'mischief after attaining peace on earth' and 'killing of life made sacred by Allah' cannot suffice without describing the punishment for these violations and committing sins of persecution and unjust killing.

Such a shortcoming is possible in human education, but divine laws cannot have such flaws. The divine command explicitly states that human life is sacred as long as it does not have somebody else's *haqq* on it. It can retain the right to life only within specific permissible limits. However, if a person violates those limits by instigating persecution [fasād] or attacking the lives of others unjustly, he loses the sanctity of his own life. The sanctity of his blood changes into fallibility, and his death becomes a guarantee of humanity's existence. Therefore, the Almighty has said: killing is bad but tumult and oppression are worse than killing. If a person commits such significant wrongdoing, the best solution is to bring an end to the bigger crime. Similarly, when someone kills another unjustly, God has issued the following verdict: O you who have believed, legal retribution [*qiṣāṣ*] is prescribed for you for those murdered. This divine command removed the difference established by ignorant nations based on higher or lower status. Hence, the Almighty said: 'a life for a life'. It is not possible to let a rich person who kills a poor person or a free person who kills a slave go unpunished. Instead, as humans, all of them are equal. Only one life can be an alternative to another life, regardless of whether it belongs to the rich or the poor. To avoid confusion, since some might consider it unnecessary bloodshed, the Almighty said: do not consider *qiṣāṣ* to be only about death. There is security of life for you in the law of *qiṣāṣ*, O people of reason. It guarantees the security of life for the society, which is attained by removing a festering boil from the body. The Holy Prophet (peace be upon him) has perfectly described the concept of life in the law of retaliation [*qisās*]. He said: help your brother, whether he is an oppressor or a victim. The listener felt surprised, as helping the oppressed seems right, but how could one help an oppressor? Therefore, he asked: O messenger of God, we will certainly help the oppressed. However, how can we help an oppressor? The Prophet replied: you can do so by holding his hands to stop him from committing injustice. Thus, any strict action against a transgressor to stop his transgressions only implies kindness to him rather than cruelty and is an assistance to him.

For this reason, Islam strictly commands the implementation of boundaries set by Allah, and this has been declared a cause of blessing and prosperity. The Holy Prophet (peace be upon him) has been reported to have said: the blessing of establishing a divine limit [*hadd*] is more than the rain that continues for forty days. The blessings of rain are that it fertilizes the earth, increases the growth of crops and enhances prosperity. However, the blessing of establishing divine limits is greater than that of rain because it uproots tumult, suppression, tyranny and lawlessness, allows God's creation to live a peaceful and calm life, and ensures peace, which guarantees the life of civilization and the soul of progress.

Rationale of War

The Wise and Knowing God has revealed this advantage and necessity of wars in his following command:

> Had not God checked one set of people by means of another, monasteries, churches, synagogues and mosques, in which the name of God is commemorated in abundant measure, would have been pulled down.
>
> (Q 22:40)

In this noble verse, the Almighty did not only mention the mosques of Muslims. He included the places of worship of three other religions: *ṣawāmi'*, *biya'* and *ṣalawāt*. *Ṣawāmi'* refers to the places of worship of Christians, Magians and Sabians. The word *biya'* describes Christian churches and Jewish synagogues. After using these broad terms, God applied the broader term *ṣalawāt*, which refers to the place of worship of any religion. At the end of these, the Almighty mentioned mosques. The purpose is to explain that had Allah not driven back cruel people through just people, it would have caused such persecution that all the places of worship, which are known to cause no damage to anyone, would have been destroyed. Moreover, it also explains that the worst form of nuisance or persecution [fasād] is when one nation, in enmity towards another, destroys even their places of worship. Subsequently, the Almighty has very eloquently expressed His will. It is necessary to eradicate the evil of such mischief-makers at the hands of another group.

19

While relating the story of the aggression of Goliath [*Jalūt*] and his death at the hands of David [*Hazrat Da'ud*], God Almighty described this wisdom behind wars in the following words:

> Had Allah not repelled a group of people by the might of another, persecution would have become rampant on the earth [*la fasadat al arḍ*], but Allah is Gracious to all (as He has arranged this system of eradication of nuisance [fasād]).
>
> (Q 2:251)

At one place, God mentions mutual enmity and hatred among nations and says:

> Whenever they kindle the fire of war and bloodshed, Allah puts it out. And they strive to spread persecution [fasād] in the land. And Allah does not like such people.
>
> (Q 5:64)

Jihad in the Path of Allah

It is this war of persecution, lawlessness, greed, bias, enmity, jealousy and narrowmindedness that Allah Almighty commands His servants to extinguish by picking up their swords. He commands:

> To those against whom war is made, permission is given to fight, because they have been wronged. And verily, God is Most Powerful for their aid. They are those who have been expelled from their homes without fault. Their only fault was that they declared, 'Our Lord is Allah.'
>
> (Q 22:39–40)

This is the first verse of the Quran dealing with fighting [*qatal*]. It does not command fighting a people because they have fertile land, own a big trade market or follow a different religion. Instead, the crime clearly attributed to them is that they are oppressors, they force innocent people out of their homes, and are so biased that they harm and persecute others just for calling Allah their lord. Allah has not only commanded defence against such people but also support and aid for those facing oppression by them. He stresses saving and protecting such weak and helpless people from oppressors.

And what is it with you, that you do not fight in the cause of Allah for oppressed men, women and children who cry out, 'Our Lord! Deliver us from this town of which the people are oppressors! By your special grace appoint for us a protector and a helper!' (Q 4:75).

God calls war against oppressors and tyrants in self-defence and in support of the weak, the helpless and oppressed people as war particularly fought for the cause of Allah. The wisdom behind this specification is that such a war is fought purely for the sake of God, not people. It is not fought for the objectives of humans but to win the pleasure of God. It has been commanded that this war must continue till the process of oppression and coercion of the innocent, carried out owing to the base motives of oppressors, comes to an end. For this reason, Allah Almighty has said: 'Fight against them until there is no more persecution [*fitnah*]' (Q 8:39). He also says: 'Fight until they lay down their weapons, and nuisance and persecution are wiped out completely so that there is no need to fight against them.' In addition, He has also explained the outcome of avoiding this war, considering it bloodshed or fearing the loss of wealth and lives.

Drawing the Boundaries of Truth [*Haqq*] and Falsehood [*Batil*]

Moreover, Allah Almighty did not remain restricted to describing the need for and rationale of the war in support of truth and justice. He has also explicitly stated:

> Those who believe fight for the cause of Allah. And those who are recalcitrant disbelievers fight for the cause of oppression and rebellion. So, fight against Satan's friends. Indeed, Satan's cause for war is weak.
>
> (Q 4:76)

The above is a decisive verdict setting the boundaries between good and evil. Those who fight for injustice and transgression are the friends of Satan. Those who fight to put an end to oppression instead of promoting it are fighters in the path of God. Every battle is a battle of evil rebellion [*tāghūt*] if its objective is to inflict pain on innocent people, while militating against truth and justice, depriving humans of their rights, forcing them out of their legitimate properties and persecuting people who glorify the name of Allah. It is completely cut off from God. Believers must not indulge in such a war. However, the war of the people who support and protect the oppressed against such oppressors, who

21

seek to eradicate oppression and rebellion in order to establish justice and truth, is war in the way of God. They strive to uproot the transgressors and mischief-makers to help God's creation live in peace and satisfaction and progress towards the higher objective of humanity. In helping the suppressed, they help God in a way. The promise of divine support is specifically extended to such fighters.

Excellence of Jihad in the Path of Allah

This is the jihad in the path of God, the blessings of which have been spread on many pages of the Quran. The Almighty says about it:

> O believers! Shall I guide you to a trade that will save you from a painful punishment? This trade involves having faith in Allah and His Messenger and striving in the cause of Allah with your wealth and your lives. That is the best thing for you to do if only you knew.
>
> (Q 61:10–11)

The Quran praises the fighters for this cause in these words:

> Surely, Allah loves those who fight in His cause in solid ranks as if they were one solid structure.
>
> (Q 61:4)

The glory and high status of this jihad have been testified in these glorious ways:

> Do you consider providing the pilgrims with water and maintaining the Sacred Mosque as equal to the act of those who believe in Allah and the Last Day and wage a war in the cause of Allah? They are not equal in Allah's sight. And Allah does not guide the oppressors. Those who have believed, emigrated, and fought in the cause of Allah with their wealth and their lives are greater in rank in the sight of Allah. It is they who will triumph.
>
> (Q 9:19–20)

In addition, this is the same fight for truth in which staying awake for a night is better than staying up to worship for thousands of nights. It has been declared that remaining steadfast on this battlefield is better than offering constant prayers for sixty years at home. The fire of hell has been prohibited to the eye that stays awake in this battle for truth. The feet that gather dirt in this battle have been promised never to be dragged to the fire of hell. At the same time, the Almighty has issued a stern warning to those who sit back and avoid participating in the battle and shake at the call to war. He says:

> Tell them, O Prophet, 'If your father, son, brothers, wives, and relatives, and the wealth you have acquired, and the trade you have established and the homes you cherish – are more beloved to you than Allah and His Messenger and waging jihad in His way, then wait until Allah brings about His Will. Allah does not guide the rebellious people.'
>
> (Q 9:24)

Reasons for the Excellence of Jihad

Now ponder why jihad for the cause of Allah merits this excellence and praise. Why is it repeatedly explained to the participants in this jihad that they are on the path to success and that their ranks are the highest? Why are the people who avoid participation in jihad and sit back at home so sternly warned? To find the answer to this question, you can have another look at the verses that command jihad, describe its excellence and condemn avoiding it. In no part of these verses are success and glory explained as attaining wealth, rule or power. Unlike what Krishna told Arjun, 'If you won this great battle [Mahā Bahārat], you would enjoy the kingdom on earth' (Gita 2:37), the Quran never encourages fighting in the way of Allah by promising the fighters worldly riches and power. On the contrary, the Quran only promises the pleasure of God, the highest ranks in the court of God and safety from the painful punishment (of hell) against jihad in the way of Allah. Allah declared leaving home and business to fight in the way of Allah more excellent than providing water to the pilgrims and inhabiting the Sacred Mosque, an act that secured great influence and income in Arabia [at that time]. He did not mention any reward for jihad other than a greater rank in the eyes of God [a'ẓamu darjatan 'ind Allāh]. On another occasion, the Almighty refers to a trading benefit, which might suggest the possibility of gaining wealth. However, if you study the relevant verse, you can see that the reality of that trade is this: spend your life and wealth in the path of God and, in return, secure salvation from punishment. On another occasion, the people are chided because they shirk jihad owing to love for their wives and their children. They also fear loss of the wealth they have earned, recessions in their businesses and loss of their beloved houses.

However, those who conquer countries through war get a lot of money, see trade expand and get grand buildings they snatch from the vanquished nation.

If the aim of jihad is not to get wealth and annex territories, what does all this bloodshed give to God that in return for this fighting He extends such huge ranks? What does this dangerous activity carry that the dusty feet of a person is declared to be the object of generosities and blessings? What success is implied in jihad that the participants in this dry and unpleasing war are repeatedly told that 'they are the triumphant' [*ulā'ika hum al fā'izūn*]? The answer to these questions lies in the following verse:

> Had Allah not repelled a group of people by the might of another, corruption and persecution would have become rampant on the earth [*la fasadat al arḍ*].
>
> (Q 2:251)

Allah does not want anyone to spread nuisance and oppression on his earth. He does not tolerate the persecution and destruction of His innocent people. He does not like that the powerful people feed on the weaker ones, ruin their peace and calm, and cause the destruction of their moral, spiritual and material lives. He dislikes that sins, crimes, oppression, injustice, killings and lawlessness persist on his earth. He does not like to see His special servants turned into slaves of His creatures, and thus have their human dignity stamped by humiliation. Therefore, who can be more deserving of Allah's love and pleasure than a group of people that stands up to purify the earth from this persecution only for the sake of Allah and without greed for wealth and riches and without a wish for personal gains? Those who stand up to eradicate this oppression and establish in its stead justice. Those who are eager to sacrifice their life, wealth, economic benefits, love of family and the peace and comfort of home in this noble task. Who else can enjoy the lap of success but them?

This is the excellence of jihad in the way of God that makes it stand above all good deeds, except having faith in Allah [*īmān bi-Allāh*]. A little deliberation reveals that only this deed is the soul of all the virtues and perfect morals. It is human spirit [transliterated in Urdu *ispirit*] to refuse to tolerate evil and be ready to sacrifice everything to eradicate it. It is the highest spirit of human nobility. The secret of success in practical life lies in this very spirit. The moral weakness of a person who stays unmoved seeing others being subjected to evil can ultimately lead him to tolerate being treated the same way. When he develops such a level of tolerance for evil, he enters the level of humiliation that God calls His wrath, as expressed in the following the following Quranic verse:

> And humiliation and wretchedness were stamped upon them and they were visited with wrath from Allah.
>
> (Q 2:61)

Having fallen to this level, a person loses any feeling of nobility and humanity. He falls not only into physical and material slavery but also into mental and spiritual slavery, landing in the depths of lowliness from where he cannot escape in any condition. On the contrary, a person who has the moral strength to dislike wrongdoing precisely because it is wrong, and tirelessly strives to protect human brethren from it, he is an honest and honourable man. His existence becomes a source of mercy for mankind.

Such a person may not hope for a reward from the world. However, despite all the ingratitude stamped on its forehead, this world is not so ungrateful as to refuse accepting such a person as their leader, their crown and imām who serves humanity fearlessly, without asking for any return and renumeration, and sacrifices everything to protect people from evil, to help them attain material, psychological and spiritual freedom. This explains the meaning of the following Quranic verse: 'The earth shall be the inheritance of My righteous servants.' It leads to the conclusion that the divine statement 'they are the triumphant' [*ulā'ika hum al fā'izūn*] does not merely imply success in the Hereafter but also that success in this world shall also belong only to the people who wage jihad purely for the sake of Allah and the well-being of Allah's servants without mixing personal objectives.

****

Reformed War

War against Fitnah and Fasād

To clearly distinguish the second type of evil, against which Islam calls its followers to raise their swords, from the first type and to make its nature more explicit, God describes it with the terms fitnah and fasād. Therefore, all the verses that permit or prescribe fighting against evil or command its removal through the use of force invariably employ the terms fitnah and fasād instead of *munkar*, evil.

> Fight against them until there is no more fitnah.
>
> (Q 8:39)

Had Allah not repelled a group of people by the might of another, fasād would have become rampant on the earth [*la fasadat al arḍ*] (Q 2:251).

> Unless you do this, there would be fitnah on earth, and fasād.
>
> (Q 8:73)

> And fitnah is worse than slaughter.
>
> (Q 2:191)

If anyone slew a person, unless it be [as punishment] for murder or for spreading fasād in the land, it would be as if he killed all humans (Q 5:32).

> Indeed, they had sought fitnah before.
>
> (Q 9:48)

> Every time they turn towards fitnah they succumb to it.
>
> (Q 4:91)

In all these verses, the Almighty has described evil as fitnah or fasād. The reality is that, among all evils, only fitnah and fasād are the wrongs that cannot be undone without using a sword.

Research on Fitnah

Generally, the term *fitnah-o-fasād* is taken to mean that two parties start fighting. They begin by exchanging verbal abuse, and then the physically strong among either party start a fight using stones, bricks, sticks, daggers, swords or guns. They beat each other, break their opponent's skulls and satisfy their anger by killing and injuring their rivals. Although the words *fitnah-o-fasād* apply to such activities too, the meaning of these terms in the Holy Quran is not as restricted. Instead, the Quran uses this word to refer to many other crimes against ethics. We do not have to look up the variety of meanings of these terms in other books because the Quran itself explains what it means by the term *fitnah-o-fasād*.

In the lexicon, the verb *fatan* refers to the process of heating gold to check whether it is fake or real. By extension of this literal meaning, the verb is used for putting a man to the fire, as stated in the following Quranic verse:

(It will be) a day when they will be roasted [*yuftanūn*] over the Fire!
(Q 51:13)

Figuratively, it has been employed to refer to everything that puts a man to the test. Hence, wealth and children have been called fitnah:

Your riches and your children are a trial (fitnah).
(Q 64:15)

Wealth and children have been called fitnah because they become an instrument of testing a man's preference for truth over these entities.

Ease and difficulties have also been called fitnah in the following verse:

And We test you by evil and by good by way of trial [*fitnatan*].
(Q 21:35)

The reason is that, through these two conditions, man is tested.

The revolutions and changes in times have also been called fitnah as they test nations and put them to trial.

See they not that they are tried [*yuftanūn*] every year once or twice?
Yet they turn not in repentance, and they take no heed.

(Q 9:126)

Burdening someone more than his capacity is also called fitnah.

Among them is [many] a man who says: 'Grant me exemption and
draw me not into trial [*taftinnī*]'.

(Q 9:49)

All these examples prove that the real meaning of fitnah is test and trial
regardless of whether it happens through greed for benefits, desires for
pleasure and attainment of beloved things, or fear of loss, the appearance of
hardships and infliction of pain. If such a test comes from God, it is
justified. God is the creator of man and has the right to test His servants.
His purpose in testing men is to raise them to a better and higher level of
being. However, if such a trial is perpetrated by other humans, it is
injustice because man has no right to put another man on trial. A person
puts another person to the test to deprive him of his freedom of conscience,
forcibly enslave him and put him in a state of moral and spiritual degradation. In the latter of the above two senses, the word fitnah corresponds to
the English word 'persecution' [English word in text]. However, the
English word does not carry as much depth and breadth as the
word fitnah. The practical examples of the term given in the Holy Quran
are as follows:

1 Oppressing the weak, depriving them of their due rights, snatching
  their homes and properties, and torturing them.

   Then your Lord, to those who leave their homes after being tried
   [*futinū*], (tortured), and who thereafter strive and fight for the
   faith and patiently persevere, is Oft-Forgiving (Q 16:110).
   (To fight during the sacred months surely amounts to violation
   of the sanctity of the Sacred House.) But graver is it in the sight
   of God to drive out from the Sacred Mosque those who live
   there. Fitnah is worse than slaughter (Q 2:217).

2 Suppressing the truth and preventing people from embracing it.

   But none believed in Moses except a small group of youths of
   his nation, because of the fear of Pharaoh and his chiefs (who
   worked to appease Pharoah), lest they should put them into trial
   [fitnah] (Q 10:83).

3 Preventing people from the path of God. This term has been explained in the previous chapter. Hence, in Surah Al Anfal, the Almighty first ascribed the crime of diverting people from the cause of truth to the disbelievers.

> The unbelievers spend their wealth to hinder [men] from the path of God (Q 8:36).

Later, God foretold their defeat (at length they will be overcome, *yughlabūn*). Afterward, He referred to their actions as fitnah. Finally, He commanded His servants to fight against these disbelievers.

> Fight against them until there is no more persecution [fitnah], and the faith is devoted entirely to God (Q 8:39).

4 Misguiding people and striving against the truth through deception, cheating, bribery and coercion.

> And they had decided to tempt and coerce [*yaftinūnaka*] you away from this revelation which We had sent to you, so that you leave it and ascribe lies to Us. (In that case), behold! They would certainly have made you their friend! (Q 17:73).
> But beware of them lest they beguile you from any of those commands which God has sent down to you ... Do they then seek a judgment of the days of ignorance?
> (Q 5:49–50).

5 Fighting for the cause of untruth, killing, shedding blood and forming alliances for impermissible/illegitimate objectives.

> And if (during the Battle of Ahzab) the enemy had breached Madinah from the sides of the city, and these (hypocrites) had been incited to join the turmoil [fitnah], they would certainly have embraced it, without a slight hesitation! (Q 33:14).
> Others (among these hypocrites) you will find that wish to be at peace with you as well with their people: but every time they are sent back to temptation [fitnah] they side with those inciting it
> (Q 4:91).

That is, they become part of the party perpetrating the persecution.
6 Dominance of unbelievers over the followers of the truth.

> Unless you [protect the followers of the truth], there would be a turmoil [fitnah] on earth, and a great mischief [fasād] (Q 8:73).

29

That is, due to the domination of the evil, life would become hard for the followers of the truth.

Research on Fasād

Now note how the Holy Quran uses the word fasād in different senses.

Linguistically, the word fasād signifies a thing that deviates from a balanced course. It is the antonym of justice and *ṣalāh*, or reform. Going by the linguistic interpretation, any action that deviates from the moderate or just (*'adl*) state is called fasād. However, the Holy Quran employs this term to connote distortion of collective moral conduct and the civilizational and political system. For example, the Holy Quran charges that the pharoah, as well as 'Ād and Thamūd, had committed fasād. It reads:

> Did you not see how your Lord dealt with the 'Ād [people], of the [city of] Iram, with lofty pillars, the like of which were not produced in all the lands? And with the Thamūd [people], who cut out rocks in the valley? And with Pharaoh with his large armies? These people transgressed beyond bounds in the lands and spread fasād in them.
>
> (Q 89:6–12)

Subsequently, the Quran mentioned the crimes they had committed for which they were declared *mufsid*.

1 About the pharoah, the Almighty says that he was arrogant. He discriminated among his subjects on racial grounds. He would divide them and rule over them. Moreover, he would suppress the weak and shed their blood unjustly.

> Truly Pharaoh elevated himself in the land and broke up its people into sections. He weakened a group among them and started slaughtering their sons. And left alive their females; for he was indeed one of the *mufsidīn*
>
> (Q 28:4).

The pharoah used force to prevent people from embracing the truth. When the magicians embraced faith after witnessing the miracles of Moses (peace be upon him), the pharoah said:

> 'Did you believe in him before I gave you permission? Surely this must be your leader who has taught you magic! I will get

your hands and feet cut off on opposite sides, and I will have you crucified on trunks of palm trees; so shall you know which of us can give the more severe and the more lasting punishment' (Q 20:71).

Finding a nation weakened, he had enslaved them. Hence, when he reminded the Prophet Moses (peace be upon him) of his favours, the latter replied:

> And this is the favour with which you reproach me, that you have enslaved my nation, the Children of Israel!
>
> (Q 26:22).

Intoxicated by his power and authority, he chose to act as God above humans like him. The only basis of his rule was his power, whereas the actual right to rule comes from justice, fairness and empathy.

> Pharaoh said: People, no god do I know for you but myself . . . and he and his armies were arrogant and unjust [*baghair haqq*] in the land, they thought that they would not have to return to Us! (Q 28:38–39).

He had corrupted the mental condition and moral conduct of his people and turned them so lowly that they had acceded to submitting their will to his rule in slavery.

> Thus did he make lowly/light [that is, made them low in reasons and morals] his people and consequently they obeyed him: Truly were they corrupt people (Q 43:54).

His government was based on unjust and wrong laws.

> But they followed the commands of Pharaoh, although the command of Pharaoh was not on the right path (Q 11:97).

2 Similarly, we have been told about the *'Ād* that they obeyed oppressive and transgressive rulers.

> And they followed the command of every powerful enemy of the truth (Q 11:59).

They were unjust oppressors and had nothing to do with justice and fairness. Therefore, condemning their behaviour, the Prophet Hūd (peace be upon him) would tell them:

And whoever you assault, you assault in tyranny!
(Q 26:130).

They forced their rule upon weaker people unjustly.

They assumed grandeur on the earth without right, and they said, 'Who is stronger than us in might?' (Q 41:15).

3 Explaining the crimes of the nation of Thamūd, the Holy Quran states that their rulers and chiefs were tyrants and characterless men. Still, the nation obeyed them. Hence, the Prophet Ṣāliḥ (peace be upon him) would advise them in the following words:

And follow not the bidding of those who are transgressors, who spread fasād [*yufsidūn*] in the land, and do not reform (Q 26:151–2).

They were so arrogant and rebellious against the truth that they chose to kill a person who stopped them from bad deeds and advised piety. To execute this heinous task, they used the worst tricks of cheating, lies and deception without feeling any sense of guilt.

There were in the city nine men (leaders of groups) who spread fasād in the land and would not reform. They said: Friends, swear a mutual oath by God that we shall make a secret night attack on Ṣāliḥ and his household, and that we shall then say to those of his heirs who will seek vengeance: We do not know anything about the slaughter of Ṣāliḥ and his family, and we are positively telling the truth (Q 27:48–9).

4 The Holy Quran calls the nation of Lot *mufsid* and explains their fasād in the following words:

You who commit wrong acts, such as no people in the world committed before you. Do you indeed lust after men, and commit highway robbery and openly practise wickedness in your gatherings? (Q 29:28–9).

Such was the fasād of Lot's nation that it involved normalizing unnatural acts, blocking trade markets and looting travellers. Their collective moral conduct had fallen to the extent that they openly committed crimes, and nobody was there to stop them.

5 The people of Madyan have also been declared *mufsid*. The Prophet Shu'aib (peace be upon him) would advise them in the following words:

32

Measure correctly and weigh accurately, do not hand over to people less than the actual quantity bought; and do not spread fasād on earth after it has been set in order: that will be best for you if you have faith. And squat not on every road breathing threats (that is, do not rob people). You hinder from the path of God those who believe in Him and seek in it something crooked (Q 7:85–6).

When the Prophet Shu'aib (peace be upon him) guided them to righteousness, they replied:

Were it not for your people, we should certainly have stoned you to death! For you cannot be difficult for us [to defeat]! (Q 11:91).

It shows that the fasād the nation of Madyan indulged in was cheating. Their cheating in business and trade was rampant. They raided trade routes passing through their region. They stopped the faithful people from the cause of God. They had such a grudge against the truth that when a pious person tried to stop them from their misdeeds and called them to the right path, they could not bear his existence among them and intended to stone him to death.

6 Theft has also been described as fasād. When the brothers of Joseph (peace be upon him) were charged with stealing the bowl, they said:

'By God! Well you know that we came not to make fasād [*li nufsida*] in the land, and we are no thieves!' (Q 12:73).

7 The destruction caused by the expansionism of monarchs and the impact they have on the moral conduct of a nation has also been termed fasād. When Queen Saba received the letter of the Prophet Soloman (peace be upon him), she said to her courtiers:

When kings enter a country, they fill it with fasād [*afsadūhā*] completely, and make the noblest of its people its meanest: Thus do they behave (Q 27:34).

8 One comprehensive definition of the term fasād, as mentioned in the Holy Quran, involves spoiling and severing those relationships and connections that form the foundation of human civilization. Allah Almighty says:

But those who break the covenant of God, after having pledged their word, and cut asunder the relationships which God has commanded to be joined, and spread fasād [*yufsidūn*] in the land, on them is the curse of Allah; for them is the most terrible abode! (Q 13:25).

Most Quran commentators have taken the words 'yaqṭaʿūna mā amara Allāhu bi hī an yūṣala' (and cut asunder that which God has commanded to be joined) in a very limited sense. They take it to mean severing blood relationships only. However, the reality is that it refers to all the permissible relations established among individuals and groups on different civilizational and cultural grounds. For example, they include relationships between family members, husband and wife, friends and neighbours, business and transactional relationships, relationships of promise and mutual trust, and international relations between different governments and countries. These relationships form the foundation of human civilization. Their healthy bond guarantees global peace and prosperity, and their disconnection causes disagreements, conflicts and feuds. This is why Allah declared breaking these relationships a form of fasād and condemned those who break them.

9 A form of governance that allows the use of authority for injustice and tyranny instead of achieving positive objectives has also been called a fasād. Hence, Allah Almighty says in the Holy Quran:

> When he assumes rule, he seeks to spread fasād [*li yufsida*] through the earth and destroys crops and peoples. But God does not love *al fasād*
>
> (Q 2:205).

10 The term fasād has also been used to describe the previously discussed act of preventing people from the path of truth [*ṣadd ʿan sabīl Allāhi*]. Hence, the Almighty says:

> Those who chose disbelief and hinder [men] from the path of God, for them will We add penalty to penalty; for that they used to spread fasād [*yufsidūn*] (Q 16:88).

11 Fasād has been ascribed to those in Surah Maida who 'strive with might and main for mischief [fasād] through the land'. About them, He said: 'And God does not love those who do fasād [*mufsidīn*].' The Quran describes the characteristics of these as follows:

> Many of them you will see hastening to commit sin and transgression and to eat that which is forbidden (Q 5:62).

34

Among them, We have seeded enmity and hatred till the Day of Judgment. Every time they kindle the fire of war, We extinguish it (Q 5:64).

It means that any sin that destroys personal moral conduct, and sins that have a negative impact upon others, and bribery, practice of usury, depriving people of their rights unlawfully, having enmity for others for individual desires and kindling the fire of war for such objectives, are forms of fasād.

The Need for Divine Sovereignty [*Ḥakumat-e-Ilāhī*] to Eradicate Fitnah and Fasād

The above discussion of fitnah and fasād makes it clear in what sense the Quran uses the terms. An overall look at all those evils that have been termed fitnah and fasād reveals the fact that all those evils result from a system of governance that does not recognize truth/justice [*nā haqq shanās*], is ungenerous and is without principles. Even if an evil's existence is not the direct creation of such a system of governance, it continues to exist and remains immune to correction only because such an evil system of rule protects falsehood. To begin with, such a government is in itself fitnah because it is against the original objective for which a political system is established. Moreover, the evils it generates do not remain contained within a particular realm. Instead, such a form of governance [*hakumat*] becomes the fountainhead of all the evils and the main source of principles and expansion of fitnah and fasād. It is through such a government that the path of truth is hindered, justice and truth are suppressed, wrongdoers and oppressors are granted the power to commit their crimes and such laws are implemented that destroy moral conduct and demolish social justice [English term in text; Urdu *'adl-e-ijtimā 'ī*]. It is this government that seeds hypocrisy and discord in the unity of humans, kindles the fire of war and bloodshed on the earth and causes adversities to befall people. To sum up, this [form of governance] is the power that, in one way or another, becomes a source of wrongdoing and injustice or plays a role in allowing these evils to persist and survive. To suppress evil and ward off and uproot wrongdoings, Islam stipulates a successful strategy of organized struggle [*jid-o-jehd*], that is, jihad. And maybe even war [*qatal*] can be waged to remove such governments and replace them with a just and fair system based on the principle of the fear of God and the permanent principles issued by Him. The sole and pure objective of such a government should be to serve humanity instead of chasing personal, class or national objectives. The purpose of the formation of this system of government should be the promotion of goodness and suppression of evil. Such a government would not be motivated by individual, class or national interests but a keen sense of service to all humanity, and a commitment to eradicating evil and supporting good, all to earn God's pleasure.

Take a look at the Holy Quran. You will see that it repeatedly prohibits believers from obeying oppressors and tyrants. It stresses that a human [*insān*] must not put himself on course for destruction by following falsehood and obeying oppression and arrogance. On some occasions, it commands:

> And follow not the bidding of those who are transgressors, who make mischief [*yufsidūn*] in the land, and do not reform.
>
> (Q 26:151–2)

Elsewhere, it commands:

> And do not obey him whose heart We have made neglectful of Our remembrance, the one who follows his own sensual pleasures, and whose command is based on excesses.
>
> (Q 18:28)

At certain points, the causes of the destruction of a nation are identified as follows:

> And they followed the command of every powerful enemy of the truth. Therefore, they were cursed in this world, as they will be on the Day of Judgment.
>
> (Q 11:59–60)

On other occasions, the Holy Quran clearly informs us that a country faces destruction only when its wealth and authority fall into the hands of wrongdoers:

> And when We intend to destroy a community, We command its wealthy men (to obey and do good). But they commit disobedience and wrongdoing. Then the community deserves the penalty, and We destroy it.
>
> (Q 17:16)

The reason is obvious. Of all the factors [English word in text; Urdu *'awāmil*] that affect human morality and civilization in the collect-ive life, the strongest and the most effective factor is the government. If the system of governance is flawed and is in the hands of people who use it to promote corruption and self-service, instead of using it for reformation and to serve humanity, it becomes difficult for virtue to flourish, reformation to yield fruit, and ethical and moral values to spread. It is because such a government naturally acts as a protector of evil. Not only is it in itself an evildoer, it uses its power and authority to promote all forms of moral evils. Its opposite is a government based on a fair and just constitution and laws, aiming to establish justice, and run by pious and God-fearing people who utilize their energy and skills to serve humanity instead of their personal, racial or national objectives. The effects and influence of the reformative powers of such a [just govern-ment] will not remain restricted to its immediate sphere. Instead, all aspects of collective and individual life will be positively impacted by it. The reformative movement will produce positive results in every sphere, including religion [*mazhab*], the economy, society, ethics, culture, sci-ence and philosophies. Not only will it lead to restricting evil-doing, but the very sources of the wrongdoing will become dry and barren. Thus, in fact, the most important and effective method to prevent collective persecution and corruption and to purify human life of all evils is to abolish all corrupt governments and replace them with a government that should be based on piety and goodness in its principles and practice.

Islamic Laws of War and Peace

Barbaric Forms of War

Since ancient times, at least at the level of theory, there has existed in the world a very basic idea of the rights and obligations of any two groups fighting against each other. The legislatures of Ancient Greece had formulated the law that those killed in war must be buried. They prohibited killing people from the losing side who took refuge in places of worship. They also proscribed killing sportsmen and the servants of places of worship.[1] However, firstly, these laws did not apply to international wars [*bayn al millī*].[2] The lawmakers had introduced these laws to regulate their internal strife and battles. Secondly, seen from a practical perspective, it transpires that the empires of that time neither accepted these injunctions as laws nor implemented them. The Roman empire, in particular, did not accept the legal status of any non-Roman country, and had no concept of dealing with them on the basis of any rights and obligations. The same was the case with the Persian empire. They considered non-Persian [*ghair Irānī*] nations barbaric. To them, the non-Persian empires were in fact traitors who had rebelled against the Persian empire. Therefore, when at war with any such nation, the Persians did not feel any ethical obligations binding on them.

The military systems of the Roman and Persian empires were also structured in such a way that they did not allow the following of ethical rules. They had no system of maintaining military training, education in the principles of war, and military discipline. In time of war, throngs of

---

[1] Grote, *History of Greece* [English name in text].
[2] It should be clarified that the term *bayn al millī* has been used to denote 'international' [*bayn al aqwamī*].

common citizens would gather on the open battlefield. They only participated in such games of blood and murder to satisfy their eagerness to loot their neighbouring countries, destroy their opponent nations, gather wealth for a happy life, collect slaves to force them into servitude and obtain beautiful girls for their own pleasure. Their rulers, too, did not have a specific ethical objective in war-making. They would raise their sword to humiliate their enemy or to destroy them. That is why, when they invaded a country, they did not spare children, women, the elderly, animals, trees, places of worship, temples or anything that came before them. They looted whatever they could and burnt to ashes whatever they could not.

The Vandals of Africa and the Goths of Europe continuously fought against the Romans. History is replete with accounts of the barbaric treatment they received from the Romans. When the Romans attacked the Vandals in the era of Caesar Justinian, the entire nation of the Vandals was wiped out. Before the battle, the nation had 160,000 fighters. They were also accompanied by a large number of children, women and slaves. However, when the victorious Roman armies vanquished the Vandals, they did not spare a single living soul. Gibbon writes that a foreign visitor could walk through the region for days without seeing a single human being anywhere. When Procopius first landed there, he was mesmerized to see the abundance of the population, trade and agricultural activities. However, in less than twenty years, this bustling land had turned into ruins and desolation. A mighty population of over 5 million became victims of the cruelty and arrogance of Justinian.[3]

The same barbaric treatment was meted out to the Goths of Europe, to the extent that we find that when their king, named Totila, got injured and escaped the battlefield only to die in a far-off place, Roman soldiers went to search for him. They found his dead body, stripped him naked and sent his blood-stained clothes and the crown to Caesar Justinian as a gift.[4]

When Titus, the Roman, conquered Jerusalem in AD 70, we are told that tall and beautiful girls were picked up for the conqueror. Thousands of men aged 17 and above were moved to labour in Egyptian mines. Thousands of men were arrested and sent to different cities of the empire, where they were either put before wild animals in amphitheatres and colosseums to have them killed by swordsmen or made to fight each

[3] Gibbon, vol. V, ch. 43.   [4] Gibbon, vol. V, ch. 43.

other to the death. During the war, around 97,000 people were arrested, of whom 11,000 lost their lives just because their guards did not provide food for them. In addition, the number of people killed during the war and the bloodshed is said to be over 133,749.[5]

Similar barbaric crimes were committed in the wars between the Roman and Persian empires. When Shapur Dhū al Aktāf invaded al Jazira and conquered Amida (currently known as Diyār Bakr) after much resistance from its dwellers, the angry invader entered the city and ordered mass killing. He destroyed the place to the extent that it could never recover. When Anūshirvan attacked Syria in AD 540, he wreaked havoc on the capital city of Antioch. He killed ordinary people mercilessly, demolished their buildings and, finding no satisfaction, set the entire city on fire. In 572, Anūshirvan again invaded Syria and looted and burned Fāmia, Antakya and other cities. He sent 292,000 Syrians to Persia and offered many beautiful young girls to Ilkhan Atrak to appease him and encourage him to abandon Justinian. In AD 576, he attacked Armenia. Having faced resistance from Theodosiopolis, he entered Cappadocia (Qabāziq) and destroyed everything that came his way. He even burned Malaṭiyyah [the English name is also given in the text as Meltine] to ashes. Towards the end of his reign, Khosrow Parviz launched a fierce attack on the Roman empire. Nothing less than hell was wrought upon Syria, Palestine and Asia Minor. The oppression done to Jerusalem has been mentioned earlier. In addition, the treatment meted out to Damascus, Antioch, Aleppo and other cities was no different.[6]

Such barbarism sometimes appears in the form of the worst deception and cowardly plots and conspiracies. There is a famous story of Ardashir. When he could not defeat the Khosrow of Armenia on the battlefield, he dispatched a military officer and assassinated him.[7] Such gruesome acts are not rare in the history of Rome and Iran.

Condition of Prisoners of War

The worst treatment was reserved for the prisoners of war. Ancient Romans and Persians considered all other nations barbarian [English word in text; Urdu *muḥūsh, barābirah*]. Their laws did not offer any

---

[5] Farrar, *Early Days of Christianity*, 488–9.
[6] All these details have been taken from the works of Gibbon, Sykes and Ford.
[7] Sykes, vol. I, 427–8.

options to the wretched prisoners except death or slavery. Even the preachers of ethics, like Aristotle, frankly state that nature has created barbarians for slavery.[8] Elsewhere, he states that one of the natural and permissible means to acquire wealth is to wage war to enslave certain human groups as they are created by nature for this purpose.[9]

On the one hand, such beliefs made the Romans see no value in the lives and possessions of non-Roman nations; on the other hand, Roman society had developed in such a barbaric atmosphere that the people enjoyed witnessing gruesome violence in plays and demonstrations. They would prefer witnessing such scenes in reality, not in allusions and metaphors. When the audience wanted to see a burning house, they would like to have a real house burnt down. Likewise, if there was a need to demonstrate the burning of a person or the gruesome death of a culprit by the jaws of lions, they found satisfaction in a person actually being burnt alive and another being put before the lion cages. Meeting the demand for participants in these inhumane spectacles required individuals who could be sacrificed. Obviously, no free Roman citizen could be put to use in this way. Therefore, prisoners of war were used for this bloody entertainment. Sometimes such sport was held on so large a scale that thousands of prisoners were put to the sword at the same moment. Titus, known as the 'darling of the human race' [English phrase in text; Urdu *nasl insāni kā dulārā*], once gathered over 50,000 beasts in a walled place. Then he put thousands of Jewish prisoners in the same place as the wild beasts. In Trojan sports, over 11,000 beasts and 10,000 prisoners were set to fight simultaneously. Once, Claudius handed over swords to 19,000 men in a war show and made them fight with one another. Caesar Augustus left some writings along with his will. He records that he had witnessed sports involving 8,000 swordsmen and 3,510 beasts. All such entertainment was possible only because of prisoners of war.

Besides this, another use of prisoners of war was that they were forced to become slaves of Roman citizens. In that society, these slaves were the lowest in rank. They had no specific rights. Their lives carried no value. The only purpose of their lives was to serve their masters and fulfil their desires in all conditions. According to Farrar, in their journey from birth to death, they passed 'from a childhood of degradation to a manhood of

---

[8] *Politics*, book 1, ch. 2, vi.   [9] Ibid., book 1, ch. 8.

hardship, and an old age of unpitied neglect'.[10] The Roman laws concerning slaves were so strict that if a slave tried to raise his hand against his master, he, and at times his entire family, was given the death penalty.[11] When the wife of Heraclius, Eudoksia, died soon after her husband's ascent to the throne in AD 611, a slave woman accidently spat on the ground while her dead body was being carried to the graveyard. She was immediately arrested, and orders were issued to behead her.[12]

According to Farrar, once the Roman empire expanded through conquest, a great number of prisoners of war came to the state. At one time, their aggregate number crossed the figure of 60 million.[13]

Similar to Rome, the Persians did not offer any relief to prisoners of war. Not to speak of ordinary prisoners, when the caesar of Rome, Valerian, was arrested by Shapur the First, the Persian king made him walk around the city with his hands tied in chains. He was forced to serve his masters for life like a slave, and, after his death, his skin was peeled off and stuffed.[14] According to a famous legend, in order to take revenge on Arab prisoners of Bahrain and al Ḥasā, Shapur Dhū al Aktāf had commanded the making of holes in the shoulders of the prisoners and threading them with ropes to tie them together.[15] For this very reason, he earned the title of Dhu al Aktāf [Shapur of Shoulders] in history.

These incidents of bloodshed appear more horrific when we learn that such cruelties against human beings were committed not to achieve any great objectives but just to earn fame and demonstrate kingly aggression and power. Sometimes, the blood of hundreds of thousands of people was spilled just to gratify the base personal desires of kings. Even during the era of the Prophet (peace be upon him), when Khosrow Parviz heard about the beauty of Nu'mān bin Mundhir's daughter, he ordered Nu'mān to produce his daughter in the king's court. Nu'mān's Arabian sense of honour did not tolerate this demand, and he refused to send his daughter to be part of the king's harem. In response, Khosrow decreed that the state of Ḥīrah be annexed and Nu'mān be arrested. Nu'mān left his children and wife in the protection of Banī Shaybān and presented himself before the king to seek pardon for his failure. However, the king had him beheaded and sent a powerful military of 40,000 worriers to recover Nu'mān's family from Banī

---

[10] Farrar, *Early Days of Christianity*, 2.   [11] Rev. Cutt, *Constantine the Great*, 57.
[12] *Byzantine Empire*, 99.   [13] Farrar, *Early Days of Christianity*, 2.   [14] Sykes, vol. I.
[15] Sykes, vol. I.

Shaybān. This army had a furious battle with the Arabs at a place called Dhūqār. The two armies lost thousands of their men in battle, and all these precious lives were lost just because the king wanted a beautiful girl sitting next to him.

This brief historical narration illuminates the fact that, during that era, there were no moral limits, rights and obligations of combating armies, tolerance in enmity and a balance between mercy and anger during battle. Indeed, there was no idea of these practices. As far as war is concerned, the most civilized nations were at the initial stage of beastliness and barbarism. During those days, war only meant bloodshed, tumult and plunder, undertaken to fulfil the desire of powerful kings. Hard-heartedness, barbarity and beastliness were the essence of war. The word 'war' brought to mind something that guaranteed bloodshed and the destruction of populations using all possible means. The heedlessness of centuries had so deeply connected war with barbaric activities that nobody could think of a war that did not include plundering, bloodshed, the burning of property, mass destruction and the murder of women, children, elders, patients and injured people. It also necessarily implied sacrilege, and violation of the sanctity of places of worship and the religious relics of other nations and followers of other religions. There was no concept of a war that could be fought with complete adherence to moral limits.

Islamic Reforms

Such was the world where Islam raised the banner of reformation. It changed the reality of war and introduced an entirely different perspective with which the world of that time was not familiar. Islam's idea was that war and bloodshed are, in their essence, a form of oppression that one should try one's best to avoid engaging in. However, when a transgression bigger than this oppression appears on the land in the form of cruelty, tyranny, persecution and corruption, and the transgressors have put the lives and peace of God's creation in danger, it becomes necessary or even obligatory to wage wars to prevent harm.

The Islamic Concept of War

In this Islamic concept of warfare, the primary objective of war is not to kill and harm the opponents. Instead, the sole objective of war is to remove the evil perpetrated by the opponents. Therefore, Islam sets forth the principle that, in war, one should use only that amount of power that is unavoidable for repelling evil. Moreover, this power should be used against only those who are practically involved in fighting or against those who we fear would create evil. Other than these, all classes of that community should be protected from the effects of war. Moreover, war efforts should not extend to those aspects of the opponents which are not associated with their military power. This concept of war was totally different from those occupying the minds of the non-Muslims. For this reason, Islam set aside all the contemporary terms and concepts that described war and coined the concept of jihad for the cause of Allah [*jihād fī sabīl Allāh*]. This term perfectly indicates the objective for which it is coined. It separates jihad [in the path of Allah] from the barbaric conceptions of war. Linguistically, the word *jihād* means making the best effort to do something or achieve an objective. Unlike the term *ḥarb*, jihad does not carry the meaning of anger, plundering and destruction. Nor does it reflect fear or terror, like the term *rowʿ*. It does not signify evil and mischief, like the word *sharr*, nor does it allude to the inhumanity and barbarity denoted by the word *nitāḥ*. Finally, it does not mean hardship and extreme intensity, like the word *karīhah*. In contrast to all these, this term vividly indicates that the true objective of the *mujāhid* is to repel harm. One makes only as much effort as would suffice to prevent harm. However, the term 'effort' [*koshish*] alone could also not convey the intended meaning, because it did not identify the direction of exertions. Efforts can be made in the direction of virtue as well as wrongdoing. For further clarity, the condition of *fī sabīl Allāh*, that is, in the path of Allah, was added. Therefore, jihad cannot include wars waged for the fulfilment of personal desires, the conquest of a country, winning over a woman's company, revenge for personal grudge or the acquisition of wealth, money, authority and fame. The restriction imposed by the addition of *fī sabīl Allāh* dictates that jihad should only apply to a struggle made for the pleasure of God that is completely free of any inclination to personal desires and is waged only to fulfil objectives approved by Allah Almighty.

Under this pure concept, Islam introduced a comprehensive code of conduct for war, which includes the etiquettes of war, its ethical boundaries, the rights and obligations of combatants, and the separation between combatants and non-combatants, as well as the rights of both groups, the rights of allies, representatives, prisoners of war and the subjects of the vanquished nations. Islam established foundational principles for each of these and, when required, introduced applicatory subrules. Furthermore, Islam provided a rich treasure of examples from the life of the Prophet (peace be upon him) and his four guided caliphs as a practical guide to how these general principles are implemented in particular cases.

Purification of the Purpose of War

Islam did not aim merely to provide the entire code of conduct on paper. Instead, the real purpose was to correct the practical flaws and to implement this civilized code of conducting war by eradicating barbaric war strategies. For this purpose, the first requirement was to remove the wrong concept of war that had been firmly fixed in people's minds for centuries. People failed to understand what purpose a war could serve and why a man should sacrifice his life if not for wealth, property, land, country, fame, revenge, group feeling and honour. They could not imagine a war that had nothing to do with personal gains and desires. For this purpose, the first thing the Holy Prophet (peace be upon him) did was to explain the meaning of jihad for the cause of Allah [*fī sabīl Allāh*]. He set the boundaries that distinguish it from jihad for the cause of transgression/evil [*fī sabīl al tāghūt*]. He adopted different techniques to engrave this pure concept of war on people's minds. Many prophetic hadith have been reported about this concept, of which some are mentioned below.[16]

Abu Mūsā al Ashʿarī reports:

> A man came to the Prophet and asked: One man fights for booty, another fights to win fame, and the third fights to show off his bravery. Which of them is fighting in the cause of Allah? The Prophet replied: The War in the cause of Allah is the war of only him who fights so that the Word of Allah be exalted.

---

[16] [Editor's note: Each of the hadith in this section is narrated first in Arabic in Maududi's text.] All the hadith reports included in this chapter have been taken from *Ṣaḥīḥ* of Bukhārī (*Kitāb al Jihād* and *Kitāb al Maghāzī*), *Ṣaḥīḥ* of Muslim (*Kitāb al Jihād wa al Siyar* and *Kitāb al Imārah*), *Sunnan* of Abu Dāwūd (*Kitāb al Jihād* and *Kitāb al Fayʾ wa al Imārah*), *Sunnan* of Nisāʾī (*Kitāb al Jihād*), *Sunan* of Ibn Mājjah (*Abwāb al Jihād*), Tirmidhī (*Abwāb al siyar* and *Abwāb al Jihād*) and *al Muwaṭṭā* of Imām Mālik (*Kitāb al Jihād*).

Abū Mūsā al Ash'arī also narrates:

A man came to the Prophet and asked: O Allah's Messenger! What kind is fighting/killing [*qatāl*] in Allah's cause? Some of us fight out of anger, and some for the sake of his pride over his nation. The Prophet raised his head and responded: He who fights so that Allah's Word should be upheld, he alone fights in Allah's cause.

Abu 'Umāmah Bāhilī narrated:

A man came to the Prophet and said: 'What do you think of a man who fights seeking material reward and fame – what will he have?' The Messenger of Allah said: 'He will not have any reward.' The enquirer found this answer strange. He came again and repeated the same question. The Prophet gave the same answer. The enquirer did not get satisfaction. So, he returned a third and a fourth time and put the same question. In order to satisfy him, the Prophet said: 'Allah does not accept any deed, except that which is purely carried out for his pleasure and agreement.'

'Ubādah bin Ṣāmit narrates that once the Prophet said:

He who fights in God's path but intends to get just a tethering rope for his camel will have no reward other than what he intended.

Mu'ādh bin Jabal reports that the Prophet (peace be upon him) said:

There are two types of battle. The one who fights purely seeking God's pleasure, obeyed the leader [during the battle], spent his wealth and avoided discord [fasād], his staying awake and sleep deserve reward. The one who fights to show off and earn fame, disobeyed the leader [during the battle] and spread corruption in the land, he will not even salvage himself (that is, he will be chastised instead).

Abu Hurayrah reports that the Prophet (peace be upon him) once said:

On the Day of Judgment, the fates of three types of people will be decided first. The first person will be the one who fought and was martyred. God will count His blessings that He showered upon him, and he will confess to having benefited from them. Then, God will ask what he did for Him. The person will reply that I fought for You till I was martyred. God will say: You are lying. You just fought to make people remember you as a brave man. You achieved your objective. Then God will order for him to be punished, and he will be dragged on his face and thrown into hell.

46

'Abdullah bin Mas'ūd narrates that the Prophet (peace be upon him) said:

> On the Day of Judgment, a man will come, holding another man's hand, and will say: O Lord, this man had killed me. Allah will say to him: Why did you kill him? The man will say: I killed him so that glory would be to you. Allah will say: Yes, glory belongs to Me. Then another man will come holding another man's hand and will say: This man had killed me. Allah will say to him: Why did you kill him? He will say: So that the glory would be to so and so. Allah will say: Glory and honour did not belong to him [*haqq tau na thā*]. Then the man will be caught for that sin.

These teachings purify war of all worldly ambitions. War has not been permitted for any worldly purpose, including the desire for fame, yearning for honour and rule, acquisition of wealth and property, greed for booty, appeasing personal or national revenge, or any similar objective. In fact, there is no mundane objective for which war is permissible. Separated from these elements, war remains an unenjoyable and unpleasing moral and religious obligation. Considering the dangers and harms associated with such a war, nobody can possibly ask for it. If others start to persecute, even then, a person will raise his sword only when he has no other option to correct the course and prevent the damage. The Holy Prophet (peace be upon him) himself has said:

> You people must not desire to face the enemy but must ask God for safety and peace. But when you have to meet them, show endurance and know that paradise is under the shadow of the sword.

Purification of the Methods of War

In addition to correcting the objectives of war, the Prophet of Islam also reformed the methods of achieving those objectives. He gradually stopped all the barbaric activities performed during pagan wars. Many prophetic teachings prohibit barbaric activities in totality as well as individually.

Sanctity of Non-combatants

The first thing in this regard is the division of belligerents [English word in text; Urdu *muḥāribīn*] into two groups, combatants [English word in

47

text; Urdu *ahl-e-qitāl*] and non-combatants [English word in text; Urdu *ghayr ahl-e-qitāl*]. Combatants are the people who engage in war in practice or have the power to fight according to reason and custom, such as young men. Non-combatants are the people who cannot be taken to be participants in war rationally and practically or those who generally do not fight. These include women, children, the elderly, sick, injured, blind, crippled, mentally ill, tourists, ascetics in temples and places of worship, the caretakers of places of worship and temples, and other harmless people. Islam has permitted the killing of individuals who fall into the first category and prohibited the killing of persons who belong to the second category.

Once, the Holy Prophet (peace be upon him) saw the dead body of a woman lying on the battlefield. He became angry and said: This woman was not among the fighters. The Prophet sent a message to the leader of the army, Khālid bin Walīd, commanding him not to kill a woman or a hired servant.

According to another report, the Prophet announced a general prohibition on killing women and children.

A hadith report tells us that the Prophet once said:

> Do not kill an old man, or a young child, or a woman. Do not steal from the spoils of war. Whatever you collect in spoils, gather all of it together. Do right and be generous, for God loves those who show generosity.

At the time of the conquest of Mecca, the Prophet had issued commands even before the assault not to attack an injured fighter, not to follow a person who tries to escape and to guarantee the safety of those who sit behind their closed doors.[17]

Ibn 'Abbās narrates that whenever the Prophet sent his armies on an expedition, he would clearly advise them to avoid killing harmless servants of places of worship and the worshippers who seclude themselves and remain within temples.

The jurists of Islam have derived the following general principle from these particular rulings: all such people as are unable to fight or who normally do not participate in war as combatants are exempted from being attacked and killed. However, this exemption is not absolute. Instead, it is conditional that they do not, in fact, participate in the

---

[17] *Fatūh al Buldān*, 47.

battle. If any of them participates in the war – for example, a sick person suggests war strategies to soldiers right from his bed, a woman spies on the enemy to become a recipient of spoils, a child tries to get secret information and a religious person tries to incite people to participate in the war – then killing such persons is not prohibited. It is because such an individual took part in the war as a combatant and deprived himself or herself of the rights granted to non-combatants.

Islamic law on this subject summarizes that anyone who is a combatant can be killed, whether he physically participates or not, and killing any non-combatant is impermissible unless they physically engage in the war or perform such actions as are usually done by combatants.[18]

---

[18] *Al Hidāyah, Bāb Kayfiyyah al Qitāl, Fatḥ al Qadīr*, vol. IV, 290–2, Badā'i' al Ṣanā'i', vol. VII, 101.

War in Other Religions

While researching and defining the plausibility or implausibility of something, the first thing to observe is it in itself. Then, we proceed to analyse it in comparison with other things. It can only be declared worth accepting if it proves better on both counts. From this perspective of research and investigation, we have completed the first phase of inquiry. We now need to undertake the second phase. In this phase of the study, we shall start by comparing Islam with other religions and then compare it with laws of the modern period to investigate how they relate to the Islamic norms. If they permit war, then the question is whether their objectives and methods [English term in text; Urdu *manāhij*] are better or worse than those of Islam. If they prohibit war, are the teachings of these schools in harmony with human nature, or do the teachings of Islam do that?

Principles for the Comparative Study of Religions

In fact, the comparison of religions is a very difficult task. A person with a belief in one specific creed or viewpoint can seldom do justice to the rival creeds and viewpoints. This weakness is a very common trait of human dispositions. Moreover, in religious groups, this weakness has assumed an even worse shape in the form of bias and narrow-mindedness. When followers of a particular religion criticize another religion, they only search for flaws in that religion. They either avoid looking for positive elements in it or, if they manage to find any, deliberately try to avoid pointing them out. Their purpose behind such religious criticism and comparison is not to find the truth but only to defend their stances, which they had already embraced before starting their study. Such a method nullifies all the benefits of a comparative study of religions.

It does not even benefit the religion of the practitioner of such a critique, for which he adopts such an ignorant approach. If the purpose of comparison is nothing more than finding and establishing the truth, then certainly it is not the right approach to adopt a sternly opposing stance about other religions and embark upon this study only with the intention of hiding their positive elements. He seeks to find flaws in them to prove his religion superior to the rest. Such dishonesty and cheating carried out to establish the superiority of one's own religion do not prove one religion better. Such a success does not even earn a true religion any honour. In the eyes of the truth, such a religion cannot become more authentic. If such dishonesty encourages a seeker to embrace that religion, his belief will be entirely untrustworthy, because it would have a false foundation.

In order to reach a correct conclusion in our comparison of religions while avoiding these evils, it is imperative to establish certain principles governing comparison and strictly adhere to them throughout the study. In our opinion, the following should be these principles:

1. In order to prove a religion sound, it is not necessary to conclude that the teachings of other religions are wrong in their entirety. That one religion contains truth and veracity does not necessarily mean that other religions are void of all truth. Truth [*haqq*] is universal, and its particulars remain its integral parts regardless of where they are found. Change in their condition and location does not alter their essence and reality. If a religious truth of Islam is found in another religion, that does not mean either of the two religions is deficient. Therefore, one does not need to cover the truth in the other religion. On the contrary, it means that both religious traditions issue from the same true source and have kept elements of that truth. Therefore, any quantity and form of the truth deserve to be valued. We should not stretch the matter and put all our efforts into making it seem valueless.

2. A person insisting that truth resides in his religion alone, and that there is no trace of truth in any other religious tradition, wrongs not only other religions but also truth itself. The fact of the matter is that the light of truth and righteousness is found in almost every tradition to varying degrees. However, researchers prefer one religion over the others because they view the preferred religion as the perfect manifestation of the truth. Thus, a student of comparative religion should never decide beforehand that all religions except his preferred one are

devoid of the light of truth. Rather, he should appreciate that a mixture of truth and falsehood will appear before him. His task is to use his intellect and discernment to see the truth as truth and falsehood as falsehood, and to distinguish one from the other.

3 While investigating religious traditions, one must specifically avoid the writings of biased opponents and exaggerating followers of a particular religion under study. In preliminary research, a researcher can never come to a sound conclusion by studying the writings of such extremist writers. The reason is that before a person can see the true face of the religion under study, he wears a lens of a certain colour which interdicts his ability to look at the religion's true colours. If this investigation is to reach a sound conclusion, it is necessary to look at the religion not as others see it, but how it manifests itself. Due to this reason, one should study the original sources of each religion to the best of one's ability and, after studying these sources, one should decide, using one's reason, to what extent that specific religion is true and to what extent it is false. Then, when a person has formed his opinion, he may engage in studying the thoughts and opinions of others, because, at this stage, he can easily distinguish between right and wrong.

In the following pages, we discuss the teachings of different religions on war in the light of these three principles. We have made every effort to prove the truth as truth and falsehood as falsehood while removing ourselves from a zealous support for our own religion.

The Four Major Religions of the World

It is not possible to review the teachings on war in every great and small religion there is in this short book. This type of exhaustive study is neither easy nor necessary. Generally, the discussions of comparative religion are limited to the religious traditions acknowledged as the great religions of the world owing to the number of their followers, the extent of their influence, and their past and present greatness. Following this conventional rule, we will confine our discussion to four major religious traditions: Hinduism, Buddhism, Judaism and Christianity.

On the question of war, these four religions divide into two groups, those allowing war and those not allowing it. The first group comprises

Hinduism and Judaism. The second group includes Buddhism and Christianity. We will begin our discussion with the first group.

Hinduism

The first difficulty one finds in discussing this religion pertains to defining what Hinduism is exactly. Hinduism is not a religion in the conventional sense of the word 'religion' [*mazhab*]. It is necessary for a religion to be qualified as one having a central creed on which it is founded. But we cannot find such a central belief in Hinduism. Different classes and groups, each of which has different beliefs, rituals, worships, symbols and holy books, are called Hindus.[1] This is why, when we need a Hindu religious edict on an issue, we find it difficult to decide which subtradition to turn to.

However, this difficulty has lessened to some extent owing to the modern religious inclinations of the Hindus. Though differences among schools and traditions still exist, the Hindus are increasingly inclined to base their religious devotion on a few specific holy books. A great majority recognize these books as the foundation of their religion. These are three books: the Four Vedas, Gita and Manusmriti. Our discussion in this work on Hinduism will be based on these three books.

The Three Periods of Hindu Mazhab

These three books belong to three different historical stages of Hinduism. They present three aspects of Hindu teachings regarding the issue of war. The Vedas belong to the period when the Aryan nation came out of Central Asia, attacked India and warred with the original inhabitants of that country whom they found different in colour, race and religion. What were the feelings of these invaders against their alien

---

[1] Due to this fact scholars and researchers found it difficult to define Hinduism. One scholar says: 'Hinduism is what a Hindu practises' (Guru Parsad Sen, *Study of Hinduism*, 5). Another scholar says: '[Hinduism] is the collection of rituals, worships, beliefs, traditions and idol worship which are sanctioned by the rulings of the Brahmanas and their sacred books and which have been propagated by the Brahminic teachings' (Lyall, *Religious Systems of the World*, 114). Yet another researcher defines it by saying, 'All such people are Hindus: those who do not ascribe to Islam, Jainism, Buddhism, Christianity, Zoroastrianism or any other religious tradition of the world, whose worship spans from monotheism to idol worship, and whose religious discourses are coded exclusively in Sanskrit' (*Census Report*, Baroda, 1901, 120).

enemies? In what way did they see them? What was the reason for their mutual enmity? What were their objectives in the war against them? And how did they like to treat them? The poetic narratives of the Vedas throw sufficient light on these questions.

The Gita is from the time when the Aryans had established their dominance over North India and there was a struggle between two powerful Aryan branches for superiority and domination. This book provides us with the knowledge of Hindu philosophical thoughts on war through the words of such religious leaders of theirs as Krishnji.

Manusmriti is a collection of religious, political and moral laws of the period when India had completely become a country of the Aryans [*Arya Vart*]. Non-Aryan nations had lost power, and the Aryan civilization was at its peak in the country. In this book, we can find details about the rules and regulations of war and the rights and duties of vanquished nations.

The discussion below follows this order of presentation.

Vedic Teachings about War

The word Veda applies to four books, all of which are famous in their distinct titles. The oldest of these is Rigveda, followed by Yajurveda, Samaveda, and the Atharvaveda. It is difficult to thematically organize the hymns of these books because, often, many subjects surface in a single hymn. We will ignore the thematic discussion of the books and quote hymns of each book that relate to war in some way.[2]

Rigveda

The hymns in Rigveda which relate to war issues follow:

> Indra, bring for our protection riches endowing joy, the source of eternal victory of the victor, wealth that may help us. The wealth by which we may repel our enemies, [encountering them] hand to hand.
>
> (1.8.1, 2)

[2] I consult here the English translations of the Vedas produced by Mr Griffith. I have also consulted Max Müller's translations. I regret my lack of knowledge of Sanskrit and resultant inability to read the original books. Our experience with the European translators of the Quran does not allow us to fully rely on them. Therefore, I request scholars to critically see what I write based on these translations of the Vedic poems and intimate to me any mistakes in translation that might have led to incorrect conclusions.

Resplendent Agni, the one invoked by oblations of sacred oil, consume our adversaries, who are defended by evil spirits.

(1.12.5)

Through the protection of (Indra and Varuna), we enjoy riches and heap them up, and still there is abundance. O Indra and Varuna, I invoke your various forms to bestow wealth upon us. Keep us conquering!

(1.17.6–7)

Slay each reviler and destroy him who in secret injures us (probably through magic). O Indra, give us hope of beauteous horses and of kine, in thousands, O most wealthy One!

(1:29:7)

Discern well and differentiate between Āryas and Dasyu;[3] punish the creedless, give them up to him whose grass is strewn (to be offered to the deities).

(1:51:8)

Well pleased with these bright flames and with these Soma drops, take away our poverty with cattle and horses. Due to these drops, O Indra, scatter the Dasyu. May we obtain abundant food freed from their hate. O Indra, let us heap plenteous wealth and food ... We gather the strength of heroes, special source of cattle, rich in steeds.

(1:53:4–5)

---

[3] Dr Rajendralal Mitra seeks to prove, in his work *Indo Aryans*, that the term 'Dasyus' signifies the worthless Aryan tribes (see vol. I, 210). However, a study of the Vedas clearly shows that the Aryan invaders used this term to mean those of the indigenous Indian people with whom they were fighting. It is not my personal understanding. Other students of the Vedas also appreciate this. Griffith writes: 'The name Dasyu is used for the indigenous nations who had hindered the Aryans' migration to India. Later on, the usage extended to cover all the people that did not follow the worship rituals prescribed by the Vedas and specific Brahiminic rituals' (translation of Atharvaveda, vol. I, 9). Professor Bloomfield says: 'During an undefined era, estimated to begin probably by 1,500 BC, or even older times, the Aryan tribes started migrating from the upland of Iran, situated at the north of the Hindu Kush mountains, to southwest Indian lands, that is, the Indus and its tributaries. The aboriginal non-Aryan people of the land, who were called Dasyu to distinguish them from the Aryans, were easily defeated' (*Encyclopedia of Religions*, vol. VIII, 107). Professor McDonald writes: 'The terms Das and Dasyu in Rigveda are generally used to refer to the dark-skinned ancient population defeated by the Aryans' (*Encyclopedia of Religions*, vol. VII, 610). William Crooke writes: 'Great deities are generous gods of their worshippers. These deities lead Hindu Aryans in their combat against the Dasyu or the dark-skinned aboriginals' (*Encyclopedia of Religions*, vol. VI, 691).

So give us, Indra, bliss-increasing glory, give us great sway and strength that conquer people. Preserve our wealthy patrons, save our princes; vouchsafe us wealth and food with noble offspring.

(1:54:11)

O Agni, may your wealthy servants secure food and the rich be endowed with long life! May we win booty in war against our enemies and offer the deities their due share. O Agni, we may, through your support, secure horses through horses, men through men, and the valiant through the valiant.

(1:74:5–9)

The mighty Indra conquered land, sunlight and water, with the help of friends of beautiful colour.[4] May Indra be our protector and may we loot wealth without fear.

(1:100:18–19)

O Indra, you have shattered ninety forts, for Pūru, for Divodāsa your servant, for your worshipper. For Atithigva he, the Strong One, brought Shambara from the mountain down. He distributed the mighty treasures with his strength, parting all treasures. Indra helped his Āryan worshipper in battles, the one who has a hundred helps at hand in every fray.

(1:130:7–8)

O Indra Maghavan, by your support in war of old, may we subdue in fight the men who strive against us, conquer the men who war with us. This day bless him who pours the Soma juice. In this our sacrifice may we divide the spoil, showing our strength, the spoils of war.

(1:132:1)

[Editor's note: some verses have been excluded for brevity.]
You have wrecked seven autumn forts of Das tribes,[5] their shelter. You have slain them and aided Purukutsa.

(6:20:1)

---

[4] The friends of fair and beautiful colour refer to those fair-coloured Aryan tribes that came from Transoxiana and invaded India. In contrast, the aboriginal Indians were people of colour. See Griffith's translation of Rigveda, vol. I, 130.

[5] Just like Dasyu, the term Das is also used to refer to the local Indian people who resisted and fought against the Aryan invaders. Some scholars have sought to prove that Dasyu and Das refer to evil spirits. However, this interpretation needs supportive arguments. According to Griffith, 'this term was originally specifically applied to the evil spirit thought to be the enemies of Indra and humans. Generally, it was used to refer to the barbarian aboriginal people, against whom the earliest Aryans fought' (Griffith's translation of Atharvaveda, vol. I, 172). At another place the same author says, 'these were the

Rulings on War in Manusmriti

The Laws of Manu is the best collection of Hindu religious laws.[6] Its rulings have remained in practice in the Hindu nations and states for about fourteen hundred years. The identity of its author is still unknown. The period of writing of this work is also not yet identified.[7] However, it is an acknowledged fact that the work originates in a period of Aryan history when their civilization had developed and there arose a need for organized laws to manage the affairs of the states. For this purpose, other than Manusmriti, other laws were also composed. However, Manusmriti enjoys domination over all of these writings because the other works are either based on Manusmriti or have been rejected by Hindu clerics as contradicting Manusmriti. Hindu religious literature has a general acceptance of the rule that 'whatever Manu says is sound' and 'any legal code that contradicts Manu's is not reliable'.

barbaric and misshapen locals that the Aryan refugees included in their definition of evil spirits' (Griffith's translation of Atharvaveda, vol. I, 174). It is similar to our use of the term *shaitan* which is used to refer to *djins*. However, when the word *shaiyatīn* is used for those humans about whom we have a poor opinion, then it is clear from the context that the term here refers to humans, not supernatural beings. That the Dasyu were human is indicated in different places within Rigveda. They are referred to as being without religion and areligious in various instances. They do not believe in the Aryan gods, follow alien rules, are bereft of rational thought and have many cattle. They have forts that the Aryans conquer. The most compelling evidence is that they are mentioned as having flat noses, broad jaws and dark colouring. These are the features of Dravidian people even today. Rigveda says, 'O fearless, you have conquered, through magic, these people with jaws as wide as bulls' (7:49:4). At another place it says, 'you have slain the flat-nosed Dasyu with your weapons' (5:29:1). There is a mention of Dasyu being given in slavery: 'Yado and Torwa have given us Devdas to serve us and many cattle' (10:26:10). Then there is the mention of their women being given in slavery, 'We see Tarasdev giving us fifty women as a gift' (8:9:1:36). In the face of these multiple testimonies we don't need to imagine that a reference to Dasyu means evil spirits and not actual human beings.

[6] I have before me two English translations of Manusmriti. Sir William Jones' translation, published by Fort William College, Calcutta, in 1794, and Dr Burnell's English translation of Manusmriti, along with a commentary on the text, which was edited and published by Professor Hopkins in 1894. The first of these works was completed under government direction and is considered to be very authentic.

[7] Sir William Jones maintained that the work was composed between 1250 and 500 BC. Professor Monier dated it to 500 BC. The German Orientalist [*mustashriq*] Johann Tegen believes the correct date of the work is 350 BC. Schlegel believes the book was written around 100 BC. According to Professor Crooke, the work is not older than 200 BC. However, Professor Burnell's research shows that the work was compiled somewhere between AD 100 and 500. Probably a ruler of the Chalukya dynasty had it written to promulgate it as the constitution of his state.

Therefore, in our search for knowledge of the laws of Hinduism we have no better source.

Since this collection of laws was established in a period when the Aryan nation had established their states in India and progress in civilization and culture had taught it the need to follow a specific law in administering their affairs, we find in this book laws and rulings on all necessary aspects of war.

Objective of War

The first question pertains to the objective of war. Manu has not offered a detailed discussion on the subject. However, the following clarifications within it clearly indicate the objective for which war can be waged in Manu's view.

> Those kings who, seeking to outmatch (or slay each other) in battle, fight with the utmost exertion and do not turn back, go to heaven.
>
> (7:89)

> Of the king who is always ready to strike, the whole world stands in awe and fear; let him therefore make all creatures subject to himself even by the employment of force.
>
> (7:103)

> This way when, after having prepared himself for conquest, he should subdue all the opponents by reconciliation and peacemaking or (if they do not accept obedience to him) by other means such as bribes, forming and breaking alliances and military power.
>
> (7:107)

> Of the four means of victory, the learned always prefer using conciliation and military power to expand the empire.
>
> (7:109)

> A king who thus duly fulfils his duties in accordance with the religious edicts may seek to gain countries which he has not yet gained, and shall duly protect them when he has gained them.
>
> (9:251)

> A peculiar duty of the (king following the religion) is conquest, and he must not avoid war.
>
> (10:119)

These verses show that Manu's thoughts on the question of the objective of war do not rise above Krishna's level. He too does not extract any moral objective of war and remains confined to the ambition to have universal rule through expansion of the empire, conquest and the subjugation of countries and neighbouring opposing nations. Just like common mundane men, he sees government and rule as the ultimate objective of the powerful. He encourages the powerful to permanently engage in and use their power in the service of expansion of rule. This idea of the right to rule and use of power cannot emanate from a high moral stance and purification of thought. From the perspective of morality, the blood of humans, the freedom of nations, and the peace and security of peoples have more value than kings' greed for rule. It can never be the requirement of morality to satisfy kings' greed and desire for power. Morality is concerned with the collective welfare and progress of all of humanity. It allows destructive acts like war only in cases when there is no other option left to protect the material, spiritual and moral life of humans at large from greedy powers. However, apparently no Hindu philosopher or law deviser, not just Manu, could access this moral principle. Those who tried to rise above this [material approach] crossed the mean level and touched upon the limit of Ahimsa, a concept that is no less harmful to the collective welfare and betterment of humans than the full allowance of shedding blood. Rather, in practice both approaches lead to the same result, that is, the destruction of nations and the domination of evil and corrupt men.

The Moral Limits of War

However, with respect to the practical aspect of war, Manu has shown significant progress. He has prescribed limits in order to regulate and discipline war. His proposed limits greatly resemble the limits prescribed by Islam. In what follows we quote Manu's rulings verbatim.

> Someone taking part in a battle and fighting with his foes should not strike with weapons concealed, nor with a barbed or poisoned arrow, nor with hot spears.
>
> (7:90)

> Let no (one riding a chariot or horse) strike the one who is on foot, nor a eunuch, nor one who joins the palms of his hands seeking life security, nor one whose hair has become untied, nor one who sits

59

down, nor one who says, 'I am your captive,' nor one who sleeps, nor one who has lost his coat of mail, nor one who is naked, nor one who is disarmed, nor one who looks on without taking part in the fight, nor one who is fighting with another [foe].

(7:91-2)

Remembering the duty of an honourable warrior, he should not kill the one whose weapons are broken, nor one afflicted with sorrow, nor one who has been grievously wounded, nor one who is in fear, nor one who has turned to flight.

(7:93)

Chariots and horses, elephants, parasols, attire (except for the jewellery on it), grain, cattle, women, all sorts of valueless and solid metals (except for gold and silver) belong to him who wins them in the war.

(7:96)

Of these, the part of the valuable things the looting soldier shall present to the king; what has not been taken singly must be distributed by the king among the soldiers.

(7:97)

When he has besieged his foe, let him destroy the kingdom of the foe only after being encamped. He should continue to spoil the rival king's grass, food, fuel and water.

(7:195)

Likewise let him destroy the tanks, ramparts and ditches, and let him assail the foe and alarm him day and night.

(7:196)

When he has gained victory, let him duly worship the gods[8] and honour righteous Brahmins. Let him grant exemptions, and let him proclaim and declare safety from oppression and injustice.

(7:201)

But having fully ascertained the intentions and behaviour of all the (conquered) people, let him place there a relative of the

---

[8] Kullūka, the commentator on Manusmriti, holds that 'gods' in this context refers to the deities of the vanquished nations. However, the word 'Brahmana' in the text indicates that this ruling does not pertain to the gods of the non-Aryan nations. One cannot expect Manu to command the Aryan nations to worship the deities and gods of the non-Aryan nations.

vanquished ruler on the throne, and let him issue specific guidelines to him.[9]

(7:202)

Let him make authoritative the laws of the inhabitants, just as they are stated to be, and let him honour the [new king] and his chiefs with precious gifts.

(7:203)

Some of these rulings certainly cannot be observed on the battlefield. For example, the ruling that a rider may not kill a soldier on foot. If the hair of the enemy comes loose, he may not be attacked. If an enemy has no coat of mail, he should be left alone. A naked, armless, grieving or frightened person should not be killed. When an enemy soldier is fighting with another, he should not be attacked. In such directives, one finds ostentatious morality overshadowing the objective of reform. Therefore, these rulings do not observe a balance between the necessities of war and moral boundaries. It is very much obvious that in the heat of battle a soldier cannot observe these rulings, and if he does follow them, he cannot fight. On the other hand, Manu has sacrificed moral responsi-bility for the purposes of war. For example, the ruling that all the resources of the enemy should be destroyed and the people of the country be left to die of hunger does not match up to moral sensibilities in any aspect. However, collectively, the rulings of Manu are civilized and reflect a disciplined sense of morality that considers the human duties of combatants fighting a battle. It is a sensibility that reaches the higher moral imagination, where it can appreciate that man as a human

---

[9] This ruling is also specifically related to the wars among the Aryan nations (and more correctly Hindu Aryan nations). The reason is that verse 202 is not an independent and isolated statement. Rather, it forms part of the group of instructions running from verse 26 to verse 203. This understanding is supported by other sources as well. Professor Hopkins writes: 'It is interesting to note that both Manu and Vishnu state that when a king has conquered a foreign foe, he shall make a prince of that country (not of his own) the king there, and he shall not destroy the royal race of his foe unless that royal race be of ignoble birth' (*Cambridge History of India*, vol. I, 290 [in English]).
Another expert in the history of ancient India, Professor Havell [in English], a great admirer of Hindu civilization, writes in his history: 'Wars between the different Aryan tribes, as well as struggles with the non-Aryan "barbarians", the Dasyu or Das, were frequent, but as in the former case it was a fixed principle that war should not be made merely for acquisition of territory, and that a conquered Aryan king should not be deposed but should become the tributary of his conqueror, tribal quarrels probably did not greatly disturb Aryan social order' (E. B. Havell, *The History of Aryan Rule in India*, 33).

being owes rights to others, including his enemies, that cannot be set aside in any circumstances. In this regard, Manu's rulings are closer to Islamic teachings on the issue, though they are not so balanced and advanced as those of Islam.

Treatment of Vanquished Nations

It was discussed earlier that Manu's law was compiled at a time when non-Aryan nations had lost their political power. There was not a single state in India to fight against the Aryans. Therefore, it would be fruitless to search for laws of war that regulate the wars between Aryan and non-Aryan nations. During this era all the non-Aryan nations, referred to as Das, Dasyu, Rakshas or Ussar in the Vedas, had either abandoned their settlements and sought refuge in the mountains or had merged with the main population of the country after being defeated and dominated. Collectively, these were all called Shudras. Therefore, what we can learn from Laws of Manu is confined to this: how does Hindu law regulate the treatment of one Hindu group by another Hindu group? These laws do not tell us anything about how the non-Aryan vanquished nation should be treated by the conquering Aryan nation. In order to learn about such guidance, we need to study Manu's rulings about the treatment of the Shudras.

1 Manu declares Shudras to be a low class by their nature. They are not low due to their actions. Rather they are lowly merely because of their low birth:

> The Lord created Brahmana from his mouth, the Kshatriya from his hand, the Vaisya from his thighs, and the Shudra from his foot.[10] [More examples follow in the original text.]

2 Manu considers Shudras impure, filthy and mean in nature. He commands the twice-born castes, that is, the noble Aryan castes, to avoid contact with these:

> A Brahmana who takes a Shudra wife to his bed will sink into hell (3:17).

---

[10] The same theme has been mentioned in Rigveda (10:9:12) and Bhagavata Purana (2:5:37).

He who explains the sacred law to a Shudra or teaches him the performance of religious rites and rituals will sink together with that Shudra into the hell called Asamvrita (4:81).

Let him not recite the Veda texts in the presence of Shudras[11] (4.99).

Let him not take the food of a Shudra[12] (4:211).

If there is no one from the caste of the dead Brahmana, his corpse may not be carried by a Shudra because the rituals of passages defiled by a Shudra's touch cannot proceed to heaven (5:104).

The offspring of a Shudra man and a Vaisya, Kshatriya or Brahmana female will be mixed race. They will be called, correspondingly, an Ayogava, a Kshattri and a Chandala, and all of these are the lowest of human creation (10:12).

But the dwellings of Chandalas and Svapakas shall be outside the village. They must not use unbroken utensils. Their wealth shall be dogs and donkeys. Their dress shall be the garments of the dead. They shall eat their food from broken dishes. Their ornaments must be of iron. They must always wander from place to place like nomads. A man who fulfils his religious and mundane duties shall not interact with them. Their relations should be confined among themselves. They may marry only with their equals.

3 Manu forces the Shudra to slave for the twice-born castes. According to him, it is the natural and birth duty of a Shudra to serve the twice-born:

The Almighty has assigned only one occupation to the Shudra: he should serve, without hesitation, these castes [Brahmana, the Kshatriya and the Vaisya] (1:91).

A Shudra, though emancipated by his master, is not released from servitude; since that is innate within him, who can set him free from it?

(8:414)

---

[11] 'A Shudra who by choice hears the Vedas being recited, molten metal should be poured into his ears. If he recites the Vedic text, his tongue should be cut off. If he memorizes it, his body must be slashed and cut into two' (Gautam, 12:4–6).

[12] 'Food prepared by a Shudra, regardless of whether he has touched it or not, is prohibited' (Apistamha, 1:5:16–22). 'If a Brahmana dies while having some food in his stomach prepared by a Shudra, he will rise to life as a swine in the next incarnation' (Vasishtha, 6:27). 'If a Brahmana is touched by a Shudra, the former should leave the food' (Apistamha, 1:5).

4 Manu refuses to grant Shudras the right to possess even the wealth and property they earn rightfully:

> A Brahmana may confidently seize the goods of his Shudra slave; for, as that slave can have no property, his master may take his possessions (8:417).
>
> Even if a Shudra is able to earn wealth and property, he may not make collection of wealth; for a Shudra who has acquired wealth gives pain to Brahmanas (10:129).

5 Manu severely discriminates between the twice-born castes and Shudra in devising laws of inheritance. In some cases, he completely deprives the Shudra of the right of inheritance. In other instances, he gives the Shudra a share lesser than that granted to the twice-born.

If there be four wives of a Brahmana in the direct order of the four castes, the rule for the division of the estate among the sons born of them is as follows: the tillers, workers, the bull kept for impregnating cows, horses for riding, and the vehicles, the ornaments and the house shall be given to the Brahmana son. After setting this share aside, he shall again have an additional share owing to his noble caste.

Of the remaining property, the Brahmana's son shall take three shares, the son of the Kshatriya two, the son of the Vaisya a share and a half and the son of the Shudra may take one share.

Alternatively, someone who knows the law makes ten shares of the whole estate, and distributes them according to the following rule:

The Brahmana (son) shall take four shares, the son of the Kshatriya wife three, the son of the Vaisya shall have two parts and the son of the Shudra may take one share.

Whether that [deceased] Brahmana has sons or has no sons by wives of the twice-born castes, the heir must, according to the law, give to the son of a Shudra wife no more than a tenth part of his estate.

The son of a Brahmana, a Kshatriya and a Vaisya by a Shudra wife receives no share of the inheritance; whatever his father may give to him, that shall be his property.[13]

---

[13] The content of this verse clearly contradicts the statement of the previously mentioned verse. The commentators (Kāluka and Medhātithi) have realized this contradiction. They explain it away by saying that the share of the Shudra woman's son depends on his actions. He can have a share if he is righteous and his mother was properly wed by his father.

All the sons of twice-born men, born of wives of the same caste, shall equally divide the estate (9:149–56).

6 In the criminal laws, Manu becomes particularly hard upon the Shudras. He is extremely miserly in granting legal protection to Shudras' life and honour. In comparison, he is very generous in ascertaining and granting the rights of the twice-born and protecting them. As a result, the legal status of the Shudras falls to almost nothing.

> If a Shudra insults a twice-born man with gross invective, he shall have his tongue cut out; for he is of low origin (8:270).
>
> If he blasphemes against the twice-born by their names and castes, an iron nail, ten fingers long, shall be thrust red-hot into his mouth (8:271).
>
> If he arrogantly teaches Brahmanas their duty, the king shall cause hot oil to be poured into his mouth and into his ears (8:272).
>
> A low-caste man [that is, Shudra] who tries to place himself on the same seat as a man of a high caste [Brahmana] shall be branded on his hip and be banished, or the king shall cause his buttock to be gashed (8:281).
>
> A Shudra who has illicit intercourse with a woman of a twice-born caste, and the woman is unmarried, he loses the [body] part used in the offence and all his property. If the woman is married, then the offender shall be deprived of everything, including his life (8:374).

Racial Distinctions (nasli imtiaz)

Today, some Hindu writers, under the pressure of modern thinking, have declared that the division of castes is not by virtue of birth or race but on the basis of virtue and actions. Indeed, if it had been that, it would have given us much pleasure. But sadly this is not a claim supported by the original books on Hindu law in both letter and spirit. From these, what is apparent is that the Hindu religion has the least concern with virtue and actions. The stratification here is not on what we do but on the caste we are born into.

Initially, the local people were known as Das and Dasyu and later came to be called Shudras, not on account of their actions but only because they were non-Aryans. A glance at the laws of inheritance, and criminal and social laws mentioned above, will make this fact obvious. We can observe that the most pious and righteous of Shudras do not possess the rights that a Brahmana, who might conduct himself most disgracefully, does. The Brahmana's son, born of a Shudra woman, regardless of his abilities and righteousness of character and actions, does not have rights equal to his brother, born of his father's Brahmana wife. A Brahmana mother's child born of a Shudra father, on the other hand, will be termed a Chindal just on account of his birth and would have to go through life in the disgraceful conditions reserved for the Chindals, according to Manu. Why should this be so? Is this linked to anything they have done? Does being born a Shudra's son naturally make a person guilty of moral turpitude, and being born of a Brahmana naturally righteous? This in fact is not discrimination on account of character or conduct. It is outright racial discrimination at its worst. The righteousness or immorality of a person and his status in life have been predetermined on account of his lineage, not his conduct.

In this regard Manu himself has been quite lucid and states:

> A person born of a righteous man and an ignoble woman has a chance of becoming righteous by his conduct. However, a person born of an ignoble father and a respectable woman will always remain disgraceful.
>
> (10:67)[14]

> Like the growth of a tree of high quality is dependent on the quality of the seed and the land it is planted on, only the man born of a respectable father and respectable mother can attain the status of a full-fledged Dawaij.
>
> Brahma has himself judged that those Shudras who act righteously, as the Dawaij should, and the Dawaij who act in the lowly fashion of the Shudra are neither equal nor unequal. That is, the degree of the respectability of their actions does not change their status, but neither are the actions of both such that they cannot be compared.
>
> (10:73)[15]

---

[14] He can never attain the full status of respectability equal to the person born of parents of respectable lineage. See Manu, 9:149–56 and 11:127.

[15] Inequality in status means that the Shudra and the Dawaij will remain at the same level in society, as was preordained. The righteous actions of a Shudra are no doubt more

After consideration of the above, none can deny that the stratification of humanity in the Hindu religion is based on racism and not on our actions.

Modern commentators have even tried to establish that Shudras are not the non-Aryan locals but, in fact, lower-ranking members of the Aryan race. Unfortunately, in the light of scholarly research, this claim remains unacceptable. No doubt, Aryans who had been expelled from their caste and society for violation of religious edicts were counted among the Shudras.[16] However, in general the title Shudra is reserved for those of the local inhabitants who chose not to seek refuge in the mountains but accepted subservience to the Aryan conquerors. Historical and linguistic research has in fact established that Shudra was the name of the Indian tribe that the Aryans overpowered first, in the Valley of Attock. After that, whichever tribe in India accepted subservience to them were called by this name, and those who remained fighting were called Dasyu and Malich.[17]

One of the basic Brahmanic teachings is 'Brahmana is a caste born of gods, while Shudras are born of the evil spirits'.[18]

This saying removes all doubt that Shudras are considered the progeny of evil spirits. Scholars of ancient Indian history are in agreement with this interpretation. Some of the scholarly conclusions are reproduced here.

Raguzan writes:

> This is to differentiate between the Aryans and Dasyu; we are aware of the former, of the latter we have reached the conclusion that they were the local non-Aryan inhabitants and no one else. These were the people that the Aryan immigrants found when they came to India. These were the people brought down after extended warfare to a very ignoble condition. There is very little doubt that it is here that the caste formation initially started. The present-day division of Hindus into Dawaij and Shudras bears a striking resemblance to the original differentiation.

respectable than the unrighteous actions of a Dawaij. Thus, some actions can be superior to other actions, but some actors cannot be superior to other actors.
[16] *Vedic Index of Names and Subjects*, vol. II, 265 and 393 [in English].
[17] Wilson, *Indian Castes*, vol. I, iii [in English].
[18] Muir, *Sanskrit Texts*, 14 [in English].

Apart from anything else, the word 'waran' has been used in the context of caste difference in the Sanskrit language. The word means 'colour', and later we will see that this differentiation based on colour, between the fair-skinned Aryans and dark-skinned Shudras, has been oft repeated in the Vedic poems. Moreover, the word 'Dasyu', with the many changes it has undergone, tells us a tale in itself. This is an ancient Aryan word, which the Persians used in its original meaning, to depict a nation or group ... In India, it took on the meaning of 'enemy'.[19] Then the word progressed to assume the meaning of 'evil spirits' or 'ghosts' in the Vedic discourses of the supernatural, and generally it began denoting the evil forces of darkness and famine. Inder was always ready to combat these evil forces with the powers of light. This adoption of the word 'Dasyu', though natural and logical, creates some complexity in the interpretation of Vedic texts. Wherever, in Vedic words, Inder is requested to rid the Aryans of the Dasyu, and to kill them, or where it is stated that 'Inder put an end to the Dasyu', it is often difficult to determine which enemy is intended, and whether it is a real or an imagined one.

In a last twist to its meaning, the word just indicated a servant or slave. With a little alteration of the word itself, it became 'das', that is to say, a slave or a servant. In this way, the process of changes in the word indicates to us the journey to complete Aryan victory over the locals. The word itself became close in meaning to the term 'Shudra'. Accordingly, the correct sequence of the equivalence follows this pattern:

Aryans – Dasyu = Dawaij – Shudras

If further evidence is required to confirm that the Shudra race was made into a caste of servants through conquest, we should refer to the collection of the Laws of Manu. In Manu's laws, it is declared that a Dawaij should under no condition accept the servitude of a Shudra, even though the Shudra be a raja. In this, the Shudra raja can be no other than of local origin.

Although the terms 'Aryan-Dasyu' or 'Das', 'Dawaij' and 'Shudra' follow a pattern, it is incorrect to assume that Shudras or Dasyu were any particular race. In fact, these terms apply to all races that were not Aryan. Just like the Romans or Greeks termed as Barbarians [English word in text] all those who were 'not them'.[20]

---

[19] In the Arabic language, too, the use of the word 'nation', without qualification, often denotes 'enemy nation'.
[20] *Vedic India*, 282–5 [in English].

Professor Rapson writes:

The poets of Rigveda were not thinking of the limited meanings of caste that those terms have acquired now. They only knew that there were different classes (*tabqat*) of humans. The religious class known as 'Brahmanas', the ruling and fighting class that is Rajnia or Kashtris, the tillers of land the Vesh, and those who served, known as Shudras. There was a huge gap between the first three and the last class. The highest class is of Aryans and the lowest of the conquered Dasyu. The difference between these is in colour (*waran*). Generally, the Aryans were fair-coloured and the Dasyu dark-coloured.[21]

Dr Bradel Keith writes:

The big and important difference between the Aryans and the Dasyu was in colour. One of the main factors behind the Hindu caste system is the 'Arya Waran' and the dark colour. The over-powering of the dark-skinned and forcing them into subservience was one of the most important undertakings of the Vedic Hindus ... Although Rigveda mention wars and advances against the Dasyu and the capturing of new lands, it is confirmed that the Aryans did not attempt a total eradication of the locals. Some of the local inhabitants fled into the mountains of the Northwest, and took refuge there, but others (who remained there) were enslaved.[22]

Professor Hopkins writes:

The Shudra slaves had been accepted as a part of the total social structure. The name itself indicates that they were a part of a conquered nation. Just as the word 'Karian' [English word in text] came to mean slave in ancient Athens, similarly the word Shudra assumed the meaning of slave. The Shudras, however, were not pariahs, that is, they were not exempt from the collective. They came to be included in the domestic affairs of the home and were also included in certain domestic functions.[23]

The same writer later writes:

If we compare Gautam's ruling (12:2) regarding the situation where an Aryan woman has an illicit relationship with a Shudra man, with

---

[21] *Cambridge History of India*, vol. I, 54 [in English].
[22] *Cambridge History of India*, vol. I, 84–6 [in English].
[23] *Cambridge History of India*, vol. I, 234 [in English].

the ruling of Apsthumbh Dharm shastar (2:26, 20, 27 and 9), we find ample proof of the belief that the Aryans were a superior race to the dark-coloured people ... Mr Ketkar has been a little careless in his book, *The History of Caste Divisions in India* [sic] (p. 82), where he states that there 'appears to be no racial difference between the Aryans and Dravidians'. It is true that those people who were expelled from their castes and their society were thereafter not called Aryans. But no Shudra has ever become an Aryan. The Aryan race has, since the period of Rigveda till much later, been the proponent of this racial discrimination.[24]

From studying these pieces of evidence it becomes amply clear that, in Hindu law, those who have been termed Shudras are actually the vanquished non-Aryan nations. Therefore, the laws prescribed for them in the books of Hindu religious texts and the attitude of the Hindu *dharam* [moral obligations] demonstrate the attitude of the conqueror in relation to the vanquished.

Judaism

Searching for and researching the Jewish laws is not of the same level of difficulty as we face in finding out the Hindu laws. We can find out the Jewish teachings and laws from a single book, the Torah. Judaism in its true colours can be accessed from the Torah alone. The Jewish scholars from later periods of time have penned many works containing the Jewish law. These works predominantly discuss the details. Examples include 'Aqībah b. Yūsuf's Mishnah and Midrash, written during the second century of the Christian era. Similarly, the Talmud, which combines the Mishnah and Gemara, was written in the sixth century AD. The Halakha, by Isaac Alfasi, completed in the eleventh century AD, is considered the best commentary on the Talmudic laws. Mūsā Maymūnī's (Maimonides) Mishnah Torah was written during the late twelfth century AD. Ya'qūb b. Ashhar's Ṭūr is a work of the fourteenth century AD. Shulchan Aruch, by Joseph Karo, was penned during the sixteenth century AD. In all these works, the Jewish laws are compiled in the light of the ancient tradition. However, it is not at all beneficial to argue on the basis of these works, because these works do not contain any such thing as is agreed upon by all the Jewish sects. Nor does any of these books hold such significance that it

---

[24] *Cambridge History of India*, 246 [in English].

can be considered the basis and foundation of the Jewish religion. Moreover, at times the Jews themselves express distrust in these books and refuse to accept anything other than the Torah. For example, in a session held in Indianapolis in 1905, the Central Conference of American Rabbis openly rebelled against the universalization of the religious laws. Therefore, we set these works aside and base our study of the Jewish views on war on the teachings of the Torah.[25]

Objective of War

The Torah mentions war very abundantly and enjoins fighting frequently. Yet we do not find any trace of the objectives of war other than

---

[25] It needs to be appreciated that our statement about the teachings of the Torah here does not pertain to the Torah revealed to Moses (peace be upon him). Rather, our statements refer to the Torah which exists as the Old Testament [in English in text] in the world today. Our research shows that the Pentateuch [In English in text] of the Old Testament does not correspond to the original Torah. The original Torah is no longer extant. This idea is affirmed by the Old Testament itself, which tells us that Moses (peace be upon him), with the help of Joshua (peace be upon him), compiled the Torah towards the end of his life and put it in a box [Deuteronomy 31:24–7]. After his death, when, during the sixth century BC, Nebuchadnezzar [Urdu *Bakht Nasr*] set the Sacred House on fire, the sacred box was burnt, along with hundreds of other books compiled by the reformers of Moses' sharia. About two or two and a half centuries after this incident, the Prophet 'Uzayr (according to the Biblical account), with the help of Israelite Levites and prophets, compiled the book a second time based on divine inspiration (Drawson, vol. II, ch. 14). However, the accidents of time did not allow this new script to survive in its original form. Alexander's great international conquests not only spread Greek (Latin) [Urdu *ūnānī*] rule over the Near East, it brought with it the Greek (Latin) disciplines of knowledge and tradition. Therefore, in 280 BC, all the books of the Torah were translated into Greek (Latin). Gradually, the original Hebrew material was abandoned, and the Latin translation gained currency. So the Torah in our hands is not directly traceable back to the Prophet Moses [peace be upon him]. However, by no means does this imply that the current Torah contains no part of the original book or that it is wholly fabricated. What we want to say is that the current version of the Torah contains a mixture of the original and many other things. There is a chance that some parts of the original have been lost. A reader who studies the Torah with the eye of a researcher will clearly discern that in this version the word of God is mixed with the interpretations of Jewish scholars, the national history of the Israelites, the legal deductions of the Israelite jurists and many other things. It is difficult to separate it from the original divine speech. We also want to clarify that, according to the Quran, the religion of the Torah is the same as that which the Quran presents. Moses, peace be upon him, was a prophet of Islam like the Prophet of Islam, Muhammad, peace be upon him. Israelites were originally followers of the religion of Islam. Subsequently, they altered the original religion according to their desires, adding things to it and deducting others. This is how they introduced a new religion called Judaism. Therefore, our discussion here pertains to this Judaism rather than the religion brought by Moses, peace be upon him.

71

the one described in Deuteronomy 2 and Numbers 33. The objective of war has been described thus in Numbers:

> On the plains of Moab by the Jordan across from Jericho, the Lord addressed Moses saying: 'Speak to the Israelites and say to them: "When you cross the Jordan into Canaan, drive out all the inhabitants of the land before you. Destroy all their carved images and their cast idols and demolish all their high places. Expel the inhabitants of the land and settle in it, for I have given you the land to possess, so take possession of it."'
>
> (Numbers 33:50–4)

In Deuteronomy we find:

> Set out now and cross the Arnon canal. See, I have given into your hand Sihon the Amorite, king of Heshbon, and his country. Begin to take possession of it and engage him in battle.
>
> (Deuteronomy 3:24)

> But Sihon, king of Heshbon, refused to let us pass through. For the Lord your God had made his spirit stubborn and his heart obstinate in order to give him into your hands, as it is now. The Lord said to me, 'See, I have begun to deliver Sihon and his country over to you. Now begin to possess his land so that you be its owner.' Then Sihon and all his army came out to meet us in battle at Jahaz. The Lord our God delivered him over to us and we struck him down, together with his sons and his whole nation. At that time we took all his towns and killed all the men, women and children. We left no survivors except the livestock that we captured from the towns as booty for us and wealth that we had captured in the towns.
>
> (Deuteronomy 2:30–5)

> Next, we turned and went up along the road towards Bashan, and Og, king of Bashan, with his whole army marched out to meet us in battle at Edrei. The Lord said to me, 'Do not be afraid of him, for I will deliver him into your hands, along with his whole people and his land. Do to him what you did to Sihon, king of the Amorites, who reigned in Heshbon.'
>
> So, the Lord our God also gave into our hands Og, king of Bashan, and all his people. We struck them down, leaving no survivors. At that time, we took all his cities ... We completely destroyed them, as we had done with Sihon, king of Heshbon, destroying every city – men, women and children. But all the livestock and the plunder from their cities we carried off for ourselves.
>
> (Deuteronomy 3:1–7)

These passages clearly say that the objective of war in the Torah is territorial conquest. The Torah holds it allowable to subjugate the inhabitants of a country by the sword and possess their wealth, property and life through power. According to the Torah, this subjugation and occupation are the meaning of the inheritance of the land which God Almighty promised to the Israelites. [The Quran says:]

> The earth shall be the inheritance of My righteous servants.
>
> (Q 21:105)

On another occasion, He says:

> Surely the earth is God's and He bequeaths it to whom He will among His servants. The ultimate success will go to the god-fearing.
>
> (Q 7:128)

However, this perception of inheritance is entirely different from the one proposed in the Torah. As is clear from Numbers 33:50, the Torah deems the earth to be the inheritance of the Israelites. On the contrary, the Quran does not give this right to a particular nation. Rather, in it, the right of inheritance [of the earth] belongs to the pious. The meaning of inheritance of the earth as depicted in the Torah is that one nation possesses the dwellings, property, wealth, life and honour of another nation, and that it destroys the other nation and settles in its place. The Quranic understanding of the inheritance of the earth is that God has selected a people, owing to their righteousness, to be His deputies and representatives. They are made responsible for the management of worldly affairs on His earth. Their duty is to uproot oppression and transgression and replace them with a just and equitable system. Secondly, the Torah commands fighting for possession of the land. However, the Quran does not state anywhere that such-and-such a country is your national inheritance and therefore you should go, fight and conquer it. Thus the 'inheritance of the land' in the Torah is an open form of occupation of the land. Contrary to Islam's concept of jihad in the name of Allah, war in the Torah is fought merely for the sake of obtaining wealth and land and establishing the superiority of one nation over others.

****

The Impact of Ahimsa on Followers of Buddhism

As a result of the teaching of Buddhism, this religion failed to establish a powerful civilization in the world. It never gained such power as could enable it to defeat any civilization and bring it under its influence. No doubt Buddhism impacted a negative change in the moral life of the countries it reached. However, it failed to change and replace their political approaches and civilizational system with a new one. Nor did it try to affect such a change. Undoubtedly Buddhism spread in the world. The rise it enjoyed in Central Asia [Urdu: *sharq-e-awsat*] and the Far East [Urdu: *sharq-e-aqṣā*] could not be parallelled by any other religion. The human populations embraced it in such great numbers that the followers of this religion, even today, exceed any other religion in the world. However, there is not a single example in history to show that Buddhism caused a major revolution within a nation or that a Buddhist nation has any major achievement to its credit. In contrast, we notice that wherever it struggled against a powerful civilization, it was badly defeated. India, the birthplace of Buddhism, remained its follower for a long time. During the first century AD, almost the entire population was following this religious tradition. During the third century AD, more than three-fourths of the population was Buddhist. When Fa-Hien travelled to India during the fourth century AD, Buddhism was on the rise in the country. But as the Brahmanic religion gained salience, Buddhism had to give way within three centuries. Subsequently, Buddhism came to an end in India. Today, we see that among the 32 million-strong population of India, there are only three to four lac [3–400,000] Buddhists.[26] Similarly, Buddhism flourished in Afghanistan owing to Ashoka's influence. During the second century AD, the king of Kabul, Mināndar or Mlindā, converted to Buddhism.[27] However, when this religion faced the powerful civilization of Islam, it could not survive for a moment. The survival and establishment of

---

[26] Rhys Davids discusses the causes of the downfall of Buddhism in India in his work *Buddhist India*. He seeks to establish that the followers of the Brahmanic religion did not uproot Buddhism by the sword. If we accept this explanation, that would prove the weakness of Buddhism even more. A tradition that is destroyed by the sword means that the uprooted tradition lacked material power. However, going extinct without being attacked by the sword and giving way in a peaceful struggle clearly means that the vanquished religion, that is, Buddhism, was intellectually weak against Brahmanic religion.

[27] Smith, *Early History of India*, 225.

Buddhism in China were due to the support of Taoism [English word in text]. Otherwise, Confucianism would have almost destroyed it in that land.[28] In Japan, Buddhism had to be reconciled with Shintoism after much give and take. In its struggle with Shintoism, Buddhism had to change its basic beliefs to survive the opposition.[29] As for the other countries, for example, Ceylon, Burma, Tibet, etc., there was no powerful civilization that could oppose Buddhism. Therefore, the religion spread there. However, history witnessed that this religion did not infuse the spirit of culture and civilization in any of these countries during any era. They remained as lifeless and unmoved during the Buddhist era as they were previously.

Moreover, it is an undeniable fact that nowhere did Buddhism dare to confront the rulers and mend the corrupt system of society. In Buddhist ideology, there is no place for politics. The religion commands obedience to the rulers rather than taking part in government or changing it for the better. This command applies regardless of whether the ruler is oppressive or just.[30] Not only this, it also teaches such humility and humbleness before Satanic powers and bearing of oppression that no staunch follower of Buddhism can say a word against the harshest form of oppression. This religion dictates that all the trials and tribulations a man suffers in this life are the result of his sins in the previous life. Therefore, when someone wrongs a Buddhist, the victim should appreciate that the oppressor is not guilty. Instead, the Buddhist himself is the cause of the infliction, as he must have committed such a sin in the previous incarnation that it led to the current punishment.[31] This religious belief kills all sense of honour and retaliation and creates in a believer such a passive state that he readily swallows every kind of humiliation and every form of oppression.

There is no doubt that there is nothing more welcome to the oppressive state than such a religion. Such a religion does not pose oppressive powers any threat. Rather, it lends strength to the oppressive regime. A subject accepting such a belief can be very easily forced to bow before every sort of oppressive law and injunction. This subject can be looted through every form of taxes and bribes. Their life, wealth and honour can be attacked in any way. They can be put to serve any kind of Satanic wishes of the oppressive rulers. This is the reason that Buddhism has

---

[28] Hackman, *Buddhism as a Religion*, 83.   [29] Hackman, *Buddhism as a Religion*, 90–1.
[30] *Vinaya Texts*, part I, 301.   [31] *Buddha and His Religion*, 150–1.

rarely needed to confront governments. Instead, in most countries, the rulers supported it rather than opposed it. Immediately after the preaching of Buddha, Bimbisara, the king of Magadha, embraced him with great zeal and issued a royal injunction favouring Buddhism.[32] Ajatashatru, his son and successor, was also a believer in and a warm supporter of Buddha. The king of Kosala, called Pasenadi (Agni Datt), invited Buddha to his kingdom and accepted his creed. To strengthen his relations with Buddha, Pasenadi married a Sākya woman.[33] Traditions reveal that Avanti-Putta, king of Sūrasenas, and another king from Eleyya were also disciples and supporters of Buddha.[34] When we go beyond this era and look at the third century BC, we see that Ashoka protected this religion and used all the royal means and resources to spread Buddhism to the corners of India and far-off countries. During the first century AD, King Kanishka earnestly supported this religion. Subsequently, during the third century AD, Wikrmajit I protected and strengthened Buddhism even though he himself followed the Brahmanic religion. During the seventh century AD, Buddhism obtained support from another powerful king, Harash. He supported the religion so vehemently that the followers of Brahmanic religion initiated a secret plan to assassinate him.[35] Outside India, Qublai Khan from Tibet and Mongolia invested all his power in propagating this religion. He believed that this religion was useful for him in political terms.[36] The Chinese king Mang Ti invited Buddhist priests to his kingdom and came forward to welcome them.[37] Many Chinese kings after him supported this religion. The same remained the case with other countries, the circumstances of which can be better appreciated after thorough historical research.

To conclude, the propagation Buddhism enjoyed in this world and the fact that it survived continuous revolutions over the centuries are not owing to this religious tradition having a specific, powerful civilization or its life energy being so strong. Instead, the reason for its survival lies in the fact that it surrenders before coercive political power. It has never tried to face oppression squarely. It never thought of liberating humans from the oppressive clutches of the rebellious rulers, never mind being practically involved in such an effort. Therefore, governments always

---

[32] *Vinaya Texts*, part I, 136–97.   [33] *Buddhist India*, 10–11.   [34] *Buddhist India*, 16.
[35] Smith, *Early History of India*, 349.   [36] *Buddhism as a Religion*, 73–4.
[37] *Buddhism as a Religion*, 177.

supported it and found its presence useful to maintain their power and coercion.

The above brief comment brings to light the difference between Islam and Buddhism on the issue of war. In the sight of Islam, every human being has been created for a great purpose. His success in the afterlife lies in being able to deal with the world in the best possible way. Therefore, Islam commands every human being to adopt such an approach, which is necessary and useful for the moral and material success of his fellow humans and of himself, and is better for the best management of worldly life. In contrast, Buddhism does not see any objective to human life. For this religion, a man's success lies in cutting himself off from all worldly relations, and even from his own self. Therefore, Buddhism does not allow its followers to engage in any such practical effort or mental engagement that can lead to his interaction with any aspect of the world. Now sound intellect can appreciate whether Islam's jihad or Buddhism's Ahimsa is useful for humanity.

Christianity

The other religion that has a fundamental difference with Islam on the question of war is Christianity.[38] The source of our knowledge about this religion, along with Judaism, is a single book which all the Christian world believes to be the foundation of their religion. This book is the Gospels. However, before we turn to the book to know about its stance on the question at hand, it is necessary to explain that, from the current form of the Gospels, we can learn only the beliefs of the current Christian faith. As for the question about the original teaching of Jesus Christ, that cannot be solved on the present form of the book. Since a proper understanding of the following discussions rests on this proposition, it is imperative to cast a look at the historicity of the Gospels.

---

[38] In fact, Christianity does not refer to the religion which Jesus (peace be upon him) had taught. Rather, it is the religion which is ascribed to Jesus (peace be upon him). We have strong arguments to prove that Jesus did not teach Christianity we currently know. Rather, Jesus brought with him the religion of Islam which all the previous Messengers had taught, and which was later preached by Muhammad, peace be upon him. Below we will discuss a few such arguments. Here we intend to make it clear that our discussion on Christianity is not related to the real religion of Jesus. Rather, it rests on the religion which has been carved in the name of Jesus.

Research regarding Sources

The collection of books which we now call the Gospels consists of the four major books, Matthew, Mark, Luke and John. However, none of these is the writing of Jesus Christ. We do not find the revelations sent by God upon Jesus collected in a single book, the way the Quran contains all the verses revealed by God and their surahs, which were revealed to the Messenger (peace be upon him). We do not find the original addresses and advice of Jesus, which he delivered on different occasions during his prophetic mission, in his own words. The books that we have are neither the speech of God nor of the Prophet Jesus. Rather, in their origins, these Gospels are the books of the disciples of Jesus or, more correctly, the disciples of His disciples, in which the authors have tried to collect the events of the Prophet's life and his teachings, according to their own understanding and knowledge.

But these books are of so unknown an origin that we cannot put much reliance upon them. The first Gospel is attributed to Jesus' disciple Matthew. It is historically proven that the book is not the writing of Matthew. The original work of Matthew, called Logia [English name in text], is no longer extant. The book attributed to Matthew is the writing of some unknown author. This unidentifiable person penned this book using the sources available to him, including Logia. The book mentions Matthew in the third person.[39] Moreover, a careful study of the Gospel of Matthew shows that it is based on Mark's Gospel. This is clear because out of the total of 1,068 verses, 470 are the verbatim reproduction of Mark's Gospel. But if this book had been authored by Matthew, he would not have needed to rely on the work of Mark, who was not a companion of Jesus (peace be upon him) – nor had he ever met him. If it was authored by Matthew, the disciple of Jesus, he would not need recourse to the work of a man who was neither a disciple nor had he met Jesus ever. The scholars of Christian studies believe that the Gospel of Matthew was penned around AD 70, about forty-one years after Jesus, and, according to others, it was written in AD 90.

The second book is attributed to Mark. It is generally accepted that it is in fact the writing of Mark. However, it is historically established that

---

[39] Matthew 9:9 reads: 'As Jesus passed on from there, he saw a man named Matthew sitting at the tax office.' Obviously, an author cannot refer to himself in his writings in these terms.

Mark never met Jesus. Nor was he a disciple of Jesus.[40] He was in fact a disciple of St Peter [English name in text; Urdu *Patras Hawari*], the disciple of Jesus. He would record everything he heard from Peter in the Greek language. This is why Christian authors usually refer to him as the interpreter of Peter. It is believed that this book was written somewhere between AD 63 and AD 70.

The third Gospel is attributed to Luke. It is a recognized historical fact that Luke never saw Jesus; nor did he benefit from his teaching. He was a disciple of St Paul [English name in text]. He was always in the company of Paul. In his Gospel, Luke has presented the views of Paul. This is why Paul himself calls Luke's Gospel his own Gospel. It is also established that St Paul remained deprived of the company of Jesus. According to the Christian tradition itself, he embraced Christianity six years after the event of the crucifixion. Therefore, there is a missing link in the chain between Luke and Jesus. The dating of Luke is also not determined. Some scholars claim that it was written in AD 57, and others say that it was penned in AD 74. However, according to researchers including Harnack, McGriffit [Griffith Thomas] and Plomer, Luke's Gospel was not written before the year AD 80.

The fourth book, attributed to John, too is not the work of John, the disciple of Jesus. Rather it is the work of some unknown person whose life history we do not know. He was called John. The book was written much after Jesus, in the year AD 90, or after. According Harnack, it was written in AD 110.

Obviously, none of these books can be traced back to Jesus Christ. Therefore, based on these books, one cannot confidently claim that Jesus really made a certain statement [recorded in these works] or not.[41] However, a deeper investigation casts further doubt on the historicity of these works.

First, the four Gospels differ among themselves in their statement of the facts. So much so, the Sermon on the Mount, the first principle of

---

[40] Some people believe that Paul was present among the spectators who watched the crucifixion of Jesus. However, this report has no authentic basis in the historical sources.

[41] The fact of the matter is that these books, in terms of authenticity, do not match the authority of the weakest compilation of the hadith, to say nothing of the Quran. The best level of authenticity is the one which is enjoyed by the Muslim books on the birth of the Prophet.

79

the Christian faith, has been presented in different, even contrasting, ways in Matthew, Mark and Luke.

Second, the views and impressions of the authors of all four Gospels are clearly observable. It appears Matthew addresses the Jews. He seems to clarify the argument against the Jews. Mark's addressees are the Romans, whom he intends to introduce to the Israelite tradition. Luke is the representative of St Paul and is seen trying to prove Paul's claims against the other disciples of Jesus. John seems to be impressed by the mystical and philosophical thoughts that had spread among the Christians during the last part of the first century AD. This is how the thematic differences in the four Gospels overshadow the verbal differences among them.

Third, all the Gospels were written in the Greek language. However, Jesus and his disciples spoke Syriac. The difference in language naturally causes differences in the ideas expressed.

Fourth, there was no effort to record the four Gospels before the second century AD. Before AD 150 the common belief was that oral narration was more useful than writing. The idea of recording things appeared towards the end of the second century AD. Still, however, the writings of that period are not acknowledged as authentic. The first authentic text of the New Testament [English term in text; Urdu *'Ahd-e Jadīd*] was approved at the Council of Carthage [Urdu *Qarṭājanah*] held in AD 397.

Fifth, the oldest manuscript of the Gospels found in the world today dates to the middle of the fourth century AD. The second oldest belongs to the fifth century and the third, an incomplete one found in the library of the pope, is no older than the fourth century. Therefore, it is difficult to ascertain how much the current four Gospels match the Gospels that existed in the first three centuries.

Sixth, there has never been an effort to memorize the Gospels in the way [Muslims] memorize the Quran. At the earliest stage, the dissemination of the Gospels relied on transmission by meaning. In this process, it is very natural that effects of lapses in memory and the inclusion of the personal views of the transmitters exist. Later on, after the commencement of the practice of committing these books to writing, they remained at the mercy of the copyists. While copying a manuscript, it was always easy for a person to omit anything that went against his creed. He could add something that he thought was missing.[42]

---

[42] This discussion is based on the following works: Dummelow, *A Commentary on the Holy Bible*, T. K. Cheyne, *Encyclopedia Biblica* and Millman, *The History of Christianity*.

Due to these reasons, we cannot be sure whether we find the true teachings of Jesus in the four Gospels. Therefore, what will be said about Christianity over the forthcoming pages does not relate to the religion taught by Jesus Christ. Rather it relates to the religion that the current Christian world believes in.

Reasons for Not Supporting War in Christianity

After the discussion above, it is not necessary to state that in Christianity all instructions regarding war, treaties, conflicts, government, politics and so forth given in the Torah have been kept intact, without a word being changed. This was because, at the time of the birth of the religion, there was no occasion to refer to them or to implement them.

We have discussed above that by the time of the arrival of Christianity, their nation, the Jews, had suffered slavery for some seven to eight hundred years. Twenty years before the birth of Jesus (peace be upon him), the Romans had attacked Palestine, and their troops had conquered all its territories. When Jesus (peace be upon him) was born, his entire nation was under the yoke of Roman slavery. Their particular homeland, Yahudia, came under direct Roman administrators in AD 2 who were called 'procurator' [English word in text]. When Jesus (peace be upon him) declared his prophethood, Jerusalem was under a very unjust and unconscionable procurator named Pontius Pilate [English words in text]. The slavery of these sacrilegious and unconscionable rulers had brought the moral and ethical conditions of the Jews to a very low level, such that they were not ready to listen to the truth. In front of Jesus (peace be upon him), a noble of Galilee, Herod, had had killed John the Baptist [in English in text] (Hazrat Yahya, peace be upon him) just to please a dancing girl. The Banu Israel, his own people, even failed to value the life of Jesus over that of a robber named Barabbas. In such circumstances, how was it possible for Christ to stand up with the banner of war even at the start of his preaching mission? How could he fight and establish an independent religious state? He was conscious of the fact that the Jews had lost spirit. There was no strength in their character and no life in their nationhood. Therefore, the first task before Jesus was to rescue his nation from the depths of moral degradation into which it had fallen. He needed to inspire in the nation such a spirit of high morals, without which no nation can unchain itself from the clutches of slavery and become able to remain free in this world. This is why initially he turned his efforts to the building of the national character of his people. While trying to achieve this constructive task, Jesus continuously tried not to cause an event leading to a clash with the government. Confrontation with the government at the beginning would hinder the reform work. Before completion of the moral reform of the nation, there was no chance of success in the struggle against the government. This is why Jesus avoided confrontation with the government. When the disciples of the Jewish scholars wanted to trick Jesus and get him arrested by the government, they asked him the question whether they should pay taxes to caesar. Jesus gave the following response, a double entendre:

> Give unto caesar the things that are caesar's, and to God the things that are God's.
>
> (Luke 20:22)

He commanded the following: Do not confront the evil man. Pray for and bless the one who wrongs you. Whoever presses you into service for one mile, go with him two. The one who seeks to take away your coat, let him have your cloak also. Whosoever shall smite you on your right cheek, turn to him the other also. The objective in issuing these commands at the beginning of the prophetic mission was to avoid a struggle against the government and enable the nation to gain power to face adversities. Subsequently, Jesus gradually instructed his nation to be steadfast, patient, forbearing and fearless. He trained them to face difficulties and adversities. He tried to remove from their hearts the fear of death, as well as the fear of oppression and the coercion of rulers. He said: When you are arrested and presented before officials and kings and you are tortured, be steadfast (Mark 13). He instructed his followers to remove from their hearts the love of life and to grow ready to embrace death. He said: 'For whoever desires to save his life will lose it, but whoever loses his life for My sake will save it' (Luke 9:23).

He taught the people to rely on God and His benevolence rather than the government and its blessing. This approach would free them from the weakness that keeps an enslaved nation enchanted by the ruling nation. He said: 'If you, having grown up, give good gifts to your children, then [know] your heavenly Father will surely give those who ask of Him!' (Luke 11:13). He tried to remove the awe of the ruling power from the hearts of the believers. He told them that those who can kill a body cannot kill the spirit. There is no need to fear them. The true entity that deserves you fear him is the one who can bring death upon both body and soul (Luke 12:4–5).

All these teachings were necessary to enable a nation to get free from centuries of slavery. This is why, at the initial stage of his preaching, Jesus confined his teachings to these matters. Having passed this phase, and near the end, he was progressing to the theme of fighting and war. Occasionally, he started expressing the wish to kill his enemies. On one occasion he said:

> Now as for those enemies of mine who did not want me as their king, bring them here and slay them before me.
>
> (Luke 19:27)

Similarly, he commanded his followers to keep swords with them. Luke writes:

> Then he said to them, 'But now, he who has a wallet, let him take it, and likewise a bag; and he who has no sword, let him sell his garment and buy one' ... So they said, 'Lord, look, here are two swords.' And He said to them, 'It is enough.'
>
> (Luke 22:36–8)

However, Jesus had only two to three years of life to guide and instruct his nation. This period was not enough to prepare and enable a nation for war in the path of God. During that limited time, he had not mustered followers in numbers enough to be put against the Romans. Nor had the people who had followed him obtained full moral training so they could, like the Companions of the Prophet Muhammad, peace be upon him, face all forms of dangers steadfastly and bravely, abandon their homes and migrate, and fight against the major powers of the time unafraid. The belief of the followers of Jesus had not yet obtained such strength that they could openly profess the truth. Even the most beloved disciple of Jesus, Peter, had as much faith, so that during the night Jesus was arrested, he was asked: 'Are you the follower of Jesus?' 'He denied Jesus thrice before the rooster crowed two times' (Mark 14:3). Another disciple, called Judas Iscariot, took thirty silver coins to help in Jesus' arrest (Matthew 26:14–16). When Jesus was arrested, all his disciples abandoned him and fled (Matthew 26:56). When this was the condition of Jesus' close companions and reliable disciples, then, obviously, he could not have dared to lead such an unreliable army into jihad. Had he, like Muhammad of Arabia, obtained enough time to teach and train people, he would have put in his disciples such a spirit of striving against evil that the Prophet Muhammad had created in the Companions, may Allah be pleased with them. However, the transgressing nation of Jesus did not tolerate his prophecy even for three years. They did not give him respite for a great achievement for their betterment and success. In this short period of time, only as much could be done as Jesus did. If we study the first three years of the Prophetic mission of Muhammad, peace be upon him, we may not find any sign of jihad and war. Muhammad's teachings contain the same exhortations to patience, perseverance, steadfastness, fear of God, reliance upon God, purification of the soul and purification of morals, just as they are found in Jesus' teachings.

****

War in Modern Civilization

In this chapter, we will analyse the objectives of war and the laws regulating it current in modern civilization. Our goal is to observe the status of these laws with the criterion of morality and humanity. A reader who has followed the previous discussion can claim that 'there is no doubt that Islam introduced great reform in the wars of that time. It guided man to objectives and paths of war with which the people of that time, religion and culture were acquainted. However, today, as a result of centuries of progress, human thought has become mature on the question of war. This progress has caused the emergence of such civilized laws of war that are beyond comparison with the laws and thoughts of a time when human thinking faculties were in relative infancy.' Therefore, we need to make another comparative analysis in which we contrast Islam and modern civilization and see whose objectives and methods are sounder, more beneficial and firmer.

Before we set out on such a comparison, it is important to settle the question of where we must turn to identify the original law of war as found in Western civilization. One can learn about the beliefs and methods of a people on a certain issue from three things: the religion, literature and behaviour of the society. As for religion, modern civilization has turned it into a personal and private affair of individuals. Religion has no control over the cultural aspect of modern life. As for literature, there is no doubt a great literary treasure in this realm exists in the West. Western jurists and moralists have written a lot about war and related issues. They have discussed every aspect of these matters. However, regardless of the matter of how greatly the views of such writers contribute towards the growth of collective thinking, and how great the share of their thoughts in the formation of the laws of society is, they do not themselves enjoy authority. They should therefore not be considered authoritative for a collectivity of people. Not even the greatest of the writers in this world enjoys such a position that his sayings become law for his nation. It is no doubt possible that his thoughts can impact his nation, which could have formulated laws for itself in the light of his writings. However, being ascribed to a specific great writer does not mean that such statements become authoritative for the nation. They are authoritative only because the nation has accepted them and embraced them by turning them into their national laws. This means that on the question of war the vast literature produced by the admirable efforts of Western scholars of different languages does not serve the purpose. Now, we are left only with the third source upon which we can base our knowledge of the objectives and methods of war in Western civilization, and this source is the practical manifestation of objectives and laws of war held in Western nations. This practical observation is of two kinds: a) written [English word in text; Urdu *mudawwan*], which in technical parlance is called International Law [English term in text; Urdu *bayn al millī qānūn*]; and b) unwritten [English word in text; Urdu *ghayr mudawwan*], which means the mutual dealings and practical politics observed by the different states. Which of the two types is the more reliable and authentic law? Which should be preferred in case of difference? Which of the two has more power to become an authority for Western nations? These are the issues contested by Western scholars among themselves. These issues have not been settled even today. But we need not enter into this theoretical discussion. The different aspects of the question of war have become divided in the two sources, such that the moral aspect of war has fallen wholly within the realm of unwritten law. However, the practical aspect has predominantly discussed within written law. Therefore, we will leave the question of preference and discuss the two aspects of war separately.

Ethical Aspects of War

The approach we have followed so far while analysing the question of war dictates that the moral aspect of the issue is discussed first. The first thing we need to investigate is the viewpoint of Western civilization on war. What status does war hold in the moral system of Western civilization? For what objectives is war lawful, and for what objectives is it not? If Western civilization has a higher and pure objective of war, then what is that objective? If it does not have any such objective, then what status does war hold in the realm of morality and civilization? Once we have found answers to these questions, we will proceed to gauge the soundness or unsoundness of the law about the method of war.

Written law in the West is totally silent on these questions. In the past, the question about the morality of war was considered a question relevant [English word in text; Urdu *muta'allaq*] to international law. Therefore, Grotius, the first compiler of international law, tried to distinguish between right and wrong objectives of war in his work *De Jure Belli ac Pacis* [Latin name in text]. However, international law in modern times has rendered this question completely irrelevant to the discussion. Professor Lawrence writes in his work *The Principles of International Law*:

> But modern international law knows nothing of these moral questions. It does not pronounce upon them: it simply ignores them. To it war, whether just or unjust, right or wrong, is a fact which alters in a great variety of ways the relations of the parties concerned. It must, therefore, be defined and its legal incidents set forth. The law will tell us how the relation of belligerency [Urdu *ḥarbiyyat*] is created, and what the rights and obligations of belligerents towards each other and towards neutrals are ... Such questions as these are worthy of the most careful consideration; but they are as much out of place in a treatise on international law as would be a discussion on the ethics of marriage in a book on the law of personal status.[1]

A German writer, Eltzbacher, writes:

> International law has always imposed only such conditions on the practice of war as can be observed and followed without significant interference with military objectives. International law limits itself to the suggestion that the enemy should be spared from unnecessary loss to the best possible level. That is, such losses should not be inflicted upon the enemy as have no role in the objectives for which the war is fought or result in losses outweighed in importance by the gains.[2]

Professor Nippold writes:

> Therefore, the question of sin in war does not relate to international law. Rather, it is a question of ethics. International law cannot

---

[1] Lawrence, 1923.   [2] Paul Eltzbacher, *Anarchism*, 1908.

differentiate between a right or wrong war because from the perspective of international law war stands in defiance of the law.[3]

These observations reveal that, as far as the written or compiled international law is concerned, there is no difference between right war and
wrong war, as well as legitimate war and illegitimate war. We cannot
learn from international law for what objectives Western civilization
holds war allowable, and for which purposes it forbids it. But as
Dr Bayi has said, 'there is also an unwritten or uncompiled international
law which is the actual [international] law'; we need to analyse the actual
conduct of the most civilized Western nations in this regard. We have to
see, when war breaks out among the nations which are believed to be the
epitome of modern civilization, whose action and inaction create civilization, and without whose word and action nothing can be proclaimed
civilized, for what purposes and objectives it is fought. What sort of war
do they consider war for justice and truth? Therefore, we would not
discuss the small wars that were fought during the nineteenth and the
twentieth centuries between the civilized nations and a small group of
nations seen by the West as uncivilized. The reason is that the practices
in these wars cannot be a valid example of the practices of Western
civilization. So, leaving all these, we analyse[4] the war fought in the
twentieth century in which all the nations representing Western civilization took part. In other words, it was the war the management committee
of which had representation from all the nations of the modern world.
The saga of this war can expose us to the moral criterion of licit and illicit
war in the eyes of Western civilization.

Causes of the World War

The World War (1914 to 1919) was originally a war among the six great
European nations. Different other small and big nations became involved
in it as secondary elements. One of the two warring camps comprised
Germany and Austria. The opposition consisted of England, France,
Russia and Italy. The members of each group themselves had remained

---

[3] Nippold, *The Development of International Law after the World War*, Eltzbacher in
Nippold, 7–8.
[4] It needs to be appreciated that this book was written after World War I. Therefore, at this
point, it is the moral aspect of World War I that is being analysed. Afterwards, the world
witnessed another world war, the moral aspects of which are many times crueller.

in a state of severe animosity with each other over the centuries. England was an old enemy of France. Even in 1899, the two nations were about to enter into a war over the question of Sudan. Similarly, Russia and England were constantly opposed to each other. This is why, until the beginning of the twentieth century, the British empire persistently remained on the alert for a Russian invasion of India. The question of Tunisia remained a constant source of opposition and enmity between France and Italy. For this reason, even until right before the start of the World War, Italy was in alliance with Germany. However, during the first decade of the twentieth century a relationship of shared interests and objectives arose among these enemy nations. This united them all, and they fought side by side against the other group. On the other hand, Germany had been an ally of England till 1904. It remained on positive terms with Italy until 1914. Russia too was a nation friendly to England. Indeed, there had been warm, friendly relations between tzar and king until the start of the World War. However, some other objectives changed this friendship into enmity. Germany had to become an ally of Austria, its historical enemy, against nations friendly to Germany in the past.

Grouping of Nations

What were these specific objectives which bound the enemy nations together? Religion played no role, as all of these were Christian nations. Similarly, there was no dispute about the defence of the motherland, as none of the states had attacked the other. There was nothing related to rights, as all were enjoying their rights fully. Then what caused them to fight against each other? A study of history shows that there was nothing other than the wish of every state to have more than it deserved. Every party desired to suppress or annihilate the other and benefit from the enemy's profits.

The first seed of enmity was sown among them in the 1870s, when Germany annexed Alsace and Lorraine, snatching it from France. Though the entire population of Alsace was of German origin, and the majority of the population of Lorraine was racially and linguistically German, France considered the annexation as an injustice to the nation. From that time on, the major objective of French politics came to be the idea of defeating Germany and taking back the two provinces.

Later on, trade and industry in Germany started to flourish, and by the end of the nineteenth century the country had a flourishing and great trade and industry. In the 1900s, Germany realized that England occupied all the sources of marine trade and England's domination could not be removed without establishing a great navy. Therefore, the country started advancing its navy at a very quick pace. England felt this growing threat immediately. First, England tried to befriend Germany. This is why Mr Chamberlain, Lord Denis Down and other British statesmen continued wooing Germany between 1899 and 1902. However, Germany was not ready to accept the naval and trade domination of England. It wanted to be a major power in the world of trade. Therefore, the two opposing countries could not become friends. It led to an immediate revolution in world politics. The first expression of this change appeared in 1904, when centuries-old enemies England and France became friends. France accepted the English occupation of Egypt. In return England accepted the French occupation of Morocco. Both nations vowed to each other to unitedly protect their objectives in future.

Russia joined this group in 1907 for two great objectives. The first objective was to capture the Dardanelles Strait and the Bosphorus. Russia had been striving to gain control over these for a century and a half. The second Russian objective was to take control over and subjugate the Balkan Peninsula so that Russia could have a naval passage to the Aegean Sea and the Mediterranean. Germany and Austria stood in Russia's way of achieving these goals. Germany desired to build a railway track between Berlin and Baghdad and develop its Eastern trade. For this purpose, Germany wanted Turkey and the Balkans to be free from Russian influence. On the other side, Austria felt that the only path to fulfil its greed for territorial expansion and the advancement of trade lay in the occupation of the Balkan Peninsula and to exploit the harbours in the Aegean and Adriatic Seas. Therefore, for this purpose, Austria annexed Bosnia and Herzegovina in 1908.

England remained opposed to the political objectives of Russia till 1907. However, having learnt that it could not strangle Germany to death without Russian support, the country extended the hand of friendship to the age-old adversary. England assured Russia of its support for the latter's occupation of the Dardanelles Strait and the Bosphorus at the proper time.

Thus two powerful groups had formed before 1907. One party consisted of England, France and Russia. The other party included Germany and Austria. The first group was united by their ambition to do away with Germany and Austria to secure territorial expansion and to maintain their trade domination. The members of the other group were bound together by their desire to expand the empire and dominate the international trade and economy, an objective for which they needed mutual help. So far Italy had not taken part in this grouping. Apparently, Italy was bound in a co-operative treaty with Germany. How then did it abandon a friendly Germany to side with France, an enemy? It is a strange story. Italy had kept its relations and agreements with Germany and France in such a way as to enable itself to demand Germany's help against France in its plan to gain control over Tunisia. Similarly, when it needed to go to war and snatch the parts of Austria (under Italy's control for some time), then it could seek the allies' support. When, at the start of the World War, Italy realized that the greatest naval force, England, was siding with France, and Germany could not help it win Tunisia, it suddenly turned towards the allies. The leaders of the country put on the garment of truthfulness and claimed that they had always considered Germany and Austria to be on the path of evil, and therefore they could not support the said two countries.

Beginning of the War

In June 1914, the crown prince of Austria was killed at the hands of a Serbian anarchist. The seeds of corruption and anarchy that had been sown and irrigated for forty-four years were suddenly ready for harvest. In order to remove the stumbling-block of Serbia, Austria capitalized on the event because it was the only hindrance to Austria's advance into the Balkans. Germany too considered it necessary to remove Serbia from its path in order to implement its trade programmes. Therefore, it too sided with Austria. On the other side, Russia considered Serbia its 'younger brother' and had staked all its hopes in the latter country for its designs in the Balkans. Moreover, it was also certain that if Austria succeeded in annihilating Serbia, then nothing could stop its domination over the entire Balkans. Therefore Russia stood by the side of its younger brother. On the other hand, France feared that, after defeating Russia and Serbia, Germany and Austria would grow so strong that there would be no longer any hope of regaining Alsace and Lorraine. Rather, it would be impossible for it to keep power in Paris itself. This realization forced France to side with Russia. After the activity of these allies, England could no longer remain neutral. This country, 'adherent to the truth'

[Urdu *haq parast*], had taken up many moral responsibilities, the fulfilment of which required that Germany's growing threat be removed forever from the Queen of the Ocean's path to the realization of naval and trade superiority. Therefore, England too stepped forward to fight, and thus the great war of the 'civilized nations' occurred, compared with which all the wars of the non-civilized world were next to nothing.

Modern Schemes for Ending War

Many proposals for disarmament, the reduction of weapons and forces, and the prohibition of war have been enthusiastically discussed in Europe and America over the last seven years. Many naïve men take it as an indication of the good intentions of the Western world. However, the fact of the matter is that all these suggestions are lip-service and have no trace of reality. Because the relentless fighting has exhausted the general population of the West, they are in dire need of peace for the betterment of the collective life and the restoration of economic and industrial activity. Therefore, at least for the sake of consolation, they like to hear such suggestions and empty talk, which may not give peace and yet can be expected to provide an imaginary satisfaction. As for action on these suggestions, there is no hope of materialization of these expectations. On the contrary, the progress the West has achieved regarding the means of war is unparalleled in history. The West had not achieved this level of armaments even in 1914, when all of Europe was engaged in preparing for war.

After the end of the World War I, it was democratic America that touched upon this issue first of all. Under the auspices of the United States, an international conference was held in Washington in November 1921. The objective of this conference was to advocate for a reduction in military power. However, the fact is that America, France, Japan and Italy desired to somehow reduce the naval force of England. The reason is that all these countries depend on maritime trade. As long as England dominates the oceans, no country can deem its maritime trade safe. On the other hand, England knew that its life depended on its domination of naval power; it desired that no other country might achieve its level of naval power. This hidden struggle surfaced in the discussions at the Washington conference. Each party wanted to impose restrictions on the others. However, as for the question of curbs on itself, every country would clearly state that their war policy was entirely free of foreign influence. As a result, the conference could not do anything beyond a treaty among the five major powers stipulating a set of ratios of allowable naval power. Later, the United States, a country that rose to be the greatest advocate of the disarmament campaign, itself started building new Dreadnoughts and resolved to equip the Panama Canal with the most modern weapons of war.

The question of submarines was also discussed at the same conference. These boats are primarily a threat to England because it is this country whose life depends on imports from foreign countries. It is the country which owns more trade and warships than anyone else. The submarines had destroyed the English naval trade and had rendered life difficult for England. England remembered this lesson. Therefore, the country put all its efforts to get the use of submarines banned. France, on the contrary, particularly resisted this proposition. The reason was that the French naval force was weaker. The submarines were France's greatest source of protection against the British naval force. The French representatives clearly stated that these boats were not a means of attack on another country but a source of defence against foreign aggression. The countries with a weaker naval force are under a compulsion to use such boats. At last, the United States introduced a middle-way solution to the contested issue, and the parties agreed to it. The solution was to ban the use of submarines to destroy the trade of an adversary country during wartime.

Another treaty signed related to the use of noxious gases in warfare. The use of noxious gases was prohibited first by the Hague Convention of 1899. England had opposed this conference. At the second Hague Convention held in 1907 England agreed to this stipulation, but the United States continued to resist it till the end. During the World War, Germany and its opponents freely used poison gases against each other. The small restrictions agreed upon previously were abolished by the consensus practice of the empires. Later on, the previous restrictions on the subject were reiterated. Still, however, no country was ready to accept it wholeheartedly. This is revealed by the fact that the French representative, M. Sarraut, thought it imperative to issue the following note while signing the agreement: 'The effort to stop the use of noxious gases does not appear to be practicable.'

Mr Balfour also thought it useful to add a caveat on behalf of Britain, that 'this agreement does not prevent nations from the demands of protecting themselves from the possibility of use of gases by a malevolent enemy'. Due to these half-hearted attempts, no state has fully signed up to this agreement, and its legal status remains that of a meaningless document.

The History of [Western] Laws of Warfare

Until the beginning of the seventeenth century, Europe had little conception of rules of warfare. Both in principle and practically, war was considered outside the realm of rules, restrictions and the bounds of ethics. The belligerents had the unrestricted freedom to cause damage to each other according to their desire and capability. Historical records of the wars of those times suggest that when two nations were at war, they did not hesitate to commit brutal and cruel acts. Not only in practice, but even in principle or conceptually, there was no difference between combatants and non-combatants. Even a commentator committed to ethics like Grotius stated:

> The law permits all those to be killed who are found in enemy territory. Women and children are no exceptions. Foreigners who do not leave the territory within a reasonable time are also not exempt from the rule.[5]

This unlimited right was used with such freedom during the Thirty Years' War, between 1618 and 1648, that Europe was brutally shaken. It led some thinkers to argue that some kind of bounds should be placed on wars. This desire was first expressed by Grotius of Holland in his famous book *De jure belli ac pacis* [Latin name in text], which is considered the foundation of international law. It was published in 1625 and was included in the curriculum of Heidelberg University. It caused an intellectual stir among other thinkers and scholars of the time who pushed for new developments in Western thought. About half a century after Grotius, his student Pufendorf published his book *De jure naturae et gentium* and started on a series of books that culminated in the eighteenth century in a system of international law. In 1780, the famous English jurist Jeremy Bentham [English name in text] called this field 'international law', and this is what it is known as today.

Practically, the effects of this progressive thought were seen first in the Congress of Westphalia [English phrase in text], when European elders agreed to end the Thirty Years' War and on Grotius' recommendation that:

---

[5] Lawrence, *Principles of International Law*, 330.

In war women, children, the aged, clergymen, agriculturists, traders and POWs should be accorded safety from death and destruction, as a concession (not as a law).[6]

This was the first ray of light after the birth of Christ to be seen in the dark skies over Europe, some 1,647 years later. After this, the level of brutality and savagery in warfare was not at the levels witnessed in the Thirty Years' War. However, as far as the practical acceptance and actual reforms of war were concerned, Europe took another 200 more years to make some progress. So that even by mid 1857, during the Indian War of Independence (the so-called Mutiny [*ghadar*]), English forces committed brutalities beyond human conscience. As far as we know, until the mid nineteenth century there was no international law in existence that compelled kingdoms or that was implemented among European armies. Among Western nations, America was the first to take a step in that direction, and in 1863 a manual of instructions [English word in text] was published for its military. Its aim was to regulate the code of conduct of armies during wars. After this Germany, France, Russia and England also started giving similar instructions to their armies. Gradually, all of Europe accepted the path that was first articulated in the 'savage' country of Arabia under the guidance of its illiterate Prophet (peace be upon him) and his unlettered Companions some 1,200 years before.

For the first time, in 1864, an international conference was held in Geneva, Switzerland, to decide on an agreement regarding the war-wounded, the sick and medics. Later these rules were expanded in the second Geneva conference, in 1868. However, Europe lacked a comprehensive legal framework until the third Geneva conference, in 1906.[7]

Until 1868, Europe had no rules or conventions governing the use of immensely destructive weapons or ammunition. That year, for the first time, an international conference of the military held in St Petersburg recommended to the leaders of Western nations that the use of exploding projectiles [English phrase in text] weighing more than 400 grams and bullets that explode inside a man's body, as well as poison gases, not be allowed in military conflicts. With the exception of the United States and Spain, the other European leaders signed a convention to this effect on 29 November 1868.

---

[6] Bernard, *Paper on the Growth of the Laws of War*, Oxford 1856, 100–4.
[7] Birkenhead, *International Law*, 207.

After this, on the recommendation of Tzar Alexander II, a conference was held in Brussels in 1874, and in it for the first time rules of warfare were compiled. However, no state was willing to ratify them. In fact, Germany and England refused to accept them at all. The Brussels recommendations remained unimplemented and unaccepted for the next twenty-five years until, in 1899, on the initiative of Tzar Nicholas II, the first Hague Conference was held. Twenty-six nations took part, and the following conventions were agreed upon:

a) Attempts at peaceful settlement of international conflicts.
b) The rules and conventions of war.
c) Application to sea battles of rules agreed upon for land battles in the Geneva Convention of 1864 regarding sick and wounded.
d) Extension to the period of applicability of the St Petersburg Convention regarding explosive projectiles. (They were initially approved for a period of five years only.)
e) Extension of the period of applicability of the St Petersburg Convention on explosive bullets.
f) Extension of the applicability regarding the St Petersburg Convention on the use of poison gases.

This conference was unable to complete its mission, and for eight years further enactment of rules was suspended. In 1907, on the initiative of President Roosevelt of the United States and Tzar Nicholas II of Russia, the Hague Conference was reconvened. Finally, Europe had, for the first time, a comprehensive set of rules and conventions regarding war. In addition to additions and ratification of the 1899 Conventions on War, other agreements were also reached. These were:

a) Limitation on the use of force for reclaiming loans.
b) The necessity of a declaration of war before commencing hostilities.
c) The rights and duties of neutral states in land wars.
d) The status of commercial shipping, including those of opposing powers, in sea warfare.
e) Rules regarding the conversion of commercial ships for military use.
f) Rules regarding exploding sea mines.
g) Rules regarding bombardment by ships during war.
h) Rules regarding the arrest of ships during war.
i) The formation of an international department of the spoils of sea warfare.
j) Rights and duties of neutrals during sea wars.

Although this conference was successful in compiling a wide set of rules and conventions, it cannot be said that these were in any way complete and all-encompassing. Soon after this conference, the need arose to address the use of submarines, aeroplanes and poison gases. These were addressed at the Washington Conference of 1922. We still cannot say with certainty how many more conferences might be required to address other unforeseen contingencies and conflicts.

From this brief description of the history, it becomes obvious that no more than sixty years have elapsed since the Western world became aware of the civilized rules of warfare. In other words, if we leave aside the earlier period of debate and consider just the period since the enactment of the rules and conventions, it can be said that, until sixty years ago, the West was ignorant of the ethics of war. In comparison, Islam had proposed a complete code of conduct some thirteen and a half centuries earlier. As far as principles are concerned, there has never been a need for any conference, agreement or convention to cancel, alter or add to these rules. Despite this, the principles are largely the same as the ones the Western world has only just adopted, and some are beyond the capacity of the West even today.

Tehrīk-e-Azādi Hind aur Musalmān

Tehrīk-e-Azādi Hind aur Musalmān, comprising *Musalmān aur Mojūda Siyasi Kashmakash* (Parts I and II) and *Masla-e-Qaumiyyat*.

Table of Contents

CHAPTER 4

The Way Forward

Now we have to dwell on the question of how we can achieve those objectives of Islamic *qawmiyyat* [nationhood; selfhood] in India which we defined in the previous publications.[1] As far as we know, no 'Muslim' individual or group disagrees with this objective. The difference, if there be any, lies in determining the correct path to achieve this objective. Now, we need to critically analyse the various paths before us. The correct path will become evident after such an analysis.

Two Statuses of Muslims in India

We have a dual status in India: as Indians and as Muslims.

In the first capacity, we share the status and conditions of all other communities [*qawmūn*] in India. If the country is plunged into poverty and hunger, we will become poor and hungry too. If the country is plundered, we will be looted along with all others. If the country is under an oppressive and unjust government, we will be devastated in a manner similar to our compatriots [*ahl-e-watan*]. In all the calamities befalling and the curses striking the country due to its slavery, we will all have an equal share. In the light of this, all the political and economic problems of the country are equally distributed among us and other Indian nations [*aqwām-e-hind*]. Just as their prosperity and progress are associated with

---

[1] [Editor's note:] There were minor differences in the edition used for translation and the original article published in *Tarjuman ul Quran* in 1938. The most noteworthy change was the addition of subheadings to the book chapters, which I have retained here and in the next three chapters. For the value of considering the differences between Maududi's writings in *Tarjuman* and later editions, see Mudabir Wani, 'Reaching the Islamic State: Maududi on Religion, Education, and Politics in Colonial India' (Columbia University: unpublished essay, 2024).

India's freedom, so is ours. Our and everyone else's betterment is dependent on the freedom of our country from the hold of the oppressive [*ẓālimūn*]. The wealth and resources of the country should be spent on the success and refinement of its own people. The people of the land need full provision of opportunities to utilize their resources to cure their poverty, ignorance, moral decadence and cultural backwardness. And no oppressive power [*qawm*] may have the power to make these resources an instrument for their unjust objectives.

In the second capacity, we have some different problems which relate only to us [as Muslims]. No other [Indian] nation shares those problems with us. Foreign occupation has greatly harmed our national [*qawmī*] morals, national culture, principles of life and collective system. A hundred and fifty years of slavery have consumed the foundations upon which our nationhood stands. Our experience has taught us, and we can see this reality in broad daylight, that if this situation persists much longer, the Islamic *qawmiyyat* [nationhood] in India will gradually die an afflictive natural death, and the nominal skeleton that currently exists will no longer retain its significance. The impact of the current government is transforming us internally into non-Muslims. The roots embedded in the depth of our hearts and minds that sustain the tree of Islam [*islāmiyyat*] are gradually withering away. We are being fed drugs [*hashish*] that affect our essence and make us destroy our mosques with our own hands. The rapid pace at which these changes are taking place among us would indicate to any commentator that this entire process will soon achieve its culmination. By the time of our third or fourth generation, at most, the majority of Muslims will automatically become non-Muslims. Maybe merely a handful of people will remain to mourn the demise at the mausoleum of this great nation. Hence, the survival and protection of our nationhood hinges upon our freedom from the current occupation and the re-establishment of a collective system anew whose disappearance is the very reason we face these current challenges.

Two Routes to Freedom for Our Homeland

Both of our statuses are mutually inseparable. We can negate them neither rationally nor practically.

It is entirely correct that freedom is our objective in both these statuses. It is also without any doubt that as Indians we must strive collectively to rid ourselves of problems common to us and other Indian citizens. It is also completely right that the freedom we want as Muslims can only be acquired when we win freedom as Indians. However, the seeming similarity between and [mutual] compatibility [of the two statuses] carries a big deception. And in reality, many people got deceived at this very point. A deep analysis of the situation will clarify that it is not a straight path you may tread relentlessly with your eyes closed. A juncture exists right where you find yourself standing. The juncture has two roads leading you in different directions, and you have to decide which road to take after thinking rationally and responsibly about where you want to go.

Nation Worship

One way we can achieve a free country is only in our status as Indians. The people who carved this path and guided Indians to it are those who follow the Western style of nationalism [*watani qawmiyyat*], and the vision of human life [*insāniyyat*] that is deeply embedded in their ideas is a Hindu one. Their eventual target is to abolish various national differences based on diversity of religions and cultures and make the entire country into one nation [*qawm*]. Then, the map of the life of that particular 'nation' in their mind is a combination of communism and Hinduism. That map not only disallows any margin for the principles of the life of Muslims but also carries no sympathy for them. The maximum margin they allow for us from this Indian nation [*hindī qawmiyyat*] is the freedom of belief and action in the personal matters between individuals and God. As for dealings between humans, they want them to be guided purely by that particular nationalism. In their opinion, 'organized religion' [*munazzam madhab*], a religion that transforms its followers into a complete nation and compels them to have a different identity from other religions on educational, economic, social, cultural, moral and civilizational grounds and follows a specific code of conduct, is in principle objectionable. Considering the current situation in India, they will tolerate such an 'organized' religion in a vague and limited form for some time. Accordingly, in a manner of indicating this tolerance for acceptance, they have promised different religious sects scattered across India the protection of their 'personal laws' [English term in text] and languages. However, they cannot accept a system that could give more strength and a permanent life for this 'organized religion' to flourish in India. Instead, they want to develop modern India in a manner where such organized religions should die their natural death after a slow decomposition. They want to make the entire population of India into a nation that would allow divisions, no matter how many, between political and economic groups but paint the country in the same colours, when it comes to educational, civilizational, traditional, social, moral, ethical and other perspectives, as those donned by the leaders of the movement.

This path, the implications of which today are visible even to the blind, we [the Muslims] can only accept when we agree to sacrifice our secondary status [*haythiyyat*]. Following this path, we cannot win the freedom we need as Muslims. Instead, this path entirely deprives us of this status [of Muslim]. Adopting this path means that the revolution that has been taking place for one and a half centuries in our nation under the English government should reach its end with more intensity and speed under the rule of an Indian government, and we ourselves will become helpers in the completion of this [destructive process]. It would be such a perfect revolution that no chance of any reaction remains. No matter how deeply we are absorbed into Western culture under the influence of English rule, we cannot fully integrate with the English nation. At any rate, our separate collective existence remains intact, and it is possible for it to return to its previous condition. However, in this scenario, the entire situation is different. Firstly, they declare every distinguishing feature, including our sense of nationality, to be 'communalism' [English word in text; Urdu *fiqrah parastī*; TQ: *tai-fayyat*] and spread hateful propaganda against it. It means that our existence as a permanent 'community' [English word in text; Urdu *jamā'at*] is not acceptable. Secondly, those among our community [*qawm*] are called nationalists [English word in text; Urdu *qawm parast*] who put their hands together to say *namaste*, chant *banda-e-mataram*, visit Hindu temples and even offer prayers there. They completely adopt Hindu culture in their physical appearance and dress and avoid even mentioning the welfare of Muslims for fear of being accused of communalism [English word in text; Urdu *firqa parasti*]. This to them is worse than being accused of being disbelievers. Thirdly, we are explicitly told to come as individuals rather than as a group [*jamā'at*] and get divided into political parties, as labourer and capitalist, landlord and farmer, rich and poor. In other words, they want us to sever the relationship between Muslim and Muslim, and instead adopt the same relationship between Muslim and non-Muslim members of a party.

Understanding the results of all these practices requires no special thought or intellect. The obvious outcome is that during the movement for national freedom [*tehrīk-i azadā-e waṭan*] itself we will lose our collective existence as a Muslim community and scatter like droplets of water that get soaked into the soil of modern nationalism. In that case, we cannot even dream about our renaissance as a Muslim nation.

Those who want freedom as Indians only and see enough value in doing so to be able to sacrifice their Muslim identity for it may take this path. However, we entirely refuse to accept that a true Muslim will deliberately want to partake in such a movement for national freedom.

Freedom For Muslims [*TQ*: What Type of Freedom Do We Want?]

The only other path to the country's freedom is one where there is no contradiction between our status as Indians and as Muslim, Hindu, Christian or Sikh, for every Indian resident. Every group has complete freedom in both statuses. The nature of this freedom should be such that on common national problems there is no religious or national imposition, and yet on their separate national issues, no nation should be able to dominate another. Every community should have enough power in a free Indian government to solve their own issues independently.

As we have repeatedly stated, going to war for our country's freedom is inevitable for us. However, the freedom for which we can fight and consider it obligatory to fight is precisely this. As for the freedom most nationalists [*waṭan parast*] eye, not only is there no meaning in fighting for it, we consider it more humiliating than being enslaved by the English invaders. In our opinion, those who promote this type of freedom movement are no better than Clive and Wellesley for Muslims. The Muslims who follow them are no different from Mir Sadiq and Mir Jafar. Though conditions and circumstances are different, no change is visible in their enmity and treachery.[2]

---

[2] Some people have objected to the harshness of the statement. For the comfort of their hearts, I want to explain that I do not intend to say this to those who are true Muslims and have committed a mistake in *Ijtihad*. I am only comparing two types of people to Mir Jafar and Mir Sadiq. First, those who are no longer true followers of Islam and, instead, disguise themselves as Muslims to weaken the roots of the Muslim *'ummah*. Second, I compare them to those who have started worshipping their interests and are ready to bow before every emerging power.

The Mistake of Those Who Call Us to Join Congress

Now the question is, how can we achieve the freedom we idealize and consider our goal? There are two prominent groups of Muslims that present different suggestions.

One group suggests presenting our demands to a party contesting for freedom, and when they accept those demands, we should support them. The other group advises being a part of the freedom movement unconditionally.

We believe both these groups are wrong. The mistake of the first group is that they want to beg like weak people. Suppose they present their demands, and the party does agree to listen to them, what will be the outcome? How long can others sustain a nation that does not have the capability to maintain its life on its own? As for the second group, excited by the idea of freedom, they forget the weaknesses of our [Muslim] community that we have discussed in detail in previous pages. We are ready to take back our opinion if someone can prove that these weaknesses do not exist, and that Muslims have enough strength such that there is no threat to their nationality and civilization from modern nationalism. However, if it cannot be proven, and we strongly believe that it cannot, then listen carefully that at this stage calling Muslims to join Congress is synonymous with persuading them to commit suicide. You cannot simply change realities by appealing to emotions. It is better to approach a half-dead patient as a doctor rather than a military commander. Check the pulse and provide treatment. Later, you may tie a sword on his back. What is the logic in approaching a patient kicking his heels on his deathbed to deliver a sermon telling him to stand up on his own, pick up his sword and enter the battlefield?

Among the people who have adopted these two paths, there are many individuals for whom our heart has the utmost respect. We do not have an iota of doubt in their faith. However, fully respecting their dignity and status, we are obliged to say that they are currently misguiding Muslims, and the reason behind this misguidance is that they have not deliberated enough on the current position and future prospects for Muslims.

Some Realities requiring Consideration

Before taking any step, our leaders should understand the following realities very clearly:

A One thing which is inevitable for retaining the national life of Muslims is establishing a state within a state, *imperium in imperio* [Latin in text] as it is called in current political language. The foundations supporting their society cannot retain their existence unless their own group has strong disciplinary power and the authority to make decisions. Without such a central power, living within a non-Muslim government set-up will result in the gradual dwindling and finally annihilation of their collective existence, and they will not be able to survive as a Muslim nation.

B The political revolution of the eighteenth century has deprived us of this element. The annihilation it has brought upon our society is visible to our naked eye. After causing a continuous decline for one and a half centuries, the revolution has taken us to a position where our collectivity is affected, our moral values are destroyed, our social life is infected with all types of diseases, the foundations of our faith and way of life [*dīn*] are shaken, and we are on the verge of death.

C Now a different revolution has begun, which carries two possibilities. If we show the same level of negligence that we showed in the face of the previous revolution, the present revolution will drive us in the same direction that the previous one led us to. It will complete the result to which the prior revolution guided us. If we succeed in establishing a Muslim government system in a non-Muslim government system (even if it is within certain limits), the revolution will change its direction, and we will get another opportunity to strengthen our collective system.

D It is not possible to establish a state within a state with a peace treaty or an agreement. Any non-Muslim political party, no matter how generous or wide-churched [*wasī'ul mashrab*] it may be, cannot simply express happy readiness for such a thing. Nor can it be made a part of constitutional law based only on dialogue. And even if we suppose that it happens, such an extraordinary arrangement lacking a powerful public opinion or a strong force behind it proves no more durable than a water bubble. In fact, the only way it can be established on strong foundations is that we should proactively establish it through the strength of our system and invincible collective determination, and make it a permanent part of the future government system of India as an accomplished fact which should be impossible for any power to undo.

E This task cannot be achieved if we allow the current revolution to continue at the same pace and try to establish a state within a state after the establishment of a non-Muslim government system in India. Only a person who is completely foreign to practical politics would think such an approach is feasible. Any sensible person would easily understand that the direction of a revolution can only be changed during it. A state within a state can be established only when its foundations are established during the formation of the state.

F The kind of organization required for this purpose cannot be achieved by joining the framework of Congress. Congress is an organized political party. Every organized party has the quality of moulding people according to its own nature and specific psychology. If Muslims possess a strong Islamic character and a powerful collective system, they can of course change the psychology, principles and objectives of Congress after joining the party. However, with their current weaknesses (as explained earlier in detail), joining Congress as scattered individuals can lead to only one possible outcome. That is, the psychology of Congress will dominate our politics, and our leaders will be forced to follow the directions of Congress. Consequently, any remaining possibility of forming a collective opinion among Muslims for Islamic purposes will be permanently abolished. Anyone God has blessed with eyesight can easily comprehend that nationalist types of Muslims cannot do any good to Muslims even if they form a strong lobby as a part of Congress and get a large share in the government. Instead, they will prove even more harmful than the non-Muslims. They will adopt the same policy and method in every matter that a non-Muslim would prefer. However, to do so, they will possess more freedom and courage than non-Muslims because, unfortunately, they will possess Muslim names.

Important Recommendations to Strengthen an Islamic Party

When you deliberate, keeping the above facts in mind, you will find that we have only one option: to overcome our weaknesses before entering the struggle for Indian freedom and strengthen ourselves to win freedom for Muslims at the same time as gaining freedom for India. For this purpose, we should utilize our energy on the following actions:

A We should spread knowledge of the principles of Islam and the laws of sharia at a vast scale among Muslims. We should acquaint them at least with an understanding of Islamic boundaries, to the extent that they should understand which beliefs and actions should be acceptable or unacceptable to them as Muslims. This education and preaching should not be limited to cities only. Instead, the Muslims living in rural areas require this education more than the ones living in urban areas.

B Apart from spreading this knowledge, we should also teach Muslims to follow in practice the teachings of Islam and emphasize the re-establishment of fundamental elements of Islam, which form the foundation of our collective system.

C We need to train the Muslim community's common opinions to make them diligent in preventing the propagation of un-Islamic values, and their collective 'social conscience' [English term in text; Urdu *ijtimā'ī ḍamīr*] should stop them from tolerating individuals revolting against Islamic teachings. In this regard, the thing that demands the most attention is the will to resemble the other [*tashabbuh bi al ajānib*] because it is the only thing that prepares us to integrate into foreign cultures.

D We should strengthen our collective system to the extent of being able to hold the traitors and hypocrites accountable who harm the Islamic interest for their personal gains or the disbelief and hypocrisy concealed in their hearts.

E We should try our best to ensure that the position of leadership of common Muslims should not fall into the hands of the slaves of the British or Hindus. Instead, it should be in the hands of a party that will be ready to interact and work collectively with other neighbouring nations for the complete freedom of India without sacrificing the Islamic interest in any condition.

F We should establish such a unity of thinking and action among Muslims that they should become like one body and move according to the commands of a central authority.

Considering the current situation of Muslims, some people may consider it impossible. Some of my friends tell me that I am daydreaming. The nation has fallen to such a level that only a miraculous power can support it. However, I strongly believe that an opportunity that may be the last one still exists to make this nation stand again. No matter how rotten our elite are, our common Muslims still carry a hidden spark of faith; that spark is our last hope. Before it also goes out, we can make good use of it on the condition that some brave believing men should stand up to strive [*jihād*] for the cause of Allah with sincere intentions.

Removing a Misconception

Nobody should think that we want a confrontation with Congress. We have no such plans. As Indians, our mission is the same as that of Congress, that is of national freedom [*mulk kī āzādī*]. We believe that, for this common purpose of freedom, we have to finally be supportive of Congress. However, for now, we want to stay away from them because, as Muslims, we do not have the moral authority and collective system to protect our interests. First of all, we want to get rid of these weaknesses. For this purpose, we need an atmosphere that is free of disputes and conflict. Thus, if Congress continues its work without arguing with us, we do not need to fight against it. Instead, on the contrary, our sympathies will be with Congress, as far as achieving our common objectives as Indians are concerned. However, if they try to integrate our unorganized party into their system, directly preach 'nationalism' and 'communism' to our people, and use hypocrites from our community for this purpose – hypocrites who, in our eyes, are no better than the hypocrites of other types (such as the agents of British rulers) – then we will have to oppose Congress. Only Congress will be responsible for such a conflict.

To prove his current policy valid, Pandit Jawaharlal Nehru argues that preaching one's creed [*maslak*] and trying to convince opponents through conversion [English word in text; Urdu *tabdil-e-khyal*] is the right of every group. We say that if you have that right, we also have a right to convert in response. To us, preaching nationalism and communism is no different from preaching Shuddhi. Both carry the same meaning. Resistance to both of these is mandatory for us. If you are ready for this clash, and consider it beneficial for India, then that is your evident naïvety.

CHAPTER 14

The National Democratic Areligious State: Can Muslims Accept It?

Before engaging in this analysis, it is imperative to explain a few terms for the convenience and benefit of general readers.

In political science, the word 'state', whose counterpart in our language is *riyāsat*, is applied to the system that controls, through its 'coercive power' [English term in text; Urdu *qāhirānah ṭāqat*], a people living in a defined geographical boundary. On the one hand, there exists a coercive power and, on the other, obedience to it. When the two coincide, the organizational arrangement that is called the state or *riyāsat* emerges.

This understanding of the definition of the term 'state' naturally leads to a question: whether the coercive power which the population obeys arises from within the collective body of the same people, or has its origin external to this population. If that coercive power ruling the people resides beyond the collective existence of the population, then this population is in bondage. If that population owns 'sovereignty' [English word in text], that is, *ḥākamiyyat*, and wilfully lends to the system the corrective power intending to organize its collective affairs, then this population is validly a self-governing group. That a people rule itself this way or, in other words, enjoy sovereignty over itself is the principle of principles in democracy. Now, when we term a state 'a democratic state', that means that the people making up this state are sovereign (own their *ḥākamiyyat*). The government that manages the affairs of the state is subject to the collective will of the people it rules, and it has no role other than fulfilling the public's wishes in forming and implementing the law.

The actual practices in the Western democratic system differ from this ideological position. Theoretically, each individual in the system owns sovereignty and has the right to exercise it. However, practically, it is not possible to make laws and run the government according to the wishes of every individual. Therefore, for practical reasons, it has been held to be part of the principle of democratic norms that the government works according to the wishes of the majority. This is the precise point where difficulties arise. The attractive ideas upon which democratic government is initiated depart at the border of practical application. As a result, one part of the population of the country practically divests the other part of the people of their right to sovereignty and imposes its wishes upon them. In every country, different groups have different forms of interests, tastes, desires and objectives. It is due to their collective action that the machinery of civilization runs. Each one of them plays its part in the country's collective well-being and welfare in one way or another. The objectives and wishes of one group are as essential to it as the objectives and desires of others are to them. However, in a democratic system, when the principle of majority rule is adopted, that means that the group in the majority would become a ruler and, through the power of government it has, achieve its objectives and desires. The minority group is enslaved, and its aims and wishes are sacrificed for the wishes and objectives of the majority, the way they could be ignored in any extremely tyrannical rule of a tzar or caesar. This is known as the 'tyranny of the majority' [English term in text; Urdu *akthariyyat ka istabdād*] and is the ugliest mark on the faces of present-day democracies.

The rule of the majority can perform correctly only in a country where the people agree on 'fundamentals' [English word in text; Urdu *asāasī umūr*] and there is no difference among them beyond mere viewpoints; they do not differ in their objectives. In such a case, it might be possible for today's minority to grow into the majority in the future and today's majority to turn into a minority tomorrow. If public opinion is mere public opinion, it can change and can be changed. If, yesterday, public opinion favoured the Liberal Party, today it can prefer the Labour Party. Under such conditions, no majority would become a permanent and lasting majority, nor would it be able to adopt oppressive and coercive means [to further its ends]. The minority would not fear that the majority would attack the fundamentals. However, the difference in objectives or self-interests, the difference in religious principles or national [*qawmī*] sentiments, or the way of life is not something that can be removed through arguments. A group in the majority, from this perspective, will remain a permanent majority. To grant such a majority the right to rule does not mean anything other than that hundreds of thousands of tzars come to replace one tzar, and millions of caesars take the place of one caesar. They are allowed to oppress and coerce a significant group of their fellow countrymen [*hammwatan*] and do what they desire only because of their headcount. This is evidently a complete negation of the foundational principles of democracy. It is incorrect to apply the term 'democracy' to such a set-up. Instead, it should be called *Changeziyyat* on a large scale.

There are countries in which populations are divided along national lines in terms of religion, race, language, colour, etc. Similarly, in other countries, people fundamentally differ in ideologies and principles of life, or where the interests of different groups collide. In such countries, the efforts to [artificially] unite different groups to form a state and democratize it has not yielded any result other than oppression. In the entire history of the world, we do not find a single example that can stand out as an exception to this observation.

Once the workers came to power in Russia, the middle class, small farmers, traders, shopkeepers and, above all, the religious groups were crushed. They are still held under the yoke of slavery. If this oppression is compared with the tyrannical rule of the tzars, tzarism would probably be forced to bow its head before communism. This fact proves that in countries where the differences among people come down to self-interests, the rule of the people sharing interests means that they would suck the blood of all other groups and put them on the altar of their self-interests.

Western Experience of the Nation-State

About twenty years ago, different small and big nations [*qawmūn*] were combined to make up the democratic state of Czechoslovakia. The outcome of this political blunder is open for the entire world to see today. Above all, the nations that were expected to unite and form a nation-state were themselves torn into pieces by this idea of artificial nation [*qawm*] formation. There are two essential building-blocks to this new state of Czechoslovakia: Czech [English word in text] and Slovaks [English word in text]. Both differ in their ethnic and national traditions. There is no trace of interrelation between the two over a thousand years of history. The only thing that combined them was that both were subjects of Austria-Hungary. Hatred for the oppressive ruling kingdom and a desire for freedom from it attracted the two and brought them together. Political pundits thought that hostility towards a common enemy and the shared passion for freedom from it lent sufficient basis for the moulding of the two different nations into one. Therefore, they combined the two nations and formed a new nation called Czechoslovak [*sic*]. They took its practical existence for granted and established a national democratic state on its basis. However, not long after founding the new state, experience showed that binding two different nations into one does not make it one [in reality]. As soon as it was tested against reality, the artificially created nation [*qawmiyyat*] proved counterfeit. Czechs were the majority. Their literacy rate was better, and they had greater capital. The atrocities of Austria-Hungary had made them loathe not only the state but religion as well. By contrast, the Slovaks strictly adhered to their faith, were far behind their counterparts in education, depended primarily on agriculture, were poor and were outnumbered by the Czechs, being one-third of the population. Taking undue advantage of this difference, [the Czech] majority was able to include the following articles in the constitution, stipulating that Czechoslovakia would be a 'secular state' [English term in text; Urdu *dunyavī*]. Though the [constitution guaranteed] that all religions would be treated with tolerance [*rawādārī*], it stipulated that no religion, or religious system, would be acknowledged at the state level. The education system would be decided and managed by the state. Only such an education system would be provided as did not contradict the findings of scientific research.[1] Benefiting from these articles of the national constitution, the Czech majority government started appointing areligious teachers in the schools in the Slovak areas. They wholly expelled religious education from the state education system. When the Slovaks tried to provide their children with religious education on their own, the state refused to fund such a set-up. The administration in the government and particularly in key positions was specifically granted only to the Czechs. Even in the Slovak areas, the Czech officers came to act as rulers. All these realities finally made the Slovaks realize that forming a national democratic state by combining a small and a big nation translates into putting the smaller nation in the bondage of the bigger nation. Therefore, they have been

---

[1] Refer to the following articles of Czechoslovak Constitution of 1920: 119, 120, 121 and 124.

demanding 'autonomous self-government' [English term in text; Urdu *hakumati-i-khud ikhtiyārī*] for their region for many years.[2]

About 3.5 million Germans, equal to a quarter of the entire population, were also included in this same democratic nation-state. Their nationality, race [*nasal*], language and historical traditions were entirely different from the Czechs' and the Slovaks'. Instead, the Czech and German races lived in open hostility for centuries. In schools, factories, churches and wherever else the Czechs and the Germans interacted, conflicts and riots would ensue. It was not possible to employ two individuals of these two races in a single shop, to the extent that it was also difficult for the two to get on a train together from the same station. Consequently, the government established two separate stations at every small place so the Czechs could get on the train at one station, and the other station could be exclusively used by the Germans.[3] Despite such significant and intense differences, the two were brought together into one nation, establishing a democratic nation-state. In this state, the Czechs were rulers, owing to their majority status, and the Germans were subjects, owing to their minority status. This occurred even though the Germans ruled the same country where the Czechs were the subjects for centuries. The outcome of all this has been witnessed by the entire world recently. It became established that merely by being bound together in a nation-state, two different nations [*qawmayn*] do not turn into one. Nor does it guarantee that forming a democratic state would produce the true democratic spirit. However, the only thing that results from artificially making the two nations into one and establishing democracy is that the majority nation practically reduces the minority to a subject, and the democratic system causes the minority to lose their natural rights to self-government. The Czech majority did the same with the German minority. They sought to assimilate the Germans into the Czech nationality through the education system. They did not leave any stone unturned in suppressing and removing the German language and literature. They never forgot the German and Czech national differences in allotting positions in the state bureaucracy. Czechs were always preferred over the Germans. They tried to suppress the Germans and promote the Czechs in every possible way by manipulating trade, business and government tenders. Even in the specific regions where the

---

[2] R. W. Seton-Watson, *The New Slovakia*. [No publisher in original.]
[3] C. D. Hazen, *Europe since 1815*.

German population made up 60 to 80 per cent, tenders for government development projects were granted to Czechs. As a result, the economic condition of the Sudeten Germans increasingly deteriorated, and their businesses started to fail. All this unfolded in a democratic nation-state, which included Germans as a constituent of this united geographical nationality [*waṭanī qawmiyyat*] in a democratic system in which they were given complete citizenship rights according to the constitution, and they were constitutionally equally a part of its ownership of the 'commonwealth' [English word in text; Urdu *dawlat-e-mushtarakah*]. However, twenty years of experience made it clear that the terms 'national' and 'democratic' have one meaning in the lexicon and another in reality. Finally, the Germans became so strongly agitated that the peace of the whole world was about to be disturbed, had it not been for the timely and reasonable decision of handing the Germans over to Germany.

There are similar conditions in other countries as well, where different nations were assumed to be a single nationality and merged into a democratic state. Take Yugoslavia as an example. In the late nineteenth century, the Croats and the Slovenes sought freedom against Austria-Hungary's merciless occupation and formed an alliance with their neighbour, Serbia. There was no other reason behind the alliance between these elements but enmity towards Austria and the need for freedom. They ignored the differences in race, religion, language and ways of life and, intoxicated with the idea of freedom, became one. They named their collective nation 'Yugoslavia', merging the names of their separate individual languages to give birth to a united national language, giving it an unusual name, 'Serbo-Croatian Slovene', of which there was no corresponding language anywhere in the world. Instead, these were three languages with different scripts and unique linguistic features, and they were just given a single name, as in the case of 'Hindustani' [in India]. During the Great War, these three nations started fighting against Austria-Hungary. At that moment, in July 1917, a joint statement of the prime minister of Serbia and the president of the Yugoslav Committee was issued, the theme of which is as follows:

> The Serbs, Croats and Slovenians are one nation. They intend to make a nation-state for themselves, which will be a democratic state. This united state will have a distinct flag, and the three constituent partners, all of whom will be equals, will have their separate flags. Similarly, both 'Cyrillic' and 'Latin' scripts will be officially

recognized as equal. In terms of religion, Orthodox Catholic [Christianity] and Islam, all will also be acknowledged as equals.

But as the war ended, and they achieved freedom, and the new state was founded in November 1920, the situation was entirely different. Of the total state population of 12 million, there were 5 million Serbs, 3 million Catholic Croats and 1 million Slovenians. Other than these, hundreds of thousands of Germans, Hungarians, Romanians, Bulgarians and Albanians also joined this state. Even though the Serbian group was a minority compared with all the other groups combined, it was a majority in the sense that it outnumbered any other group at the individual level. Because there was no perfect agreement among these minor groups, the Serbs' position strengthened even more. Taking undue advantage of this position, the Serbs took it upon themselves to be the ruling nation, turning minorities into subjects. With this, the imaginary united nationhood vanished into thin air. The Serbian nationality was imposed upon the minorities. After the foundation of the state, when the National Council met for the first time to frame the constitution, the Serbian nationalists [*qawm-parast*] discarded the garment of Yugoslav nationality. Instead of creating a federation of self-governing provinces, they established a strong central power under a monarchy, the head of which was the king of Serbia, and its capital was the capital of Serbia. Today, this 'national democratic government' openly seeks to erase every trace of the distinct national identity of all the minority groups. For almost eighteen years, all minorities have been striving to somehow escape the trap they willingly walked into.[4]

The Major Centres of Democracy

Let us put aside these small states and turn our attention to the larger nations that are considered the forefathers of democracy and constitutionalism today. Even in those nations where various religions and ethnicities have been combined to form one national identity, the setup has only been forged through coercion and oppression. The

---

[4] Refer to the following books for details:

1 C. D. Hazen, *Europe since 1815*.
2 A. H. Morley, *The New Democratic Constitutions of Europe*.
3 'Yugoslavia' in *Encyclopedia Britannica*.

formation of a national democratic state in such cases has been driven by a large and organized group within the population forcefully imposing their desires and principles upon smaller groups while erasing the distinctive existence of the latter.

How did the Swiss nation and its federal democratic state come into being? Initially, it was merely a 'confederation' [English word in text; Urdu *riyaston kā taḥāluf*] of twenty-two free democratic nations. At the start of the nineteenth century, when the winds of religious liberalism reached Switzerland, they intended to exclude religion from education and the state system. The seven Catholic states opposed this change. However, the other fifteen liberal states had a desire to forcefully impose their thoughts on the minority despite the Constitution, which did not give them such a right. Finally, in 1847, all seven of the Catholic states left the federation as, according to the terms of the federation, they fully had the right to separate. However, the liberal states [*āzād khayāl riyāstūn*], with their overwhelming majority, deemed the separation illegitimate, attacked the Catholic states and forcefully compelled them to join the federation. Then the newly drafted constitution in 1848 restricted the role of the federal states while dramatically expanding the powers of the central state. The majority could now fully enforce their will and principles on the minority, forcing the minority to lose itself to this single nationality that 'radicals' [English word in text; Urdu *āzād khayāl lawg*] wished to bring to existence.[5]

What happened in Britain? Until the first third of the nineteenth century, election rules in Great Britain were such that England attained parliamentary seats almost three times more than the collective share of Scotland, Wales and Ireland. The number of representatives for just one of England's counties (Cornwall) was equivalent to all of Scotland's, even though Scotland's population was eight times that of Cornwall. According to the constitution, any Jew or person that did not believe in the Anglican church [*TQ* Anglicans and Catholics] could not be a member of parliament, acquire any government position or enter a municipality. All groups had to pay tithes to the Church of England. They had to turn to the priest of the Church of England to solemnify their marriages. They had to register their place of worship with the Church of England. Admission to universities – like Oxford and

---

[5] *Cambridge Modern History.*

Cambridge – had such religious conditions that they could not be fulfilled by anyone except followers of the Anglican church. Therefore, the gates of both these universities were as if closed to other groups. Though people who did not believe in the Church of England had the right to vote, they could not vote for their co-religionists, as they were not allowed to enter parliament. In 1828, there was a tendency to remove or ease these restrictions. Only after sixty years of continuous and incremental reform were the rules mostly rescinded. Such was the oppressive power and such was the material and moral domination by which the people of England subjugated the various nations and religious denominations of Great Britain and assimilated them into their civilization and their nationality and created the single nation that today is the first example of those who raise the slogan of 'one country and one nation'. Perhaps, in their view, these are the ways to build a nation.

A thorough and exhaustive investigation of the examples is not intended here. Although many more such instances can be presented from recent history and events from our age, yet these examples suffice as evidence for what I wish to prove. The meaning of forming a democratic state by declaring different nations as one nation is easily understandable from these examples. And this concept, expressed in apparently guileless words, hides a less than innocent purpose within it.

Now look at the situation in India and note what it can mean to create a national, democratic, secular state in this land.

India and the Nation-State

The meaning of a democratic Indian state is that all the citizens of India enjoy sovereignty [*ḥākamiyyat*] in the state, but, in practice, this sovereignty belongs to the group that is in a majority.

The conflation of 'national' with 'democratic' effectively denies the existence of different nationalities and declares all the inhabitants to be one nation. In other words, it means that no person would have a share in the sovereignty of India on account of his being Hindu or Muslim. Becoming a member of the state would, by default, be equivalent to him negating his Hindu or Muslim identity. His separate national identity may endure for now, but he would not be able to demand any rights from the state in this capacity. In fact, he will have to accept the decisions of the lawmaking assemblies, which the majority of the nation's citizens collectively decide.

The condition of 'secularism' [*lādīnī*] adds another thing to the concept. It means no person or group following any religion can be a part of the state in his religious capacity. He cannot even enter the bounds of the state with his religious identity. Within these bounds, he has to negate this religious status by himself. Whatever his views on morality, civilization, community, the economy, education and life, he will be forced to forget these beliefs. When a majority of people adopt a different perspective on these issues, he will not be able to disagree with the majority opinion and say that his religious and cultural perspective is different. If he raises such an objection, he will face the response that his status in the state is not at all in the capacity of the follower of some religion or culture. He will be told, you have not joined parliament as a religious man, so how would you have the opportunity to make such excuses? Your capacity here is as a mere Indian. You have already accepted the principle of democracy. Therefore, willingly or unwillingly, you will have to accept the opinion of the majority of Indians. In addition, if he requests a share of the assets and resources of the state for his religious organization, he will be told, 'Mister, this is not a religious state, but a secular areligious state. If you do not have any share in sovereignty as a religious person, how could you be given a part of the government's authority, resources and assets for a religious organization? If you want to perform these religious tasks, go and pursue them using the resources of your own religious group.

These issues result merely from focusing on the meanings and implications of these three terms. Now looking at the issue practically, the picture grows even more frightening. I have stated above that whether a democratic system is right or wrong relies entirely on the question of how majorities and minorities form within it. If there is agreement among the citizens about the 'fundamentals' [English word in text] of life and their differences are confined to the 'means and methods' [English words in text; Urdu *wasā'il awr ṭarāqa hā'i kār*], the majority keeps changing into the minority, and the minority turns into the majority. No majority, nor any minority, stays permanent or eternal. In that case, there is no danger that the majority would adopt cruelty and tyranny while depriving the minority of governance, enslaving and subjugating them. However, if the conditions are the opposite – if there is disagreement among the citizens regarding the primary affairs and foundational principles of life, and this disagreement has divided them into separate and prominent groups, and these groups have a spirit of preferring their own, and the grouping has to a great extent caused their religious goals to clash with each other – then, in such a place, the majority eternally remains a majority, and the minority eternally remains a minority. The minority cannot create and promote a consistent public opinion and become the majority there. In such a place, the meaning of declaring all the citizens part of one nation and forming a democratic, areligious state on this basis is nothing but granting a licence to the majority to be cruel, to enslave and devastate the minority. There, the nation-state would be the state of the majority group and be areligious. In this state, the minority alone, rather than the majority, would have to negate their separate national and religious identity. The majority will be able to maintain their status and identity to do all they need to do, while the minority will not even be able to mention their culture, religion, language, arts or philosophy. Declaring all the citizens of such a place a single nation does not mean they really are a single nation, but it does mean that the majority group wishes to occupy all the powers of the state, erase all the minorities and assimilate them into its own nationalism.

Look at India with open eyes and a just outlook. Is the situation here not exactly the same today?

1 Everyone can observe that the nationality difference between Hindus and Muslims is more prominent than among European German, French, English and Italian nations. Those nations at least share the same moral precepts. Their civilizational principles are the same. There is no foundational difference in their norms and way of life. If there are any, they are only marginal. On the contrary, here in India, despite living together in the same climate and on the same piece of land for 800 years, the life of each nation follows different paths. Pandit Jawaharlal Nehru may judge the Muslims and the Hindus to be one nation by looking at the appearance of the Hindus and Muslims in the villages, who dress similarly and labour together in the economic sphere. Though Nehru was born in India, his mind was developed in England and has only recently gained a tint of Russian thought. Therefore, despite living among the Indians day and night, he can only look at Indians from above and outside, just like an American tourist sees them. He cannot penetrate their hearts and their lives to see how great and deep a gulf differentiates them. The feelings and passions of the two nations collide with each other so

strongly that what a Hindu finds sacred and commanding of respect is eaten by Muslims with great delight. This difference exists between Gandhi and Maulānā Abu al Kalam Azad, just like it is found between the weaver and the Pasi in villages. However, though Azad and Gandhi can show some formal respect, the villagers strike with sticks and cudgels at such differences. Similarly, Hindus and Muslims from cities may occasionally share a table at meals, but a Hindu villager does not even drink the water touched by a Muslim. A Hindu villager has to force himself to share the bench in a train with a Muslim who is eating. In his mind he continues to condemn and distance himself from his fellow passenger. The doors to enter the life of each of these two classes are permanently closed to the other. In their entire life, from birth to death, every rite, every festival, every celebration and every sad occasion, a Hindu joins a co-religionist and a Muslim another Muslim. Given these manifest mutual differences, who can call them a single nation?

2 No doubt Muslims and Hindus are found together in the markets, offices and factories. However, do their national differences not affect their economic benefits and business objectives? One may say or write anything on an abstract level, but in daily life whatever is going on needs to be observed after entering the economic life of the population. Ask those working in the field whether or not the people differentiate between a Muslim and Hindu when choosing a servant, hiring a worker and in other matters, big and small. Are Muslims not being boycotted socially and economically even in the villages? Is it not the reality that the trades traditionally in the hands of Muslims are now being taught to Hindus so that a Muslim cannot be employed for such a job? Is it not true that it has almost been made impossible for Muslims to enter the wholesale trade? Even if a Muslim wholesaler enters a market, the entire Hindu community in that market unites to expel him from the market. What is more, has the entirety of India not recently observed that the economic interests of Muslims and Hindus relating to the new agricultural laws implemented in Punjab proved to be exactly the opposite of each other? To free the landowners from the oppressive grip of the usurers was a blessing for Muslims and a curse for Hindus. Concerning this division, Muslims and Hindus opposed each other to the extent that many Muslim leaders, inclined to the views of Congress, also sided with the Muslims while the entirety of Hindu Congressmen, even Bhola Bhai Desai, sided with the Hindus.

Does this not clearly prove that in the economic field, too, the interests of the two nations are greatly at odds with each other?

3 Have these people avoided national differences and preferences for their own type in any political matter? Leaving aside countless examples, I would focus on a few obvious examples from the behaviour of leaders of the Indian National Congress, as it is the only party that proclaims Indian nationalism. Moreover, the degree of nationalist preference [for Hindus] that is found in Congress cannot be blamed on British colonialism even by Pandit Jawaharlal.

i In response to question number 669 [*TQ* 269] raised in the Bihar Assembly on 29 April 1938, the Congress government admitted that owing to the joint electorate system election, Muslims got 47 out of 299 seats in the 24 municipal committees. On the other hand, Hindu candidates got 252 seats. However, if weighed against the population ratio, Muslims merited at least ninety-three seats, because the Muslim population in these municipalities is 33 per cent. This is the status of the election seats. The Congress government itself admitted that when it came to filling seats by nomination, of the entire number of seventy-five such seats, it nominated fourteen Muslims and sixty-one non-Muslims. However, the population ratio demanded that Muslims should have been nominated to twenty-five such seats (refer to the response to question no. 270, 29 April 1938).

ii The Ta'ullaqa Board of Buldhana District of CP [Central Province] consists of seventy-two constituencies. Under the joint electorate system, not a single Muslim could be elected in any of these. (See Qāḍī Sayyid Maḥmūd 'Alī Malkapurī's letter to Gandhi, published in the newspaper *Madīnah* on 25 September 1938.)

iii In the election for the membership of the All-India Congress Committee in CP, no Muslim could be elected, owing to this joint electorate system, nor could any untouchable [*achūt*] Hindu meet the exacting standards of the Hindus in the Indian National Congress. (See the Complaint of the Muslim Members of Congress CP, in the newspaper *Madīnah*, published 28 July 1938.)

iv In this central province, there are more than a dozen such municipal committees in which no Muslim could be elected owing to this joint electorate system. The same remained the condition of most of the local and district boards, that they are completely free of a single elected Muslim member. (See Letter by Mr Taj Uddin, published in *Star of India*, 2 July 1938. Note the fact that the writer is a famous nationalist Muslim in the central province.)

v The approach of Congress' high command towards selections is exposed by a cursory look at the government set-up in Congress-run states. The Hindu-majority provinces have Hindus as prime ministers. However, in Muslim-majority states, Muslims have been elected as the minister at best. In no Hindu-majority province, not even a most staunch [Indian] nationalist [*waṭan parast*] from among the Muslims could rise to the position of prime minister, merely owing to having an Islamic name or being accused of being related to the Muslim community. So much so that even Dr Syed Mahmood remained deprived of this honour. However, if his last name were Sinha rather than Mahmood, he would certainly be made prime minister for his services to [Indian] nationalism [*waṭan parastāna*]. Then, if we look at the list of ministers and parliamentary secretaries, we see that mostly very same proportion of the population has been considered, about which it is derogatively said that it is only communalists who take it into account. Rather, in some places, Muslims have been given a share lesser than their due proportion in the population.

Do these open indications not prove that, even in the political realm, upholders of united nationalism themselves exhibit the full spirit of discrimination based on national differences [*qawmī imtiāz*] and preference for their own kind? In such a situation, what can the meaning be of creating a democratic state on the principle of a single nationality, except that where Muslims are in the majority, they expel Hindus, and where Hindus outnumber Muslims, the latter are expelled from the affairs of state? Since, overall, in India, Hindus make up the majority, they should be able to turn the nation-state into the state of a Hindu nation.

The national democratic, areligious state created on this blatantly false claim of united nationhood, as I have already indicated, will undoubtedly be a non-Muslim state for Muslims. However, it will not necessarily be a non-Hindu state for Hindus. Rather, on the strength of their majority, they can turn it into a Hindu state. The unfolding events are increasingly making it clear that the Hindus intend to do exactly that. To prove this, too, I will present only a few incidents from one province as examples.

(a) On 24 September 1938, the Hindu chairman of the Taluka Board of Chandur, under the Congress government of CP, issued a circular (no. 446) to all the schools in the administrative division. The circular commands that children and teachers in the schools jointly worship Mahatma Gandhi on his birthday on 2 October. This circular was officially sent to all the schools without differentiating between Hindu and Muslim schools. However, there was no investigation into or accountability for this action.

(b) The Congress government of the same province, CP, issues instructions to the officers of the police department, including Hindus and Muslims, that those present at any meeting or event where 'Band-e-Mataram' is sung should stand up out of respect for the general audience. In a press note, the prime minister himself admitted that such an incident had indeed happened. (See *Times of India*, 28 June 1938.)

(c) The president of the municipal committee of Sagar, from the Central Province, threatened Muslim students that if they did not participate in singing 'Band-e-Mataram', they would be expelled from the school. This incident has also been acknowledged by the prime minister of CP himself in the abovementioned press note.

(d) In a government-run school of the same province, a representative of Anjuman Taraqqī-e-Urdu himself observed that Muslim children were worshipping Saraswati [the Hindu goddess of knowledge] along with Hindu children. Children had been taught to say, 'Jai Rām jī kī' with folded hands instead of saying, '*al salām-o-alaykum*'. (See the letter of Maulvi Abdul Haq Sahib, secretary Anjuman Taraqqī-e-Urdu, to Gandhi, in the newspaper *Piyām*, 1 September 1938.)

(h) In the Constitution of the Indian National Congress itself, the Berar region has been renamed Vidarbha, abandoning its well-known name, and Central Province has been called Mahakaushal. It is as if the Ramayana era is coming back to India.

(v) The incident of Mr Sharif, the minister of the Central Province, is still in everyone's memory. The minister had released a Muslim convicted by a court for committing adultery with a Hindu girl. To atone for this crime, he was sacked from the ministry by the Congress high command. In contrast, the Hindus accused of killing four Muslims during the riots in Jabalpur were released on the orders of the Hindu ministry of CP. However, the gods of discipline filling the high command of Congress did not feel the need to hold anyone accountable. Recently, Babu Singh, a Hindu from Hoshangabad, was sentenced to death by the High Court for poisoning a young girl to death. Mr D. K. Mehta, the Hindu minister of CP, released him. Still, it did not occur to the Congress high command to investigate the issue and take disciplinary action.

(z) The Vidya Mandir scheme is being implemented in the same province only because of the strength of the Hindu majority. Gandhi and Shukla, as well as the Congress high command, are all in agreement in showing contempt for the Muslim opposition to the issue.

Other than these incidents, there are reports of banning cow sacrifices in Bihar, UP, Madras and CP, promulgating Hindi by force while deceptively calling it Hindustani, removing the very common and conventional words of Arabic and Persian from the language, coining new, unfamiliar words to replace that language stock and committing open discrimination in government jobs. These incidents are so many that quoting them all here would cause unnecessary lengthiness. The abovementioned pieces of evidence sufficiently prove the point we intend to establish.

Everyone can see for themselves and decide how a Muslim can be part of the 'war of independence', the objective end of which negates the national interests of Muslims – in fact, their existence as a nation. Why have Muslims been taken to be so obtuse that they would struggle in order to impose such a state upon themselves? One wonders if these people have lost their minds and understanding, to expect from a nation that it would knowingly strive to dig its own grave.

CHAPTER 15

Fundamental Rights

It is claimed that the fundamental rights [English term in text; Urdu *bunyādī ḥūqūq*] declared in the Karachi Congress will be sufficient to guard the interests of Muslims in this national, democratic, areligious state. But is this true?

The source of the fundamental rights lies in the declaration of the people of England formulated by a convention [English word in text] of representatives of the subjects in 1689. This declaration was concluded after a long dispute and conflict. The objective was to prevent the despotic actions of the government and to define limits between government and subjects [*rayeet*] that neither would break. Subsequently, the same rights were enshrined as general principles in the United States' 'Declaration of Independence' and 'Declaration of the Rights of Man'. Later, these rights were included in the constitution of Belgium in 1831. Since then, it has almost become a rule to specify these rights of the inhabitants in every constitution. Therefore, no constitution of the modern age is devoid of these. In fact, some rights are added in each subsequent constitution. The summary of these rights is as follows:

In the eyes of the law, all inhabitants are equal. A person cannot be punished unless he violates the law, and his punishment must also accord with the law. The government can interfere with the personal liberty and property of the subjects only as the law finds permissible. There will be general freedom of speech and press, provided it is not contrary to the Law of Libel [English term in text; Urdu *qānūn-e-qadhaf*]. The confidentiality of mail and wire messages will be maintained. People will have the right of assembly, provided they are unarmed and do not endanger public order. Elections will be free. Members of parliament will be protected from harassment. They cannot be arrested unless one is caught violating the law.

Besides these, this is one of the principles added to modern constitutions: women and men are equals.

These rights were originally designed to contain the government whenever it overstepped its bounds. Subjects would have a legal basis to demand their rights from the government and protect their freedom and personal boundaries. Or, if government fails to comply and subjects must fight, the moral aspect of the government's action remains weak. However, first of all, the revolution in political ideas in modern times has broken down every imaginable boundary between government and subjects to the extent that it is now almost impossible to say where the jurisdiction of the government ends and where the sphere of individuals and subjects starts. Secondly, this declaration of rights can only work if there is undue interference by the government against the will of the majority population and citizens stand up in large numbers to protect their rights. But where there is a majority government, and it interferes with the minority's rights, this declaration of rights proves completely useless. Thirdly, if we consider and analyse the fundamental rights mentioned in the resolution of Karachi, it becomes apparent that they are not a cure for any of our afflictions.

A brief explanation of these three points is necessary so that the general audience can easily understand the discussion.

The Scope of Government in Modern Times

What is the scope of the government? Ideas and practices of the world are now starkly different from what they were in the eighteenth and nineteenth centuries. The eighteenth century was an era of personal rule, and people were struggling to get rid of monarchical tyranny. Therefore, the people's mind was under the influence of the mechanical theory [English term in text; Urdu *mashīnī naẓriyyah*] of the relationship between government and subjects. That is, they believed that the collectivity of the individuals is a separate thing from the state. They interact with each other like a seller and a buyer, or a hirer and a worker. The same idea gave birth to the theory of individualism [English word in text; Urdu *infirādī naẓriyyah*] and the power of the state. This theory dictates that the freedom of the individual is the primary objective. It is for the protection of individual freedom that the individual enters into the social contract [English term in text; Urdu *mu'ā'idah 'imrānī*] that brought the state into existence. Therefore, the duty of the state is nothing other than to protect the personal freedom of individuals and prevent the interference by one individual in the liberty of another. Protecting life and property, maintaining peace, establishing justice and protecting the borders of the country from external attacks, these alone are the state's functions. Violating these limits, and interfering in the personal affairs of individuals, even if it is for the betterment of individuals and with any good intention, is nevertheless illegitimate. This was an idea common in the late eighteenth century and early nineteenth century. Based on this idea, some scholars of politics went so far as to list the tasks that could come under the purview of government.

These ideas persisted in the present era and lingered for a long time while democratic governments were replacing personal rule/monarchies. People failed to realize for ages that democracy and putting limits on the government are mutually exclusive practices. When society creates the state, how can society impose restrictions on itself? And why would it need to restrict itself? Society establishes the state only to fulfil such collective needs as require coercive and organizational power. Then what is the plausible reason for society to declare the use of this organizational power as legitimate for some needs and illegitimate for others? Such a division between the state and the people was necessary when the government would be separate from society and would be imposed from without. But when the government arises out of society itself, what is the need for marking these boundaries?

Organic Theory of State and Society [English term in text; Urdu *zindah nizām-e-jismānī ki tarah*] developed along with the evolution of democratic ideas and culminated in the advent of socialism. Now, everywhere in the world, the sphere of the government's jurisdiction is extending to all aspects of collective life, penetrating the foundations of culture, social life and the economy in their minutest aspects. The duties of government at present include providing a livelihood for inhabitants, creating employment for them, raising their standard of living and providing them with maximum comfort. The government is compelled to utilize the country's economic resources in the best possible manner to fulfil these duties; thus, the entire economic life, including its industrial, commercial and financial sectors, falls under the authority of the government. To fulfil these duties, the government is obliged to take over the entire management of education and make citizens useful for these purposes. Moreover, it is not always possible to fulfil these duties while observing the personal freedom of individuals or different groups of individuals and respecting their individual wishes or their specific rights. These rights can only be observed provided people do not hinder the government's actions to discharge its duties. Wherever they create a hindrance, their individuality will be destroyed. It is no longer possible for a person or a group to freely decide what kind of education to give their children. It is the government's job to prepare children as it deems appropriate from the point of view of the collective welfare. Even in cultural and social matters, the right of individual freedom is no longer granted. Government can introduce any changes in culture and society as are necessary for the collective welfare. It can even tell people to dress in a specific way and not to adopt another dress, use a specific writing script and avoid using another, marry at a specific age and not marry at another age, and so on and so forth. Similarly, being responsible for the economic welfare and development of citizens, government cannot always respect an individual's personal rights concerning trade, industry and craft, agriculture and property. It is compelled to operate the whole economic machinery according to collective ends and restrain individual rights that stand in the way. Therefore, almost all the democratic constitutions formulated after the Great War contain provisions that lend the government immense power over private property and private business. For example, it can forcibly sell a merchant's property, and confiscate personal property with or without compensation.[1] It has the right to acquire lands without compensation if necessary for the settlement of citizens or their resettlement, or the development of agriculture.[2] Government can also take into its hands inherited property, if beyond a specified limit, and distribute it[3] and determine a share of the state in the inheritance.[4] And if the government finds it necessary for the protection of the collective good, it may even interfere in the organization of private business, and access their communications and information.[5]

---

[1] Constitution of Germany, article 153, section 2; Constitution of Poland, article 99; Constitution of Czechoslovakia, article 109.
[2] Constitution of Germany, article 155.
[3] Constitution of Yugoslavia, article 41. Estonia, Latvia and Lithuania also have similar laws.
[4] Constitution of Germany, article 154; Constitution of Yugoslavia, article 39.
[5] Constitution of Yugoslavia, article 35.

Such vast and unlimited government power has, firstly, rendered fundamental rights simply meaningless – because the rights claimed to be the primary and birth rights of man can all be forcibly taken away by today's government in the name of collective welfare. Secondly and more importantly, in a democratic system it is the majority that enacts and enforces the laws of government. It is also the majority's job to define collective welfare and its requirements. Therefore, the majority's tyranny, despotism and oppression see no bounds. The door to the minority's entire life becomes open to the majority's oppressive intervention. In the name of the collective interest, the majority can interfere in the minority's culture, economy, society and religious laws in any way and to the extent it wishes. It can also try to control the education system and completely wipe out the minority's nationhood [*qawmiyyat*].

2 Benefits of Fundamental Rights

If fundamental rights can be useful to some extent, that is only when an overwhelming majority of citizens are ready to protect them and, only incidentally, come under the imposition of such a government as wants to violate these rights. In cases where the majority itself, which is running the democratic government, starts to use oppression, then a lengthy list of fundamental rights cannot protect the minority.

Take the example of Great Britain, where these fundamental rights originated. Until 1828 it was necessary for those aspiring to be members of parliament and municipal councils or government servants to partake in the Lord's Supper [English term in text] according to the stipulations of the Church of England. Until 1829 Catholics were deprived of any form of representation. Until 1867 Jews could not be part of parliament. Until 1854 the doors of Oxford and Cambridge were closed to those who did not believe in the 39 Articles of the Protestant faith, and until 1871 no such person could receive any position, distinction or academic scholarship at these two universities. Until 1881 there were various burial restrictions on those who did not follow the Church of England. Until 1888 there were inappropriate oath restrictions for those giving evidence in the courts of law. And what happened to the minority of Ireland until 1920 is known to the whole world.

The example of the United States of America is even more instructive. The African [*habshī*] population of the country is 12 million, making up a little more than 9 per cent of the total population. Under the constitution, they have full civil rights, just like white Americans. They are also equal participants in the democratic commonwealth, and there is nothing in the law on the basis of which one can discriminate between whites and blacks. But what is the actual practice? The white majority openly discriminates against the black community. Civil rights aside, even ordinary human rights are being denied to the blacks openly, and the fundamental rights granted by the constitution are of no use to them. They cannot enter churches belonging to the white population. They cannot step into white hotels, restaurants and theatres. If a black man enters places of entertainment reserved for the white population, he is expelled with humiliation. It is not permissible for a black man to sit beside a white person in buses and railway coaches. No black person can buy a house in white neighbourhoods. A black man's child cannot sit in a school with white children. Their life, property and honour carry no value. So much so that the conscience of civilized white people does not stir at the brutal treatment of the black population. And rarely does the legal machinery move against a white man for the sake of a man of African origin.

This is not the place to detail the behaviour of the American majority towards the black minority. However, I think it necessary to briefly explain what colours the government of the majority takes and what becomes of the constitution, fundamental rights, the law and its nominal articles in a country where the majority and the minority are really separated from each other by race, colour, religion or any other such element.

In the United States, they founded a theory about black people without a scientific basis. According to this theory, biologically [English word in text; Urdu *ḥayātiyātī ṭawr par*] this race was unfit for education and, socially [English word in text; Urdu *'imranī nuqtah-e-naẓar sey*], educating them would make them useless. Instead of becoming servants, they would want to become equals. Because of this theory, some states legally banned educating the black community, and in other states it was considered wrong to educate them. For many years, black people established schools and educated their children using their own resources. When they demonstrated their intellectual abilities to the world, only then, in 1905, did their schools start to get government support.

Before the law, black and white Americans are not equal in practice, though they are equal in word. The prison sentences for black

Table 1

	Black Prisoners	White Prisoners
1890	264	84
1904	278	77
1910	284	89
1923	327	77

individuals is always longer. According to the data for 1910, on average a black man was imprisoned for seventeen months, and one from among the white population faced only five months' imprisonment. Black people make up only 9 per cent of the population but, in jails, 31 per cent of the inmates are black.

In 1880, there were 244 black prisoners and 96 white prisoners per 100,000 population.

Similarly, the number of white inmates is steadily decreasing, but the number of black inmates is increasing.[6] This is not because black people commit more crimes. A commission, known as the Chicago Commission of Racial Relations [English term in text],[7] was appointed in Chicago with the purpose of investigating race relations. A judge gave the following statement before the commission: 'The evidence which the jury considers sufficient to convict a black man is not considered sufficient to convict a white man.' Another judge testified that 'in the same circumstances and events it is easy to punish a black man and difficult to punish a white man. During riots between blacks and whites, the police arrest all the black population and rarely lay hands on the whites.' Describing the results of its investigation, the Chicago Commission states:

> All testimonies almost agree that blacks are caught more frequently compared to whites. This is because the common assumption of the police is that they [black people] are mostly criminal. The police also know that there is no danger in arresting blacks, whereas caution should be exercised when dealing with whites ... Several blacks can be caught for the same crime. Therefore, merely observing a higher population of Negroes in prisons should not lead us to understand

[6] *Encyclopedia Britannica*, 'Negroes in America'.
[7] The report of this commission has been published under the title 'Negroes in Chicago'.

that they commit more crimes. Relative to white people, the chances of avoiding arrest are very slim for black people.

This is the state of the law. What is the status of the majority which is running this democratic system? In practice, such restrictions have been imposed on the right to vote, so that many blacks, despite being citizens [English word in text; Urdu *shehrī*], are automatically deprived of the right to vote. The doors of government jobs are as if closed to them. To date, no black could hold any position of power. However, they were readily sent to war to become cannon fodder. And now again they are being prepared for that very task.

The general [white] population not only considers them lowly but feels free to instigate riots on flimsy excuses in which blacks are killed brutally. In 1919, suddenly a rumour spread in Chicago that a black man had killed an Italian girl. A crowd of white men gathered and attacked a black person who was passing by. When the body of the victim was presented before the coroner's court, it contained fourteen bullets. The skull of the man was found to be broken into pieces and his ribs had been shattered. Later it transpired that the incident of the murder of the Italian girl was baseless. While President Wilson was sitting in Paris, condemning German atrocities, an African American was being burnt alive in Chicago. In the United States they have found an innovative way of serving justice. It is called lynching [English word in text]. It means that when people are not satisfied with the judgment of the court or cannot bear the slow motion of the machinery of the law, then they take the law into their hands. The person they consider guilty is punished in the way the executers believe is just. This method of serving justice is usually inflicted on black people. Therefore, the data from 1895 to 1926, published in the *New York World*, show that 3,205 blacks were openly lynched over a period of forty-one years. Lynching is usually carried out when a black man is found or suspected to be in a relationship with a white woman. But the conscience of the white American is ready to revolt only when a black man is found close to a white woman. As far as the black woman is concerned, she is the birthright of white men. The general opinion of white people about blacks is that the latter are brutes [English word in text; Urdu *wehshī jānwar*]. Their moral standards are very low. In fact, they are entirely deprived of moral sense. Attacking women and children and villainy are ingrained in their nature. In the language of Indian newspapers, a black is a congenital *ghundah* [goon].

But the Chicago Commission proved through a proper investigation that the moral standard of the blacks is loftier than that of the masters [*sāḥibs*]. The commission noted that the masters [*sāḥibs*] were very daring in attacking the women of their own kind. A poor black man does not have a fraction of this courage. However, when this offence is committed by a black man (and that, too, is often the result of invitation and incitement by white women), then the white men create a great fuss about it. And this is the real reason behind the infamy of the black population. A judge recorded his statement before the commission stating that never had a black man come to his court who really had raped underage girls. However, many such white men have been brought. Another judge testified that during his entire term in office, only one black man charged with this crime was brought to his court, although many whites were often caught and brought before him.

Since 1865, a secret society by the name of the Ku Klux Klan [English name in text] has been working in the United States. It was established with the objective of protecting the superiority of whites over blacks and to solve the 'Negro Problem' [English term in text] in the United States in such a manner that, like the Red Indian [transliterated in Urdu text] nation, this nation too would gradually be annihilated.[8] With a membership of 1.5 million in 1923, it is the most powerful association in the United States. Highly educated individuals, those from the elite and those with close connections with the government are a part of this organization. Governors of provinces, and police, prison and court officials connive with them. That is why they can commit major atrocities and horrible crimes but are never caught. They even take prisoners out of jail and the machinery of the law stands still. The author of *America Comes of Age* [title in English] states that it is possible that the decent and polite gentleman with whom you are having a conversation might have killed a man in the forest the night before. Many such men that you would honour and warmly welcome in the daytime might also be involved with him in this crime. The governor of Texas commanded an investigation into some horrible crimes. It transpired that the

---

[8] Since 1790, the white population has grown at the rate of 13 per cent. The Red Indian population has decreased by 50 per cent. It is expected that towards the end of the current century [the twentieth century] no Red Indian will remain. This was a nation that populated America before the whites.

criminals included a priest, and many of the friends of the governor were involved in the crime.

How are these civilized people solving the problem of the Negroes? Here are some examples:

They beat a black woman until she lost consciousness and left her in the forest, naked, to die of the cold. They lashed a black man and tore his skin to the point that he was forced to sell his land to a white man at a low price. They captured a black man, took him to the forest and tied him up with ropes and barbed wire. They lashed him till his skin was torn. Then they sprinkled *kiryāzot* [creosote] onto his wounds and left him in agony for hours till he died. They captured and took away a black slave woman and her son and tied them both to a railbridge. They took a poor man from the hospital and roasted him alive on a fire. They tied another helpless black man to a telephone pole, poured kerosene on him and set him on fire.[9]

The unforgiveable, grave sin of a black man is that he lives in a white neighbourhood, or that his property lies there. Between 1917 and 1921, in the city of Chicago alone, fifty-eight such houses were bombed that had been bought by a black man or rented to him by a white man. The house and office of a black banker [called Binga] was bombed six times within a year, just because he became a source of financial stability for black people. The black people could borrow money from his bank on favourable terms. They started to buy properties from this source. These are the events that have led to the reduction in the black population in the United States from 19 per cent in 1790 to 9 per cent today.[10] And the irony is that the fundamental rights of the black minority are absolutely protected in the constitution of the United States.

Another example, this one from Germany, is open to you. The German constitution guarantees the fundamental rights of all citizens. However, today the treatment of the non-Aryan race in the country is known to all. It has become almost impossible for non-Aryans to

---

[9] These events have been published in the journal *New Age*.

[10] For details, see the following books:

J. E. Cutler, *Lynch-Law*.

C. G. Woodson, *The Negro in Our History*.

E. B. Reuter, *The American Race Problem*.

M. J. Hersko[vits], *The American Negro*.

earn a living with honour within the borders of the country. To leave the country is an equal impossibility. The doors to government and private jobs are closed to them. They cannot engage freely in trade. They are being pushed out of other independent professions. They are subjected to open racial discrimination in the courts. The theory of justice applied to non-Aryans is that everyone among them is impure and a born criminal until he proves himself innocent. The common people who have financial or any other dealings with them, they too face the wrath of the government. Their children are subjected to intolerable restrictions in schools. If their children are sent to study abroad, they are given only passports that allow emigration [*hijrat ka passport*], so that they cannot return. If non-Aryan parents want to go abroad to visit their children, they are also only allowed to go as emigrants. And for those who emigrate, Germany has introduced a law that they cannot take with them more than 10 per cent of their wealth. The rest is confiscated.

Which of the rest of the European countries are devoid of fundamental rights as part of its foundational constitution? And which is the country where the constitutionally granted fundamental rights of the citizens have protected the minority from the oppression of the majority? In every case, they assumed the entire population of the country as a nation and carved out a democratic state. The fundamental rights were included in the constitution. But wherever there is a difference between the majority and the minority, of a religious, racial or linguistic nature, there the majority tries either to make the minority shed its distinct national existence and adopt the nationality of the majority, or lower their status to that of the Shudras or destroy them through different ways. When the Yugoslavian Croats demanded a separate province for themselves and sought autonomy, do you know how the Serbs responded to these demands? Note their answer [produced below] verbatim:

> In fact, Serbs, Croats and Slavs are one nation. Foreign ruling power had forcibly separated them. Now that the yoke of alien rule has fallen off our shoulders, the feeling of national unity has triumphantly emerged. This feeling has destroyed all the barriers created by political institutions, language and religion. In order to maintain and enhance this sense of unity, it is necessary that the geographical divisions of old, through which foreign rulers divided the nation, be abolished. For the

management of the local administration, the provinces should be divided anew so that previous demarcation of the provincial boundaries cannot cause racial groups to emerge [English terms in text; Urdu *naslī halqe*].[11]

Does it not sound as if Jawaharlal Nehru is giving a speech in an independent India? The nation vehemently preaching a single united nationhood is the nation whose benefit lies in such a unity. It has almost become a principle. Obtuse people who, in the earnest zeal for freedom, raise the cry of 'One nation, one country' regret it later. Once free, the single nationality starts to swallow them like a dragon. Now they are furious. The clear law of nature calls out to these fools and 'Die of your rage.' When the objections raised by the Croats in the National Assembly of Yugoslavia were responded to in the abovementioned words, it has been reported that the Croat representatives walked out of the assembly in protest. Once they left, it became easier for the Serbian majority in the assembly to pass every law that they needed. At that moment, fundamental rights stood at a good distance, laughing and saying, 'Now say what fools we made of them!'

3 Analysis of the Karachi Resolution

Now, let us analyse the fundamental rights proposed in the Karachi Resolution. On the basis of these proposed rules, many of our naïve brothers go around explaining to Muslims all over the country, saying to them: 'Brothers! Congress has already taken the responsibility of protecting your rights. Why do you not participate in building an independent democratic state on the basis of a united nationality?'

According to the first article [of the Resolution], every citizen of India is granted freedom of expression and assembly, provided these rights are used for purposes not opposed to law and morality. The condition of law and morality may annul this freedom at any time. According to the principle of democracy, lawmaking and deciding moral standards would be absolutely the power of the majority. It will be the government of the majority that will enforce it. Therefore, reducing or increasing the limits of the freedom of the minority will only be based at their discretion.

---

[11] A. H. Morley, *The New Democratic Constitutions of Europe.*

The second article [of the Resolution] grants every citizen of India freedom of conscience and freedom to believe and practise his religion if the exercise of such freedoms does not affect law and order and moral standards. Again, we find the same condition. This condition can take away freedom at any time. However, if the majority generously gives us this freedom fully, then too our objective cannot be met. Even the British government has granted us such freedoms. Despite this freedom, our religiosity is weakened and our culture is half-dead. When governmental authority is not in our hands and the majority party that does have access to it is completely unfamiliar with the principles of our civilization and is committed to completely different ideas of civilization, ethics and culture, then we do not benefit from attaining religious freedom under this government. [Religious freedom under such a government] would mean nothing more than that we will not be forcibly prevented from praying. Rather, such apostasy will gradually be inculcated in us that we will stop praying on our own. Our mosques will not be demolished, but our hearts and minds will be changed from within so that these mosques become desolate and will automatically turn into relics. Policemen will not forcefully remove the veil from the faces of our women, but schoolteachers will inculcate in their minds, with compassion and mercy, the standard of conduct on the basis of which they would rather want to be stage dancers than queens of the house. This kind of freedom is just an opium putting us in a slumber while everything around us continues to change. This is the decree of freedom about which these people believe that in the future secular national democratic state, their religion and culture will be fully protected. They should know that the nature of the promised religious protection is no different from that of ancient historical buildings. These guarantees are confined to the limited offer that those of the present generation who intend to maintain their religiosity will not be forced to embrace disbelief. This decree does not guarantee that the next generation will not be given such education and training causing them to leave Islam. The meaning of this protection is that, if you want, you can engage in studying the sayings of God and the pronouncement of the Prophet. Your beard will not be forcibly shaved. Neither will your cloak be confiscated, nor will your prayer beads be taken away. Similarly, your tongue will not be hindered from teaching hadith and the Quran. However, all this does not mean that the future generation will also be allowed to remain in this 'misunderstanding' that Islam is the true religion, superior to others and the soundest of all. Anyone willing to remain happy at receiving this licence for religious freedom, let them be happy. We do not need such a decree. The nature of our religion and our civilization does not demand passive freedom. It demands active freedom. We want the independence of the country for nothing other than that our government be in our own hands to create our own education system and reform the distorted system of our civilization with our strength. If it is not guaranteed, then it is the same for us, whether the government is in the hands of external infidels or internal ones.

The third article ensures that the culture, language and writing script of minority communities and different linguistic regions will be protected. To award Hindi the status of the 'national' language of India, and ensuring this with the government's money and power, does not go against this article. If the education system is fashioned in such a way that it excludes the civilization of minorities, and in fact if the education system is set up with the objective of letting the civilization of minorities die out slowly ... such an outcome too would not be against this article. In fact, this article does not mean that the language of minorities and their culture will be given life using the resources of the state treasury. Rather, this article only means that they will not be forcibly killed. If they die of hunger, the government will not be responsible. In fact, we are told through the words of UP's prime minister that their dying of hunger is exactly what is required so that the phoenix [Urdu *Quqnus*] of 'Indian Civilization' can rise from their ashes. Obviously, we already enjoy this kind of fundamental right under English rule. English rule has not barred us from speaking and writing Urdu (rather, the colonial state has established vernacular schools). The English did not pass any ordinances to prevent us from living according to our culture. But this fundamental right has not given life force to our language and our culture. If the same happens in this government, which is called a 'national government', then, for us, such a 'national government' will in reality be a non-national government. We need a national government so that we can feed our language and our culture on the vast resources of the government in the same way that free nations do. Otherwise, we already have the freedom to manage our own needs. We do not need a war of independence for such a freedom.

The fourth clause says that all citizens are equal in the eyes of the law. There will be no discrimination on the basis of caste, religion and gender. This is a very good clause. However, the concept of equality differs with every culture. What would be the use of this article for us, if a majority follows this democratic principle and passes a law to equalize the share of inheritance between men and women and mocks the minority that opposes it, the way those opposing Mr Dass's bill were mocked in the Central Assembly?

The fifth article guarantees that no citizen shall be barred from holding public office or any position of power or from entering any profession or business on account of his religion, caste, creed and gender. This article has both good and bad aspects. If the system of government is in the hands of a party that has no sympathy with our civilization, then the rights granted by this clause can 'elevate' honourable Muslim daughters and daughters-in-law to the position of film actresses.

The sixth article lends equal rights to citizens to use the streets, ponds, wells and madrasas etc. Unlike the first and second articles, this article has no such condition as 'if that does not violate public order and morals'. According to the second clause, cow sacrifice can be banned. But the sixth clause does not impose any restrictions on such a use of roads where Muslims are disturbed at the time of prayer by those playing a trumpet.

These are the fundamental rights the declaration of which is hailed as a supreme blessing. We are asked to repay this favour by fighting to impose upon ourselves a government whose policy formation and legislation and implementation of the laws we cannot affect, owing to the principles of unified nationality and democracy. In other words, our services are being obtained only to replace Pharaoh with his son. As for our true condition, we have the same status as that endured by the Israelites in the era of Pharaoh. The son of Pharaoh assures us that such a freedom will be available even under his rule.

Does India Need Nationalism?

[This chapter brings together a three-part essay published in the August, September and December 1939 issues of *Tarjuman ul Quran*. It was written in response to a question about Maulānā Ubaidullah Sindhī's speech that a reader quoted, claiming it had been published in the June 1939 issue of *Madina Bijnor*. The reader asked if Western nationalism and Western dress were appropriate for Muslims now that prominent ulama such as Maulānā Mahmood ul Hasan and other elders of the Deoband school had also expressed support for nationalism.]

Nationalism for Expediency

Maulānā [Sindhī]'s arguments for promotion of the European style of nationalism [in India] are put below in his own words:

1 If my country can avoid the harms of the revolution that has engulfed the entire world and continues to dominate, then it should foster nationalism on European principles.

2 The world knows how famous our country was in the past. However, we cannot benefit from this fame unless we establish our dignity among today's nations. And we can establish this dignity through the ways Western nations have [earned it].

3 The ancient age of Indian civilization is known as Hindu civilization and the modern period is considered an Islamic civilization. Both are religious schools. However, the European school today is absolutely dissociated from religion. It is entirely based on science and philosophy. Therefore, if our country does not create the ability to understand this revolution, the entire loss will be ours.

It seems that to understand it does not mean merely understanding it, but also following it, because the previous premises of Maulānā led to this conclusion.

Ponder over these three arguments. It is not being suggested that we adopt something owing to its being truth and veracity or moral soundness and correctness. Rather, an approach is being suggested merely for expediency [English word in text; Urdu *maṣlaḥat* and *ḍarūrat*]. In the light of this fact, what value does Maulānā's suggestion carry in the eyes of a Muslim, indeed, any man of principle? A man following a distinct moral and intellectual ideology cannot adopt a viewpoint or embrace a principle on the grounds that such and such opposition or a different approach are not current in the world today, or this principle he is about to choose has replaced another. It cannot be the stance of a person following a moral and intellectual perspective that he feels morally compelled to spread and establish. It is naked opportunism [English phrase in text]. It has no relation to rationality and morality. Rationality demands that we strictly adhere to the principle that research proves to be true. Morality dictates that we firmly believe in its moral truth. If a false principle has become current in the world, then we should not blindly follow the trend. Rather, our duty is to bring the world back to our principle. What serves as a test of our truthfulness in a belief lies in our bearing with patience and steadfastness the loss that we suffer if there is opposition from the world. If the world does not value us only because we do not follow its ways, then we should spurn such a world. We do not worship dignity worldly respect. If the time of concepts that we believe to be true has passed, then we should muster the power to hold time by its ear and drag it towards the truth. It is only defeated men of low spirit who think that whatever finds currency in the world today is what we need to appreciate and then, in the process, be consumed by.

One should at least show such steadfastness as was shown by the Marxists during the World War. When the World War broke out in 1914, there was a great difference among the members of the Second International on the question of nationalism. Many socialists who had come together in an international front were subdued by the feeling of nationalism as they saw their nations entering the war. They wanted to side with their nations. However, the followers of Marx said that they had risen to fight for the sake of a principle which dictates that the bourgeoisie of every nation was their enemy, and the workers of all nations were their friends. How then can we accept nationalism of this nature, which divides workers and makes them side with the bourgeoisie and fight their own kind? On this occasion, these Marxists cut themselves off from their age-old friends. They tolerated the break-up of the Second International but did not accept giving up their principles. Not only this, but the true communists broke the idol of nationalism with their very hands. The German communists went against Germany, and the Russian communists went against Russia, for the sake of their viewpoint. Similarly, all true communists from different countries worked against their national governments for the sake of their beliefs.

Just as a communist holds to an ideology, so does a Muslim. Then why should a Muslim become so low and despicable as to abandon his views to avoid a probable harm or to become dignified in someone's eyes? And even if he slides away from his stance, he should at least be conscious of what he is distancing himself from and what he is proceeding towards. The reason is that leaving one's stance is mere weakness. However, moving away from one's position and thinking that one is still in the same place is weakness, as well as obtuseness. I am a 'Muslim' only as long as I hold an Islamic view on every matter of life. If I deviated from this view and adopted another ideology, it would be total blindness on my part to continue to believe that, if I adhered to the new idea, I still enjoyed the status of a Muslim. Professing to be a Muslim while adopting an un-Islamic ideology is clearly meaningless. 'Muslim nationalist' and 'Muslim communist' are terms no different from such [contradictory terms] as 'communist fascist', or 'Jain butcher', or 'socialist moneylender', or a 'monotheistic pagan'.

Nationalism and Islam

Whoever casts a cursory look at the meaning and reality of nationalism cannot fail to appreciate that Islam and nationalism are antithetical in their spirit as well as purpose. Islam addresses man as a human being. It offers for all human beings a social system based on belief and morality, emphasizing justice and piety. It calls all humans towards this belief. Then, Islam embraces with equal rights those who accept this system. In its forms of worship, economy, politics, social norms, legal rights and obligations, and everything Islamic, there is no room for any form of national, racial, geographical or class distinction among those who enter the folds of Islam. Islam's ultimate objective is to establish a global society and world state [English term in text; Urdu *jahānī riyāsat*].

146

In this state the chains of racial and national prejudices are broken. All humans are intended to become participants in a cultural and political system, enjoying equal rights and equal opportunities for progress. Instead of hostile confrontation, friendly co-operation among people is fostered, so that the people may support each other in material well-being and spiritual advancement. The principles and the way of life Islam suggests for human welfare will attract common people only when they transcend ignorant bias, their national customs, racial pride, and the attachments of blood and soil. They are ready to evaluate what truth is and where justice and righteousness lie [not as men of class and country but] as mere human beings. They should be able to discern which path leads to the welfare of the whole of humanity rather than that of a particular class, nation or country.

On the contrary, nationalism differentiates among men on the basis of their nationality. Nationalism means nothing other than that every nationalist will prefer his nation over other nations. Even if a man is not an aggressive nationalist [English term in text; Urdu *jafākār qawm-parast*], nationalism demands that he differentiate between 'national' and 'non-national' in terms of civilization, politics and legal status. He should protect the benefits of his fellow countrymen and erect barriers of economic privileges for national interests. He should rigorously protect the historical traditions and customary biases upon which his nation is based. He should nurture sentiments of national pride within himself. He should not equally share anything in any sphere of life with people of another nationality. In situations where his nation is enjoying or could potentially gain more benefits and advantages in comparison with other nations, his heart will become blind to justice and fairness. His ultimate objective will be a national state instead of a global state. Even if it adopts a universal approach, it will necessarily take the form of imperialism or caesarism, because into his state the people of other nationalities can never enter as equals. They can enter it only as subjects.

It is precisely the principles, objectives and spirit of both schools of thought that clearly indicate that they are contradictory to each other. Where there is nationalism, Islam can never flourish. And where Islam exists, there is no place for nationalism. The progress of nationalism implies that the path of Islam's growth is blocked. The progress of Islam means that nationalism is rooted out from its very foundation. It is evident that a person can support the growth of only one of these two ideologies at a time. It is not possible for him in any way to wear two hats at the same time.

To profess one ideology and simultaneously advocate for its exact opposite clearly indicates entanglement of thought and wavering of mind. We are forced to view those who express such views as either not truly understanding Islam or nationalism, or as ignorant of both.

The Reality of European Nationalism

The above observations emerge from considering the very basic meaning of nationalism. We may proceed and delve into the nature of 'European nationalism' on the basis of which Maulānā Sindhī wants the promotion of nationalism in India.

During the ancient ignorance [*jāhiliyyat*], the concept of nationalism was underdeveloped. In those times, man was generally more emotionally attached to his tribe or clan rather than nation. Therefore, during that era, tribalism rather than nationalism ruled. This group feeling attached to race blinded many great minds and sages. Even a philosopher of great status, Aristotle, holds in his work *Politics* that 'nature has created barbaric tribes only to be slaves'.[1] To him, 'one of the natural and permissible means to acquire wealth is to wage war to enslave certain human classes as are created by nature for this purpose'.[2] This theory turns more horrifying when we also consider the fact that by the term 'barbarians' [English word in text: Urdu *waḥshī*], the Greeks simply meant 'non-Greeks'. The Greeks' fundamental notion was that the ethics and human rights of Greek people were completely different from those of other human beings.

This was the initial seed of nationalism that flourished in Europe later. The force that restrained the growth of this germ for a while was the power of Christianity. The teachings of a prophet, however distorted they may have been, still have a broader human perspective instead of racial and nationalist prejudices. Additionally, the global political system of the Roman empire at least reduced the intensity of national and racial biases by uniting many small nations under a common authority and compelling them to obey this central authority. In this way, for centuries, the spiritual power of the pope and the political authority of the emperors combined and threaded the Christian world together in a relationship. Though both these powers were united and aided each other in oppression and

---

[1] Aristotle, *Politics*, book 1, chs. 2 and 6.   [2] Aristotle, *Politics*, book 1, ch. 8.

opposition to scientific and intellectual progress, yet they were rivals and opponents when it came to the distribution of worldly power and material benefits. Their mutual conflict and struggle, their injustices and oppression, and the modern scientific awakening in the sixteenth century gave birth to the political and religious movement known as the Reformation [English word in text; Urdu *tehrīk-e-iṣlāḥ*].

This movement yielded great success by bringing to an end the domination of the pope and the emperor, enemies of progress and reform. However, this movement led to the disintegration of nations that were bound together. The Reformation could not provide an alternative to the spiritual connection among various Christian nations. With the breakdown of religious and political unity among nations, separate and autonomous national states began to emerge. Each nation's language and literature developed separately. The economic interests of each nation diverged from those of neighbouring nations. Consequently, a new concept of nationalism emerged, based on racial, political, economic and cultural foundations. This concept of nationalism replaced the old ignorant [*jāhilī*] notion of group feeling [*aṣbiyyat*]. Then a series of conflicts, clashes and competitions [English word in text; Urdu *musābaqat*] started among different nations. Battles were fought. One nation encroached upon and forcefully snatched the rights of others. The worst manifestations of oppression and misery were carried out, which further fostered bitterness in national emotions [*qawmiyyat ke jadhbāt*] day by day until the feeling of national attachment [*qawmiyyat*] evolved and transformed into nationalism [*qawm parastī*].

The nationalism that has developed in Europe in this form, since it has arisen from competition and conflict with neighbouring nations, necessarily contains four [negative] elements.

(1) The feeling of national pride. This [element] elevates the love and admiration for one's national traditions and characteristics to the level of nation worship. It implies that one's own nation is superior and lofty in comparison with all other nations. This feeling reserves all kinds of genuine and fake expressions of pride exclusively for one's own nation.[3]

---

[3] One interesting example of this phenomenon can be seen in Turkey under Mustafa Kamal. They have started teaching children that the Prophet Adam was a Turk. This claim is part of the official syllabus at the primary level.

(2) The feeling of loyalty to the nation. Such loyalty makes a person disregard the question of right and justice and stand by his nation in every circumstance, be his nation in the right or the wrong.

(3) The will to protect the nation. This factor encourages every nation to adopt measures for the protection of its real and perceived interests, which begin with defence and end with aggression. Take, for instance, increasing or decreasing taxes on imports and exports to safeguard economic interests, restricting immigration, closing doors to job opportunities and citizens' rights for others within its borders, outracing others in building military power for national defence and striving to protect the rights of its people residing in other countries.

(4) The feeling of National Aggrandizement. This factor instils within every progressive and powerful nation the desire to dominate and prevail over other nations in the world. It drives them to enhance their prosperity at the expense of others, consider themselves the superior propagators of civilization among less developed nations, and assume the right to exploit the natural resources of other countries as their birthright.

This is European nationalism, intoxicated by which some exclaim, 'Germany above all!' Another declares, 'America is God's own country!' And yet another proclaims, 'Italy is religion!' By means of another's tongue, the message 'to rule is Britain's right' is communicated to the world. And every nationalist religiously holds this belief, 'My country, right or wrong!' This fervour of nation-worship [*watan parastī*] is the greatest curse on humanity in today's world. It is the biggest threat to human civilization, as it limits the status of human beings belonging to every other nation to that of beasts in the sight of one nation.

This nationalism does not only mean that a person loves his own nation and wants to see it free, prosperous and progressing. If that were the case, it would be a noble feeling. But in reality, it is the feelings of animosity, hatred and revenge, rather than love, that create and nurture nationalism. Nationalism's essence is the fire that ignites in the heart from wounded national emotions and crushed national spirits. This fire, the ignorant sense of honour, amplifies the noble sentiments of national love and turns them into something impure. Apparently, it grows out of the objective of compensating for injustices, whether real or imagined, inflicted upon a nation by another nation or nations. However, since it is not guided by any moral directive, spiritual education or divine law to keep it in check, it goes beyond its limits and transforms into imperialism [English word in text; Urdu *qayṣariyyat*], economic nationalism [English term in text; Urdu *ma'āshī qawm parastī*], racial hatred, war and international disorder.

A contemporary author, Francis W. Coker, writes:

Some [nationalist] writers have maintained, however, that this right of independent existence belongs only to the better peoples of the world – who have spiritual and cultural values peculiarly worth prescribing and disseminating. They argue, moreover, that a highly civilized nation has the right and obligation not only to protect its independence and administer its internal affairs without interference from others but also to expand its sway, by force if necessary, over more backward peoples. A superior nation, it is said, has a world vocation: it has no right to bury its talents or to exploit them selfishly. This was the common theoretical argument supporting the movement of colonial expansion of the later nineteenth century, whereby 'low-cultured races of Africa and the Pacific islands were brought under the sway of the states of Europe and America'.[4]

Subsequently, he writes:

A 'great nation', it is said, has the right not only to defend itself against direct attack but also to resist whatever threatens interests of essential importance to its independence and prosperity. Moreover, for any nation to survive, it has more to do than preserve its territorial integrity, protect its material resources, and vindicate its honour. It must also grow – expand its domain, increase its military strength, exalt its national prestige; otherwise, it will fall into decay and succumb in the inevitable competition between nations. The nations that succeed best in protecting their interests and enlarging their spheres of political and economic influence prove thereby their prior right to survive. War, moreover, is the natural instrumentality of national expansion and its outcome is the test of the right to expand. According to Dr Bagehot, 'it is war that makes nations'.[5]

Coker goes on to write:

Darwin's theory of evolution too has been incorrectly used to support these ideas. Ernst Haeckel – first and most influential

---

[4] Francis W. Coker, *Recent Political Thought* (New York: Appleton-Century-Crofts, 1934), 443.
[5] Ibid., 444–5.

apostle of Darwinism in Germany – who was diligent in making broad philosophical and sociological applications of his biological ideas, contended that egoism, which he characterized as a universal biological law, manifested itself in human society in a sort of racial cannibalism. The earth, he said, has insufficient resources for all the racial groups that appear upon its surface. The weaker groups perish not only through their incapacity to compete effectively in the common struggle for the limited supply of the means of life but also through their inability to defend themselves against conquest and ultimate annihilation by the stronger groups. Karl Pearson likewise characterized international strife as part of 'the natural history of mankind'. A 'scientific view of life', he maintained, must recognize that human progress comes about through an eternal contest not only between individuals but also of race against race. As a superior nation increases its internal efficiency by taking steps to ensure that its weaker stocks die off, so it achieves external efficiency – and thus advances the evolution of the whole human race – by continually contending with other strong nations and crushing out the weaker nations. It can prove its equality with other superior nations only by constantly 'struggling' with them for trade routes, sources of raw materials, and food supplies. When it comes into contact with inferior groups, it either surrenders any claim to superiority by mixing with them or adapting its ways to their ways or vindicates its superiority by ejecting the inferior groups or exploiting them to its own uses.[6]

Another writer, Joseph Leighton, writes:

The history of the world, since the fifteenth century, is very largely the story of the economic rivalries of nation-states. Economic nationalism has become more and more a cause of conflict – of commercial struggles precipitating wars. The conquest and settlement of America, of Africa, and the islands of the seven seas, the conquest and exploitation of large parts of Asia, are aspects of this predatory tale. It is the continuation, on a much vaster scale, of the predatory invasions by the barbarians when Rome fell. But, whereas, out of the remains of the Roman Empire an international order was built up on a religious, ethical, and cultural foundation, as yet that has not happened in the modern world.[7]

[6] Ibid., 447–8.
[7] Joseph A. Leighton, *Social Philosophies in Conflicts* (New York: D. Appleton-Century Company, 1937), 439.

He observes:

> When cultural nationality coincides with political autonomy, when the cultural nation is an economic unity, and this cultural-politico-economic unit is imbued with the feeling of its greatness and superiority, in the competitive struggle of politico-economic national groups we get the extreme form of economic nationalism, tending towards economic imperialism, that is, nations struggling for commercial advantages against other nations. These advantages consist in capturing foreign markets and in getting backward regions to exploit.[8]

He notes:

> The [insolvable] dilemma of politico-economic nationalism is this: the nation-state is the necessary instrument for furthering the welfare of its people; not only their economic well-being, but their cultural development – their education, science, arts, and so on – depend upon the prosperity of the nation-state. But under the competitive system economic nationalism, which means the attempt to prosper at the expense of other peoples, breeds rivalries, suspicions, fear, hatreds between peoples, and from the state of economic international conflict the passage is all too easy to open warfare.[9]

The Fundamental Difference between Western Nationalism and the Divine Teachings

Instead of describing Western nationalism and its mode of thinking and procedures in my own words, I have preferred to describe the issue in the words of Western scholars. This helps illuminate the picture as intended by its painters, so that you can understand the concept clearly. The above-mentioned excerpts provide explicit evidence of how the concepts and principles upon which Western nationalism stands are totally opposed to the principles of humanity. They have degraded humans to the level of animals. They have presented them as worse than beasts. Those principles only cause disruption, tyranny, injustice and bloodshed. They hinder the peaceful spread of development and the progress of human civilization. These principles blight the pure

---

[8] Ibid., 4.   [9] Ibid., 5.

153

objectives for which the divine messengers have been striving since the beginning. These Satanic principles oppose, resist and counter the objectives of the divine sharias and the moral and spiritual teachings of the heavenly books. These dictates turn human hearts, to constrict them and render them short-sighted[10] and biased. They breed enmity among nations and make them oblivious to the values of rightfulness, justice and humanity. They strike at the very foundation of divine sharia by replacing moral truths with materialistic strength and animalistic power.

The divine sharias have always sought to build moral and spiritual connections among human beings and thus make them support each other. However, nationalism severs those connections, using race and nationality as a tool, and creates enmity and rivalry among people instead of enabling them to support each other.[11]

The divine laws seek to build more and more doors to an unrestricted relationship between man and man, as the development of human civilization and progress totally depend upon these acts of co-operation. However, nationalism puts all types of hurdles in the way of this development, to the extent that it becomes impossible for a nation under the influence of another nation to breathe freely.

The divine laws are aimed at enabling all individuals, nations and races to develop and utilize their natural qualities and skills so that they can collectively play their role in human development. On the other hand, nationalism leads all nations and races to maximize their power and authority. It makes them declare other nations and races to be lowly, contemptible and valueless. It urges them to enslave other nations and deprive them of any chance to develop and utilize their inborn skills. Rather, the powerful nation should deprive others of the fundamental rights of living.

---

[10] The extreme short-sightedness that nationalism creates is such that Indian mangoes cannot enter Japan. A blessing that Allah has created on the earth has been prohibited by a nation against itself only because it has been grown in another country.

[11] This effect of nationalism was observed by the entire world in the Burmese riots of last year. The major cause of the riots was Burmese nationalism. Burmese Buddhists not only mercilessly killed common Indians but also Buddhists of Indian origin. It means that the scissors of nationalism cut asunder the spiritual and moral connection that Buddhism had established between an Indian and a Burmese. This is the natural characteristic of nationalism. Previously, it had cut the brotherly ties among Christian nations in the very same manner. Now it is severing relations among the Muslim peoples. Therefore, the tension between the Turks and the Arabs on the Syrian border is the issue of this nationalism.

The fundamental principle of divine sharias is to establish the foundation of human rights based on moral authority rather than material power, so that a powerful individual or group upholds the rights of weak individuals and groups if sanctioned by moral law. On the other hand, nationalism promotes the principle that might is right and that the weak have no rights just because they have no power to secure them.

Just like the divine sharias do not oppose individual self-preservation within ethical limits, they do not oppose national self-preservation when it is within ethical limits. In fact, they encourage it, because development of human collectivity depends on the individual development of each nation. However, the divine sharias only promote that national love that develops through empathy with, support of and goodwill towards humanity at large [English term in text; Urdu *insāniyyat-e-'ammah*]. It should serve the purpose that rivers serve for an ocean on earth. On the contrary, nationalism lends a man the mentality to exhaust all his power and abilities only to strengthen his nation. It dictates that not only should he avoid supporting the development of humanity at large but also sacrifice the interest of human development at large for the interest of his nation. Nationalism to collective society is what selfishness is to individuals. A nationalist is naturally always narrow-minded. He finds all the good and capabilities in his nation or race. He does not see anything valuable and worth preserving in any other nation or race. A perfect example of this type of thinking is found in the national socialism of Germany. According to Hitler, a national socialist can be defined as:

> Whoever is prepared to make the national cause his own to such an extent that he knows no higher ideal than the welfare of his nation, whoever in addition has understood our great national anthem, 'Deutschland, Deutschland, über alles', to mean that nothing in the wide world surpasses in his eyes this German people and land – that man is a national-socialist.[12]

In his book, *My Struggle*, Hitler writes:

> All that we admire on this earth – science, art, technical skill and invention – is the creative product of only a small number of nations, and originally, perhaps, of one single race ... If we divide

---

[12] Konrad Helden, *A History of National Socialism* (London: Methuen and Co. Ltd, 1934), 85.

the human race into three categories – founders, maintainers and destroyers of culture – the Aryan stock alone can be considered as representing the first category.[13]

Based on this racial pride, the life of non-Aryans has been made impossible. It is upon this idea that the ideology of the German ideal of world domination stands. According to a national socialist, the mission of the German nation in the world is to enslave the low-ranked nations and use them as a tool to spread their civilization. This is not specific to Germany. The racial differences in democratic America are based on the same grounds. A white American is never ready to consider a black man as a human being. Every nation in Europe – Britain, France, Italy and Holland – holds to the same ideology.

Another inseparable characteristic of this nationalism is that it makes people selfish. The divine sharias have been given to the world to make man principled and make his behaviour subject to such permanent principles as do not change with desires and objectives. On the contrary, nationalism makes people unprincipled. There is no principle a nationalist follows other than the interest of his nation. If ethical principles, religious injunctions and civilizational ideologies help him secure his national interests, he will happily profess them. If they stand between him and his national interests, he will put them behind his back and conveniently choose different principles and ideologies. We observe a perfect example of the character of a nationalist in the person and behaviour of Mussolini. Before the World War, he was a socialist. However, he abandoned socialism during the war just because he saw an advantage for Italy in engagement in the war. When he did not achieve the required benefits in the booty of the war, he raised the flag of a new fascist movement. Within this new movement, too, he continued to change his stance every now and then. By 1919, he was a liberal socialist. In 1920, he became an anarchist. In 1921, he opposed socialist and democratic groups for a few months. For a few months, he continued trying to win an alliance with the socialist and democratic groups. Finally, he parted from them and chose a different policy. This changing of colours, this disregard of principles and of selfishness is not a trait specific to Mussolini alone. Instead, it is a fundamental characteristic of the nature of nationalism. The approach that a selfish man adopts in his

---

[13] Adolf Hitler, *My Struggle* (London: Hurst & Blackett Ltd, 1939), 120–1.

personal life, a nationalist adopts in his national life. It is impossible for him to permanently stick to the same principle and ideology.

However, the most obvious conflict between nationalism and divine laws occurs in another form. It is obvious that any divine messenger who arrives will appear in a specific nation and country. Similarly, a divine book given to a messenger will also be in the language of that nation and the country to which the prophet is sent. Consequently, all the sacred places that command honour and sanctity due to their association with the prophetic mission will lie in that region. However, despite all these limitations, the truth and the teachings of the right guidance brought by the divine messenger will not be restricted to a nation or a country. Rather, these teachings and guidance are open for all mankind. The whole of mankind is commanded to believe in the prophet and his teachings. Whether the prophetic mission of a messenger is limited, as was the mission of the Prophet Hūd, the Prophet Ṣaliḥ and many other prophets, or whether the mission is open to all of mankind, like that of the Prophet Abraham and Prophet Muhammad, in every case all the people are required to believe in, respect and follow all the prophets in all circumstances. When the mission of a prophet is universal, then it is only natural that his divine book will carry international significance. The civilizational impact of its language will also be international. The sacred places associated with this prophet's teachings will gain international status, despite being in a particular country. Not only the prophet but also his supporters and companions carrying the mission forward will be considered international heroes, despite their connection with that specific nation. All these facts go against the taste, nature, emotions and ideas of a nationalist. The pride of a nationalist does not allow him to accept as a hero someone who does not belong to his nation. It prevents him from accepting the central position, sanctity and respect of [sacred] places not situated in his country. He cannot tolerate the cultural supremacy of a language that is not his language. He may not receive spiritual inspiration [English term in text; Urdu *rūḥānī tehrīk*] from traditions that come from foreign lands. He will not only declare these elements foreign [English word in text; Urdu *ajnabī*] but also look at them with contempt and disdain, as people look at anything that comes along with the invaders. He will try to wipe off all factors external to the life of his nation. The natural requirement of his nationalistic feeling is that he should restrict respect and sanctity to his motherland, sing the praises of the rivers and mountains of his country, give life to the ancient historic traditions of his country (the same traditions declared by the foreign religion as the period of ignorance) and feel proud of those traditions. He must relate his present to his past, connect his culture with that of his pious elders, declare the real or imaginary elders of his country to be his heroes, and draw inspiration from the original real or imagined achievements of those heroes.

In short, it is the very natural characteristic of nationalism that it forces a person to reject anything that comes from outside and embrace all the elements that belong to his nation. The ultimate destination of this path is that it forces people to fully abandon a religion that comes from a different land and gives new life to the religious traditions of his nation that come down to any nationalist from the ancient times of ignorance. It is possible that many nationalists might not have reached this last stage and are still at any stage towards it, but the path he follows ultimately leads to the destination described above.

What is happening in Germany right now is the obvious explanation and description of the natural characteristic of nationalism. A group of Nazis is openly denouncing Jesus Christ merely because he was of a Jewish bloodline. That a man is Jewish suffices as an argument for the Aryans to negate the significance of the cultural, moral and spiritual values of that man. Owing to this, the members of the Nazi group openly state: 'Jesus was a proletariat Jew who idealized Karl Marx. That is why he has said that only the poor and destitute will inherit the world.' On the contrary, the Nazis who still carry respect for Jesus in their hearts try to prove that Jesus belonged to the Nordic race. Thus, a German will either not believe in Jesus because of his Jewish background, or he may believe in a Jesus of Nordic background, but not an Israelite Jesus.

In all circumstances, the religion of a German nationalist is subservient to his racism. Not a single German nationalist is ready to follow a non-Aryan as a spiritual and moral leader.[14] So much so, German nationalists are not ready to believe in a God whose concept originates in some other country. Some Nazi groups are trying to resurrect the deities worshipped by the ancient Teutonic tribes. Therefore, they have cooked up a detailed mythology derived from their ancient history. They acknowledge a deity called Wotan, known as the God of Tempest by

---

[14] The Jews of Arabia had the same mentality, as they refused to accept the Prophethood of Muhammad, peace be upon him, merely because he was not an Israelite.

Teutonic tribes of the age of ignorance, as the chief deity. This religious movement has recently started. However, the official creed currently being taught to the Nazis by the government does not give God the status of the Lord of all the worlds but as the Lord of the German people only. This creed has been worded as follows:

> We believe in God as an eternal expression of life and authority. It is natural for Germans to believe in the existence of God on earth and in the universe. Our belief in God and eternity does not carry any similarity to the beliefs and creeds of any other religion. We believe in the eternity of Germany and the German nation, because we believe in the eternity of the power and life. We believe in the national socialist ideology of life. We believe in the truthfulness of our national objectives. We believe in our leader, Adolf Hitler.

It implies that God is nothing but the name of power and the life that have permeated the German nation. The German nation is the incarnation of God on earth. In this view, Hitler is His messenger god, and the national objectives act as a religion brought by that messenger. That is the only religious concept that can accord with the nationalist's mentality.

Pardah

****

Author's Preface to the First Edition

I wrote a series of essays on the question of pardah in *Tarjuman ul Quran* four years ago. These were published over many issues. At that time I left some aspects of the debate deliberately ignored and others under-developed, as the purpose was to write an essay rather than a book. Now, these elements have been collected and, with some further additions and explanations, collated into this book. Of course, it cannot be claimed that this is the last word on the issue. However, I do expect that those who really seek to understand this issue will find largely satisfactory material and arguments here.

Abul A'la
22 Muharram 1359 Hijra

Western Conceptions and Perspectives

Arguments that are put forward against pardah are not merely negative in nature but have a positive and affirmative basis. These arguments are founded not just on a dislike for restricting women's mobility and veiling as an unnecessary imprisonment, both of which should be done away with. Proponents of these arguments have in mind a totally different way of life for women. They also have an altogether different concept of the relationships between the male and the female. They want women to follow one particular way and not the other. Thus, their main objection against pardah is that if the woman remains confined to the house and veiled, she cannot follow that particular way, nor can she do anything else that is expected of her.

Let us now find out what that 'anything else' is: what are the concepts and principles underlying it, how right and reasonable are they in themselves, and what are their practical implications and consequences? Obviously, if these concepts and principles are taken for granted, then pardah and the social system of which it is a constituent part are automatically proven to be wrongly conceived. But why should these concepts and principles be accepted without being subjected to rational and experiential questioning? Is the mere fact of their popularity and dominance in the world today enough reason to compel one to accept them uncritically?

Eighteenth-Century Concept of Liberty

As I have suggested above, the philosophers, scientists and literary scholars who raised their voice for reform in the eighteenth century had in fact to grapple with a civilizational arrangement which was bound with undue restrictions, that was inflexible and replete with senseless customs, rigid regulations and unreasonable, unnatural contradictions. Centuries of decline and decay had rendered this system resistant to progress. On the one hand, a new awakening and enlightenment stirred the middle class (the bourgeois class) to move forward. On the other, the upper classes and clergy continued to tighten the knots of custom and tradition. From churches to armies, judiciary to royal palaces, farms to financial centres, those claiming prior rights continued to reap the benefits of the hard work done by the new emerging middle classes. Every effort that aimed at reform was frustrated by the selfish and ignorant behaviour of those in power. This led to the deepening of revolutionary fervour among the people who longed for a change. Consequently, they rebelled against the whole social system and each of its constituent parts, eventually giving rise to an extremist concept of personal freedom that placed the individual against society with an absolute vision of individual freedom. Thus, it was stated that the individual has the right to do anything that he desires and has the freedom to refrain from anything that he dislikes. Society has no right to restrict his personal freedom. The government has a duty only to make sure that the individual's freedom is protected, and collective institutions exist to help men to attain their goals.

This exaggerated notion of liberty was in reality a reaction against an unjust and coercive social order, and contained within itself the germs of a bigger conflict. Those who had proposed it initially were themselves not fully aware of its logical implications. Had they foreseen the results in which the unrestricted freedom and unbridled liberty of the individual were going to culminate, they would perhaps have shuddered with fear at the selfish individuality and unrestrained permissiveness that were to follow. They were primarily concerned with removing undue hardships and illogical constraints that were prevalent in that society. But eventually these new ideas took root in the Western mind and began to grow unhampered.

Nineteenth-Century Changes in Ideas

The French Revolution came in the wake of this concept of freedom.[1] This revolution shattered to pieces most of the older moral ideas and

---

[1] The concept of individual liberty gave birth to the modern capitalistic order, democratic system and culture, and moral licentiousness [English phrase in text]. Within the next one

cultural and religious norms. When the revolutionaries saw that the destruction of the old concepts and traditions led to progress, they concluded that each one of the already established concepts and ways of life was a stumbling block which must be removed to make any headway towards progress. Therefore, as soon as they had destroyed some wrong principles of Christian ethics, they turned their attention towards the basic concepts of human ethics: what is the value of chastity? Why place restrictions of piety on youth? What is the harm in falling in love outside marriage? And even after marriage, does one not still have a heart that could fall in love again? Such were the doubts and objections that were raised in post-revolutionary society on all sides, especially by the Romantic School [English term in text] of writers. At the beginning of the nineteenth century, George Sand [French in text; Urdu *Zor Zasan*] (1804–76) emerged as a leader of this group. She herself violated all those moral principles of conduct which are associated with human, and particular womanly, nobility of character. Being the legal wife of one husband, she established illicit relations freely with others. At last she separated from her husband and changed several friends successively, but did not stay with anyone for more than two years. In her biography at least six men are mentioned with whom she had open and regular illicit relations. One of them praises her in these terms:

> George Sand first picks a moth and imprisons him in a cage of flowers. This is the period of love. Then she starts pricking him with a pin and takes pleasure in his distress ... Then starts the period of coldness, and whether soon or early, it always arrives ... Then she plucks off his wings, analyses him and adds him to her collection of moths, who then work as heroes in her novels.

Alfred de Musset [French in text; Urdu *Alfray Mussay*] (1810–57), a French poet of the Romantic School, was also one of her lovers. He was

---

a half centuries it led to such atrocities in Europe and America that humanity had to revolt against it. By allowing the individual a free licence for selfish actions against the general well-being of society, it helped ruin the collective welfare of the community and disintegrate social life. Socialism and fascism are both forms of rebellion against this extreme individualism. However, these so-called reconstructive and reparative movements have a foundational flaw. They sought to cure one extreme by another extreme. The eighteenth-century concept of freedom erred by sacrificing the community to the individual. The twentieth-century conception of the collective errs in the other direction by sacrificing the individual to the community. For the salvation of mankind a balanced and just concept is as necessary and as rare today as it was in the eighteenth century.

broken-hearted after her faithlessness and willed that George Sand should not attend his funeral. This was then the personal character of the woman who deeply influenced the new French generation through her charming and romantic works for as long as thirty years. In her novel *Lélia* [French in text], the heroine writes to Stenio:[2]

> The longer I live the more I recognise that the notions adopted by our young people, with regard to the exclusiveness of love's ardour, the absolute possession which it demands, and the eternal rights which it claims, are false, or at least fatal. All opinions should be allowed, and I would grant that of conjugal fidelity to exceptional souls. The majority have other needs and other capabilities. Therefore, it is necessary that they be allowed reciprocal freedom, mutual tolerance, exclusion of all jealous egoism ... All loves are true, whether impetuous or peaceful, sensual or ascetic, lasting or transient: whether they lead men to suicide or to pleasure.

In another of her novels, entitled *Jacques* [French in text], she presents the character of an ideal husband. The wife of the hero (Jacques) establishes illicit relations with another man, but the husband is too large-hearted to censure her and says that he has no right to trample underfoot a flower that spreads its sweet smell to others besides him. At another place she expresses through Jacques the following ideas:

> I have not changed my opinion, I have not made peace with society, and marriage is always according to my judgment one of the most barbarous institutions ever imagined. I have no doubt that it will be abolished, if the human race makes any progress towards justice and reason; a bond more human and no less sacred, will replace it, and will secure the existence of offspring who will be born of a man and a woman, without ever restricting the liberty of either. But men are too selfish and women too cowardly to demand a nobler law than that which rules them. Truly, heavy chains must bind beings who lack conscience and virtue.[3]

Such were the ideas propounded in or about 1833. George Sand did not go further. She could not dare take these ideas to their logical conclusions. In spite of her enlightened thought, she had not been able

---

[2] These extracts have been taken from Paul Bureau's *Towards Moral Bankruptcy*, published in London by Constable and Co. in 1925, p. 106.

[3] Paul Bureau, pp. 107–8.

wholly to shake off the dirt of traditional morality. Some thirty to thirty-five years later the project was taken up again by another school of dramatists, literary men and moral philosophers whose leaders were Alexandre Dumas [French in text] and Alfred Naquet [French in text]. These writers vehemently propagated the ideas that freedom and the satisfaction of the pleasures of the body were in themselves the birthright of every individual. To curb this right with moral and social restrictions was cruel on the part of society. Earlier writers had demanded freedom of action for the individual in the name of love alone. The new writers felt this emotional basis for freedom to be too weak. Therefore, they tried to establish the demand for individual liberty, moral lawlessness and unbridled freedom on the more sound basis of philosophical reasoning. Thereby they wanted to encourage young men and women to do whatever they pleased with the full satisfaction and approval of the conscience. Moreover, they wanted to educate society not to mind the lustful behaviour of the youth but to regard it as morally right and laudable.

Towards the end of the nineteenth century, Paul Adam (1862–1920), Henri Bataille (1872–1922), Pierre Louys (1870–1925) [all names French in text] and many other writers spent their efforts in raising courage among the youth to remove completely all shadow of hesitation and inhibition caused in their minds by outmoded moral ideals. Paul Adam, in his book *Le Morale de l'amour* [French in text], censured young people for the folly of trying to convince themselves and others of true love and lifelong commitment. He writes:

> All these conceal, under empty words, the healthy longing for simple bodily union at the will of a natural and innocent appetite that all men possess. It is a great evil among the Latin races that lovers refuse to admit plainly and candidly their relish for voluptuousness, and for the joyous companionship of the sexes.

He advises the youth:

> Then be refined and sensuous, not building a temple to the servants of your pleasures nor lazily falling asleep at their feet, but choosing a new guest for each moment of pleasure.

Pierre Louys went still further. He emphasized the ideas that moral restrictions in fact hindered the proper growth of man's intellectual, scientific and spiritual development. In his book *Aphrodite* [French in text] he tried to establish the hypothesis that civilization was at its zenith in Babylon, Alexandria, Athens, Rome, Venice and other centres at the time when sensuality, moral lawlessness and sexual licentiousness [English term in text] flourished unchecked. But as soon as moral and legal restrictions were imposed on human urges, the human soul was also doomed to fetters.

Pierre Louys was a prominent literary figure of his time. He set a new style of writing and established an independent school in literature. In his wake appeared a whole constellation of novelists, dramatists and writers on morality who propagated his ideas ceaselessly. He himself made every possible effort with his pen to establish that nudity and promiscuous intermingling of the sexes were perfectly justified and laudable. In the same book, *Aphrodite*, he eulogizes Greece for its best period thus:

> [T]he time when naked humanity, the most perfect form that we can know or even conceive, since we believe it to be made in God's image, can unveil itself under the lineaments of a consecrated courtesan before the twenty thousand pilgrims . . . where the most sensual love, the divine love from which we were born, was without defilement, without shame, without sin.

In another place, he has expressed himself more explicitly. He proposed:

> to combat by the most energetic moral teaching the abominable opinion that motherhood can be under some circumstances entirely dishonourable, illegitimate, or disgraceful.

Twentieth-Century Developments

Thus far had developed ideas in the nineteenth century when writers of the twentieth century appeared, who aspired to soar even higher than their forerunners. In 1908, a play entitled *Le Lys* [French in text] was published by Pierre Wolff and Gaston Leroux [names French in text], in which two girls are shown explaining to their father, in the presence of their brother, their right to free love. Their main contention is to show how terrible it is for a young girl to pass her life without engaging in 'free love'. The old father censures his daughters for having illicit relations with a young man. One daughter replies:

> Yet I could not make you understand, because you have never understood that one has not always the right to ask a girl, though

she may be your sister or your daughter, to become an old woman without having loved.[4]

World War I not only provided an impetus to this freedom movement but also took it to its extreme logical conclusions. The movement against conception had impacted France in particular. For over forty years the birth rate in that country had continually been falling. Only in twenty out of eighty-seven French districts was the birth rate higher than the death rate. In the remaining districts, the case was just the reverse; so much so, that in certain areas the average death rate was as high as 130, 140, even 160, for every 100 births. When the war started, the French nation was already in the throes of life and death. This was a rude shock for French statesmen, to learn that the nation lacked a sufficient number of fighting-fit young men. If, for the time being, they tried to save the nation by sacrificing the available few at the front, how would they counteract the next onslaught? The whole nation was galvanized by this concern. It could not survive, the leaders thought, except by raising the national birth rate by all possible means. This gave the campaign another direction. Writers, journalists, speakers, even scientists and politicians came out and raised one universal cry requiring the people to bring forth more and more children without bothering about marriage formalities. Any virgin or widow, they said, who offered her womb voluntarily in the service of the motherland deserved to be honoured rather than censured. Lovers of freedom seized this opportunity for spreading among the people all their devilish ideas. A distinguished journalist of the time, who edited *La* [*sic*] *Lyon Républicain*, wrote, while discussing the question, why is rape a crime?

> When poor people resort to theft due to hunger, we say give them bread and thefts will stop by themselves. But it is strange that the sympathy that we express towards one natural bodily need we withhold from another. This less frequent but no less important desire like hunger and thirst leads to rape, sometimes followed by murder. A healthy man, who is young and vigorous, can no more help his desires than he can manage an empty stomach with the promise of food next week. Just as we distribute bread to the hungry for free, we should make some arrangements for those who are dying of another kind of hunger.

[4] Paul Bureau, p. 117.

This article was not meant to amuse the people. It had been written in earnest and was read equally seriously in France. About the same time, the Paris Faculty of Medicine approved a doctoral thesis and published it in its official bulletin. It contained the following sentences also:

> We hope the day will come when without cynical boasting or false modesty one can say, I had syphilis at twenty years old, just as we say now-a-days, 'I have been sent to the hills for spitting blood' . . . These diseases are part of life and its pleasures. Whoever has passed his youth without contracting any such diseases is but an incomplete being who through cowardice, a cold nature, or religious misconception, has missed the accomplishment of what is perhaps the least degraded of his natural functions.[5]

Literature of the Neo-Malthusian Movement

Before proceeding further let us consider the views that have been advanced in support of the movement for contraception [*mana' haml*]. When, towards the end of the eighteenth century, the British economist Malthus presented his ideas on birth control with a view to imposing checks on a fast-increasing population, it might not have crossed his mind that his innocent proposals after just one century would be mainly used for spreading adultery and promiscuity on an enormous scale. Malthus had only advised abstinence and late marriages to check the increase in population. But when the neo-Malthusian Movement arose towards the end of the nineteenth century, its basic principle was that individual desires should be freely satisfied, and its natural consequence, the birth of children, was to be scientifically controlled. This helped also to remove the last impediment from a promiscuous intermingling of the sexes. Now a woman could freely give herself up to a man without the fear of bringing forth children and enduring responsibilities. This is not the place to describe the consequences of this move. Here we want to first discuss some instances of the views spread through the literature on birth control.

This literature presented a neo-Malthusian case systematically:

> Every human being invariably experiences three imperious and demanding needs: nourishment, rest and desire. Nature has implanted these within us, and has attached enjoyment to their

[5] Paul Bureau, p. 151.

satisfaction so that humans remain committed to their fulfilment. Logic would have man hasten to respond to this natural desire, and such is in fact his conduct with regard to the first two needs. But it is astonishing to find that with regard to the third, he has adopted a completely different attitude. Collective norms have invented the strange institution of monogamic marriage. Social morality forbids in fact every satisfaction of the sexual appetite outside of the marriage bond, and in the married state, which it declares indissoluble, it imposes the duties of fidelity and of non-intervention in the reproductive work of nature. But this sexual morality is really absurd; it defies both nature and reason, and, being false in its very principles, produces the worst consequences for humanity.

Ideas that have been deduced from these premises may also be considered. Bebel, leader of the German Social Democratic Party, says frankly:

> Man and woman are after all merely animals. Can there be any question of marriage, of a permanent bond, between animals?

Dr Drysdale [English in text] says:

> Love is, like all our appetites, subject to change. To seek to fix it in one channel is to try to modify the laws of nature. Youth is specially given to this changeableness in conformity with the magnificent logical order of nature which ordains that our experiences should be multiplied ... free union represents a higher morality than any other, because it is more conformable to natural laws, and at the same time because it proceeds more directly from feeling, passion and disinterested love for the inclination which determines it has a moral value which is lacking in those mercantile transactions which make of marriage a veritable prostitution.

It will be noted how concepts are changing, or rather undergoing perversion. At first, efforts were made to make people throw off their belief that adultery was anything morally bad so as to get marriage and illegal relationships recognized as being of equal status. Now a step further has been taken. Marriage is being regarded with disfavour and extra-marital relations as morally superior.

In another place, Dr Drysdale writes:

> We need an arrangement that would make love without marriage respectable ... It is a good thing that divorce is slowly making

marriage obsolete because now it has become a contract between two individuals who can end it whenever they want.

The famous French neo-Malthusian Paul Robin writes:

> Over the last twenty-five years we have had at least this much success that children born outside of wedlock are now considered equal to legitimate ones. Now all we need is that only the first type of children are born so that there is no question of comparison.

J. S. Mill, a famous British philosopher, demands in his book *On Liberty* [English in text; Urdu, *Azadi*] 'that the marriage of indigent persons should be forbidden by law, just as many German laws at that time only allowed marriage to those who could show that they had sufficient means'. But when the question of the eradication of prostitution arose in England, the same philosopher opposed it tooth and nail. His argument was that it was tantamount to curbing personal liberty and insulting the workers, who were being treated like children.

Note that personal freedom is meant to enable people to commit adultery. But if somebody is foolhardy enough to want to take advantage of this freedom for the purpose of marriage, his right to it should be questioned. In this latter case not only will the law be allowed to interfere with the personal freedom of the individual but such an action will also satisfy the moral scruples of the freedom-loving economist. This clearly shows that moral concepts have undergone an extreme perversion. Good has come to be regarded as evil and evil as good.

※※※※※※※※※※※※※※※※※※※※※※※※※※※※※※※※

Implications

Literature shows the way, public opinion follows the lead and, finally, collective morality, social customs and state law all give way. Such a change becomes inevitable, especially when all the propaganda devices and techniques besides philosophy, history, ethics, science, literature, art, etc., have worked together persistently for a hundred and fifty years or so to mould man's way of thinking after a particular pattern. Then, it is unlikely that the law of the land remains unaffected by the changing public opinion in a country where government and social institutions are run on democratic principles.

The Industrial Revolution and Its Impact

Other cultural factors in the West also became favourable to paving the way for such views. During this period the Industrial Revolution also took place. The impact of this on economic life reinforced the trends which the revolutionary literature had already given them. The concept of personal freedom, on which the system of capitalism is based, received an extraordinary impetus from the invention of the machine and the consequent possibilities of mass production [English term in text; Urdu *kasīr paidawari*]. The capitalist classes established big industrial and commercial concerns with the result that the new centres of industry and business soon grew into huge cities. Hundreds of thousands of people began leaving the countryside for the cities, and life became expensive. The availability of housing diminished, and the cost of clothing, food and other necessities of life soared high. Partly due to the cultural advancement and partly to the keenness shown by the capitalists, numerous new luxuries became part of life. But the capitalist system did not distribute wealth equitably so as to enable the common people also to possess the means of affording all those comforts, pleasures and luxuries. It did not even provide them with enough means to acquire easily the barest minimum necessities of life – housing, food, clothes, etc. – in the cities to which they had been attracted. Consequently, maintaining the wife became burdensome to the husband, and the rearing of children became troublesome to the father. In fact, it became difficult for individuals to maintain themselves, much less their relatives. Economic conditions forced every member of the family to become an earning member. Gradually all classes of women, married and unmarried and widows, had to come out to earn their bread, and with the increase in the opportunities for free intermingling of the sexes, natural consequences began to follow. Now the concept of personal freedom and the new ethics came forward to console fathers and daughters, brothers and sisters, husbands and wives, to say there is no need for concern, all that was happening was most desirable. This is not degradation but emancipation [English word in text; Urdu *uthān*]. This is a lack of ethics, but very much the enjoyment of life that you are experiencing. The pit into which the capitalist is throwing you is not hell but heaven, real heaven!

The Oriental 'Occidentalists'

One group [of commentators] has intellectually accepted the philosophy, moral concepts and social principles on which Western civilization and culture are based. They consider life and its problems from the same viewpoint as was adopted by the architects of modern Europe, and now they want to mould the social pattern of their respective homelands also after the same Western pattern. They sincerely believe that the real aim of education for a woman is to enable her to earn her living and to acquire the arts of appearing attractive to the male. Her real position in the family according to them is that, like the man, she should also be an earning member, so as to subscribe fully her share to the common family budget. They think that a woman is meant to add charm and sweetness to communal life by her beauty, elegance and attractive manners. She should warm people up by her sweet, musical words, she should send them to ecstasy by her rhythmic movements and she should dance them to the highest pitch of pleasure and excitement. They think that the woman's role in national life consists in doing social work, attending municipal councils, participating in conferences and congresses, and devoting her time and abilities to tackle political, cultural and social problems. She should take part in physical exercise and sports, compete in swimming, jumping and racing contests, and set new records in long-distance flights. In short, she should do anything and everything outside the house and concern herself less with what is inside the house. This is their ideal for womanhood. It leads to worldly prosperity, and all the moral concepts that run counter to it are devoid of sense and meaning-less. To suit the purposes of the new life, therefore, these people have exchanged the old moral concepts for the new ones, just as Europe did. For them, material gain and sensual pleasures are of real worth, whereas a sense of honour, chastity, moral purity, matrimonial loyalty, undefiled lineage and the like virtues are not only worthless but antiquated whims which must be destroyed for the sake of making progress. These people are indeed the true followers [Urdu *momin*] of the Western creed. They are now trying their utmost to spread and propagate it in Eastern countries also by the same techniques and devices as have already been adopted in the West.

Modern Civilization

This moral philosophy and concept of life are not working alone, they are being reinforced by the capitalistic system and Western democracy. The three forces are operating together to produce the pattern of life that has already been established in the West. Highly obscene literature on sex is being published which is falling freely into the hands of male and female students. Nude pictures and photographs of ignoble women are printed in newspapers and journals and pasted on the walls of every house and every shop. Gramophone records containing cheap, filthy songs are being played in every house and on every street. The whole business of cinema is run by playing upon base emotions, and by presenting on the screen every evening highly obscene and immoral scenes which so fascinate the young boys and girls that they take actors and actresses as models for imitation. After witnessing such exciting performances in the cinema halls the young people passionately set about looking for opportunities for love-making and romance. Owing to the capitalistic devices for making money, conditions in the big cities are rapidly changing, and it is becoming more and more pressing for women also to earn their living, with the result that the need of propaganda for contraceptive drugs and devices is becoming all the more pressing. The modern democratic system, whose so-called blessings have reached Eastern countries also, mainly through England and France, has on the one hand opened new avenues for women to participate in political and social activities, and on the other it has established institutions that have created countless opportunities for the free intermingling of the sexes. Besides, it has rendered the law so flexible that in most cases the expression of obscenity, even the practical commission of sin, is not held to be a crime. The lives of the people who have intellectually adopted this way of life have been almost wholly revolutionized insofar as the moral and social aspects of life are concerned. The dresses their women wear are such that they can easily be mistaken for film actresses. They have given up modesty. Their semi-nude attire, their fondness for showy colours and their keenness for make-up reveal that they have no other object before them than to become sex magnets. They have become so immodest that now it is no more a matter of shame for them to bathe along with men in bathing-costumes and get themselves photographed for newspapers. This is now no question of shame, for according to modern concepts of morality no part of the human body is private. If the palm of the hand and the sole of the foot can be displayed, what harm is there in uncovering the thighs and the breasts? Hedonism that manifests itself in 'art' is above morality and has a moral criterion of its own. It is on this account that fathers and brothers feel delighted when they see their young daughters and sisters give music and dance performances on the stage and win applause from excited audiences of hundreds and thousands. Material success, which for these people is the sole object of life, is more valuable than anything else in the world. A girl who has acquired this object and has mastered the art of winning popularity in society has attained great success in life, though she may have lost her chastity. That is why these people cannot understand why a young girl's studying alongside boys in a school or college, or her going to Europe by herself for studies, may be held to be objectionable.

EXCERPTS FROM CHAPTER 8

Laws of Nature

Nature has created man, like other species, as male and female, each possessing a strong natural urge for the other. The study of other animal species has shown that their division into male and female and the natural urge in them for the opposite sex is confined to the propagation of the species only. That is why their sexual urge is just proportionate to requirements to that end. Moreover, this urge has been so controlled in them instinctively that they never transgress sexually the limits set for their nature. Contrary to this, man has been endowed with this urge in an unlimited, unparallelled measure, knowing no discipline whatever. Man knows no restriction of time and clime. Man and woman have a perpetual appeal for each other. They have been endowed with a power-ful urge for sexual love, with an unlimited capacity to attract and be attracted sexually. Their physical constitution, its proportions and shape, its complexion, touch and each element, all have a strange attraction for the opposite sex. Their voice, their gait, their manner and appearance, each has a magnetic power. Moreover, the world around them abounds in factors that further arouse this sexual impulse and make the one inclined to the other. The soft murmuring breeze, the running water, the natural hues of vegetation, the sweet smell of flowers, the chirping of birds, dark clouds, the charms of the moonlit night, in short, all the beauties and all the graces of nature stimulate directly or indirectly this relationship between the male and female.

Then if we examine the physical system of man we shall find that nature has reserved in it a great store of energy which is at once the source of vitality for life, for action and sexual contact. The same glands which provide hormones for his limbs and activate them also produce for him sexual energy. Moreover, they develop in him the impulse to utilize this energy, lend special charm, elegance and grace to his body to excite this impulse, and furnish his eyes, his ears and his senses of smell and touch, even his imagination, with the quality of being stimulated and allured by these enchantments.

The same endowments of nature can be seen at work in the psychic life of man. All his mental forces seem to be governed by two main urges of his self: the urge for self-preservation, and the urge for establishing relations with the opposite sex. In youth, when the practical powers of man are at their zenith, the latter urge, being the stronger one, generally dominates the former. Sometimes it so overwhelms man that he would be prepared even to lay down his very life in order to satisfy it.

The Place of Sexual Attraction in the Construction of Civilization

The question arises: what is all this for? Is it merely for the propagation of the species? No, for the human species is not so dependent upon sexual tension for its propagation as fish and goats and other animals are. Why then has nature endowed man with an inclination to sex beyond these species and also provided the various means that excite it more? Has this all been arranged for the pleasure and enjoyment of man? No, not even that. Nature has nowhere made pleasure and enjoyment an end it itself. It has always had some higher and nobler end in view, for the achievement of which it impels man and animal to strive from within. Pleasure and enjoyment are there, but these in fact serve as an allurement, so that effort is made earnestly and with devotion. Let us then consider what that noble object before nature is in this regard. The more one thinks, the more one will be convinced that nature intends to make the human race, unlike other species, a civilized race used to communal life.

That is why the heart of man has been infused with an unusual urge for sexual love and attachment that demands not only physical union and mating but also an enduring affection and sincere spiritual fellowship. That is why man has been endowed with sexual inclination in a degree greater than what is requisite for the purpose of mating. The sexual urge in him is so great that if he begins to gratify it in the sexual act even one time out of ten, he will soon ruin his health and exhaust his energies prematurely. This is a clear indication of the design of nature, that the great purpose for which sexual urge has been placed in man is not meant to enable him to perform the sexual act more often than animals, but is meant to unite man and woman in lifelong companionship.

That is why woman has been endowed, besides sexual desire and appeal, with modesty, resistance and escape more or less generally. This quality of resistance is found in the females of other species too, but in the human female it is stronger and keener by far, and it has been rendered all the more intense by the feminine sense of modesty. This also shows that the real object of sexual magnetism in man is to secure a permanent attachment between man and woman, not the gratification of every sexual impulse in a sexual act.

That is also why the human child has been created the most helpless and weak of all young ones in the animal kingdom. The human baby, unlike the young ones of other species, has to depend on its parents for protection and upbringing for quite some years, and it takes a considerably longer time to develop self-sustenance. This also implies that the relationship between man and woman should not only be of a sexual nature, but, as a consequence of this relationship, they should develop mutual regard and co-operation in the wider sphere of life.

That is why the love of offspring is strongest in man. Animals nurse their young ones for a brief period only, and then break all relations of love and blood with them, so much so that they do not even recognize each other. Contrary to this, man remains emotionally attached to his offspring even after its early stage of development. He transfers his love even to the offspring of his offspring, and in most cases it so overwhelms his selfish animality that he gladly sacrifices his personal desires to the desires of his children. He wishes from his innermost heart that he may provide the best possible means of life for them and leave behind the fruits of his labours for their comfort and enjoyment. The existence of this intense sentiment of love in the human heart clearly shows that nature wants the sexual urge between man and woman to bind them in an enduring fellowship, to make this fellowship the basis for family life, to knit several families together by the love of blood relations, to lay the foundation for co-operation and mutual dealings by common ties of love, and finally to create a society and system of communal life.

Fundamental Issue for Civilization

This shows that the sexual desire that has been infused in each nerve cell of the human body and soul, for the motivation of which stimulants have been scattered throughout the world, aims at turning human egoism into collective channels. Nature has made this desire the chief motivating force for the purpose of establishing communal life. It leads to companionship between the sexes and persuades human individuality towards collectivity. This leads to the beginnings of social life [English term in text; Urdu *ijtima'izindagi*].

Now that we have established this, it must then have also become clear that the problem of man and woman's mutual relationship is indeed the most fundamental problem for civilization, and on its correct and rational solution depends the well-being, prosperity and stability, or otherwise, of man's communal life on earth. One kind of relationship between the sexes is of an animal or purely sexual nature; its only object is the propagation of the race. The other relationship is the human one that aims at bringing the two sexes together for co-operation in attaining the common goals of life according to the inherent abilities of each. To secure this co-operation, sexual love acts as a binding force between the male and the female. Together, these animal and human factors impel man not only to work for the advancement and preservation of civilization but also to supply more individuals to continue this function. Hence, the prosperity and stability, or otherwise, of civilization wholly depend upon a balanced and proper co-ordination of the two elements.

****

The Proper Shape of Relationship in Marriage

After founding the family and eradicating sexual lawlessness, the necessary prerequisite for a righteous communal life is to determine the correct nature of the relationship between man and woman. This implies a just determination of their rights and responsibilities, and the allocation of status and duties in the family circle strictly according to the principles of justice and balance. Intricate as this problem of man's communal life is, its solution has always baffled him since the earliest times.

Some nations have given woman the position of governor over man, but no instance is found of a nation that raised its womanhood to such a status and then attained any high position on the ladder of progress and civilization. At least history does not present any record of a nation that made a woman its ruler and won honour, glory or distinction.

Most nations in the world have made man the governor over woman, but this preference has often taken the form of cruelty. Woman has been reduced to a slave and her dignity denied: she has been deprived of her economic and social rights, made into a slave of the family and a sexual indulgence for man. Outside the family circle a section of women was decorated with the jewels of knowledge and culture, but only so that they can pleasure men in a more sophisticated and alluring manner. They were trained to provide man with the pleasure of the ear by their music, pleasure of the eye by their dances and coquetry, and pleasure of the body by their skills. This was the most disgraceful device invented by man in his selfishness, and the nations that adopted it were unable to protect themselves from damage.

Modern Western civilization has adopted a third way. This is the way of equality [Urdu *musawat*] between man and woman, of their equal and similar responsibilities, of competition in the same fields of activity, of winning one's own bread and attaining self-sufficiency in all respects. This social reorganization in the West has not yet attained all of its objectives on account of man's natural superiority in every field. Nowhere in life has the woman been able to equal the man, and neither has been able to win all the rights that should have accrued from perfect equality. But to whatever extent some equality [*musawat*] has been established, it has already destroyed communal life. The details of the tragic consequences have already been given in the foregoing pages, and therefore no further comment is needed.

All these three social systems are devoid of justice, balance and proportion, because they have not taken any guidance from nature and have thus failed to adopt a way in accordance with its will and purpose. A little straight thinking will show that nature itself points to the correct solution to these problems. It has in fact all been due to the strong influence of nature that woman could neither fall below nor exceed beyond a certain limit, in spite of her own inclination and the utmost efforts made by man in that regard. Both the extremes that man has followed are the outcome of his defective reasoning and ill-judged ideas. But nature prefers the way of justice and balance, and itself points to the right course.

None can deny the fact that, as human beings, man and woman are equal. Both make up the human race together as its equal constituent parts. Both are equal partners in building up communal life, creating and bringing about civilization, and in serving humanity. Both have been endowed with hearts, brains and the power of reasoning, and both possess feelings, desires and the other human urges. Both stand in need of mental and intellectual training and education, so that they may duly contribute to the happiness and welfare of society. In view of these facts, the claim for equality is absolutely justified, and every reformed civilization is duty-bound to afford its women all opportunities, along with men, for developing these natural abilities. They should also be provided the facilities for educational advancement; they should also be given social and economic rights, like men; and they should also be granted an honourable place in society, so that they may also develop self-respect and thereby all their humanity. The nations that have denied their womenfolk this kind of equality, that have kept them ignorant and illiterate, without dignity and social rights, have ultimately themselves been doomed. For to debase and corrupt one half of humanity is to debase and corrupt the whole of humanity. How can wretched, uncultured, ignorant and illiterate mothers rear and bring up children who will turn out to be proud, cultured and enlightened human beings?

But the other face of equality is that the man and the woman should have the same field of activity, that their activities should be similar, that they should have to shoulder equal responsibilities in all spheres of life, and that they should have identical positions in society. In support of this view it is said, on the authority of scientific observation and experiment, that man and woman are equipotential [English word in text] as regards their physical strength and ability. But their being equipotential in this respect is not a sufficient and strong enough basis for the claim that nature also requires them to have the same sorts of pursuits. For such a claim cannot be justified, unless it is established that both man and woman possess identical physiological structures, that both have been entrusted with similar duties by nature and endowed with similar psychological dispositions. The scientific research that has been carried out so far does not lend support to any of these hypotheses.

It has been established by biological [English word in text; Urdu *ilm al hayyat*] research that woman is different from man not only in her appearance and external physical organs but also in the protein molecules of tissue cells [previous five words in English in text]. From the time that the sex formation [English in text] of the foetus starts, the physiological structures of the two sexes begin to develop differently. The female physical system is evolved in order to bear and bring up children. It is to meet the requirements of this end that all physiological changes take place in the female body, from the initial genetic formation to maturity, and it is the demands of this very end that determine its future course of development also.

As soon as a girl attains maturity, menstruation starts, affecting the functioning of all her organs. The investigations made by famous biologists and physiologists show that during menstruation the following changes take place in the body of a woman:

1 The body's ability to retain heat decreases, with the result that heat is lost and there is a fall in temperature.

2 The pulse weakens, blood pressure falls below normal and corpuscles decrease.

3 Endocrines, tonsils and lymphatic glands [English terms in text] undergo changes.

4 The process of protein metabolism [English term in text] suffers a setback.

5 The release of phosphates and chlorides slows down, and the process of gaseous metabolism [English term in text] deteriorates.

6 Digestion becomes difficult, and proteins and fats are not easily assimilated by the body.

7 Respiration slows down, and the vocal organs suffer changes.

8 Muscles become lethargic, and feelings fluctuate.

9 The ability to concentrate weakens.

These changes render an otherwise healthy woman very nearly sick. Hardly 23 per cent women experience painless menstruation. Once, 1,020 women were taken at random and subjected to investigation. It was found that 84 per cent among them suffered from pain and other troubles during menstruation.

In view of these facts it can be safely asserted that a woman during menstruation is indeed unwell. This is a kind of disease from which she has to suffer every month.

These physical and physiological changes necessarily tell on her mental powers and the functioning of her vital organs. In 1909 Dr Voicechevsky carried out research and came to the conclusion that during menstruation a woman's power of concentration and her mental abilities in general suffer a setback. Professor Krschiskevsky's psychological observations led to the conclusion that a woman becomes easily irritable during this period. She becomes emotionally cold and unstable. Sometimes she even loses the ability for reflex action – so much so that her conditioned reflexes become disordered, which may even impact matters of daily habit. A lady tram conductor, for instance, would issue the wrong tickets and get confused while counting small change. A lady motor-driver would drive slowly, as if under strain, and become nervous at every turning. A lady typist would type wrongly, take a long time to type and omit words in spite of care and effort, and would press the wrong keys inadvertently. A lady barrister's power of reasoning would be impaired, and her presentation of a case would lack logic and the force of argument. A lady magistrate's comprehension and ability to take decisions would both be adversely affected. A female dentist would find it difficult to locate the required instruments. A female singer would lose the quality of her tone and voice – so much so that a phonetician would easily detect the fault and its cause also. In short, a woman's mental and nervous system is not fully under her control and becomes disorderly during menstruation. Her limbs do not quite obey her will; rather, her will and the power of taking decisions are overwhelmed by some involuntary force within her. Thus, she begins behaving as if under duress. She loses freedom of action and is thus rendered unfit to undertake any work of responsibility.

Professor Lapinsky writes in his book *The Development of Personality in a Woman* [English in text] that during menstruation a woman is deprived of her freedom of action; she becomes a slave to involuntary behaviour, and her capacity to do anything at will is considerably reduced.

All these changes take place in an otherwise healthy woman, and they can easily take a serious turn. There is evidence to show that a woman loses her mental balance during this period. She becomes easily irritable and furious, behaves at times in a wild manner and may even commit suicide. Dr Kraft Ebing writes that a woman who in her daily life is polite, polished and sweet-tempered changes quite dramatically during menstruation. During the 'low' period, women have to pass through a terrible ordeal indeed; they become ill-tempered and quarrelsome. Servants, children and husbands complain of their quick-temperedness. Even strangers sometimes receive rude treatment at their hands. Some other authorities on the subject have been led to the conclusion that most crimes by women are committed during this state. A good, righteous woman may commit theft and then feel remorse. Weinberg says on the basis of his observations that 50 per cent of women who committed suicide were menstruating at the time of their fateful decision. In view of this, Dr Kraft Ebing is of the opinion that, before trying a young woman for a crime, the court must ascertain that the crime was not committed during menstruation.

More terrible than menstruation is the period of pregnancy for the woman. Dr Reprev writes that during pregnancy a woman loses minerals and vital salts in larger quantities than during a state of fasting. A pregnant woman cannot undertake any work of mental and physical exertion that she could easily undertake at other times. If a man were made to pass through the rigours of pregnancy, or for that matter a woman when she is not pregnant, he or she would be pronounced a sick person by any standard. During pregnancy a woman's nervous system becomes disordered and remains so for months altogether. All her mental and psychic energies remain continually upset; and she remains hanging between health and unhealth, and a little carelessness can cause her serious illness. According to Dr Fischer, even a healthy woman remains subject to extreme mental stress during pregnancy. She becomes fickle, anxious and unwell, with the result that her capacity to understand and think is seriously affected. Havelock Ellis, Albert Mole and other writers on the subject are agreed that a pregnant woman, especially during the last month of her pregnancy, cannot be expected to undertake any work of physical or mental exertion.

After delivery has taken place, a woman remains exposed to various troubles, and her internal wounds may easily become septic. Her muscles begin to contract and return to their pre-pregnancy condition, and this upsets her whole system. If everything goes well, it takes her several weeks to return to normal. Thus, after impregnation a woman remains sick or nearly sick for about a year, and during this period her general efficiency is reduced to half, even to less than half.

Then comes the period of suckling, when she does not live for herself but for the trust that nature has placed in her care; the best of her body is turned into milk for the baby. Her share from the food that she takes is just so much as can keep her alive, the rest being diverted to the production and supply of milk. Then for a long time to come she has to pay the fullest attention to the bringing up and training of the child.

A substitute found in the modern age for feeding at the breast is to feed the child artificially. But this is no solution, for there can be no real substitute for the food that nature has placed in the mother's breasts for the child. To deprive the child of this natural food is to be inhuman and callous. The specialists are agreed that for the proper development of the child there is no better food than the mother's own milk.

Similarly, nursing homes and nurseries have been proposed for the bringing up of children so that mothers may wholly devote themselves to outdoor activities. But the fact is that no nursing home can provide and make up for mother love. The love, the kindly regards and good wishes so badly needed by a child in early childhood, cannot be evoked from the hearts of hired nurses. In fact, these new ways of rearing children have yet to be tried out and tested. The generations that have been brought up in those ways have not yet attained maturity and shown results. Their character, their morals, their achievements have yet to be tested by the world. It is, therefore, too early yet to claim that the world has found the right substitute for the mother's lap. Thus, the view that is still held is that the mother's lap is the best place where a child can most naturally be nourished and brought up.

Now any person with a little common sense can understand that though man and woman are equipotential as regards their physical and mental abilities, they have not been entrusted with equal responsibilities by nature. For the continuance of the race, man's only function is to impregnate the female. He is then free to have any pursuit in life. In contrast to this, the woman has to bear the whole burden of responsibility. It is to bear this burden that she is fashioned right from the time when she is a mere clot of blood in her mother's womb. Her whole constitution is so built as to meet the requirements to this end. Monthly courses that continue to recur throughout her youth render her unfit to undertake any task of major responsibility or one involving physical or mental exertion, for three to seven or ten days in every month. She has to pass through the ordeal of pregnancy stretching almost over a year, when she does not quite live her own life, then the two years of suckling are no less terrible when she feeds humanity on her blood at the springs of her breasts. She has to pass sleepless nights and troubled days, especially during the early years of the child's development. During this period she in fact has to sacrifice her comfort and peace, her ease and desires, and everything that she would dearly love to have, for the well-being of the coming generation.

In view of these facts, let us now consider the demands of justice. The question is: will it be just and fair to demand that a woman perform all these natural functions in which man is not, and cannot be, her partner, and also shoulder those social responsibilities equally with him for the carrying out of which he has been absolved from all other duties by nature? Will it be just and fair to require her to undergo all sorts of hardships set for her sex by nature and also to earn her living in the economic field? Will it be proper and right to make her take equal part with man in defending the country, establishing peace, and promoting the cause of industry and commerce, agriculture and the administration of justice? Above all, will it be just and right to require her to allure men's hearts also by her presence in mixed gatherings and provide them with means of entertainment and pleasure? This is not justice, it is sheer injustice; it is not equality, but sheer inequality. Justice demands that the one who has already been burdened by nature should be given light duties in society, and the one who has no such natural duty should be required to shoulder all the important and heavy social responsibilities, including the duties of supporting and protecting the family.

It is not only unfair to burden woman with the outdoor duties: she cannot in fact be expected to perform them to the same ability. These duties can be suitably carried out only by those workers whose efficiency does not waver, who can perform them equally well at all times, and whose mental and physical abilities can always be relied upon. But the workers who are rendered unfit, or nearly unfit, for a number of days every month, whose capacity to work falls short of the required standards time and again, cannot be expected to shoulder these responsibilities. Imagine the situation of an army or naval fleet which consists wholly of women. It is quite possible that right in the midst of war, a fair number of them might be down with menstruation, a good number of delivery cases forced to stay in bed and a fair percentage of them pregnant. One might say that military service is an extreme example to pick for this discussion. But one might ask: which service among the police, judicial, administrative, foreign, railway, industrial and commercial services does not require a steadfast, dependable capacity to work? Therefore, the people who want women to undertake manly duties want to make them non-women [*na aurat*] and finish off the human race. Or perhaps they want a certain percentage of them always to be set aside to suffer the punishment of being non-women, or perhaps they want to lower the general standards of efficiency in all affairs of life.

****

Commandments regarding Pardah

The verses of the Quran that enjoin pardah are translated as follows:

> O Prophet, tell the believing men to restrain their eyes and guard their honour. This is the path of purity for them. Surely, Allah knows full well what they do. And, O Prophet, tell the believing women to restrain their eyes and guard their honour, and not to display their decoration except what is unavoidable. They should draw their garments close onto their chests and should not display themselves except before their husbands, fathers, fathers-in-law, sons, stepsons, brothers, nephews, their own women, slaves, those men not concerned with women, or boys who are not yet conscious of the requirements of pardah. Moreover tell them that they should not stamp the ground in walking so as to reveal their hidden ornamentation through sound.
>
> (24:30–1)

> O wives of the Prophet, of course you are not like other women. If you are God-fearing, do not talk in a soft voice, lest the man with ill in his heart should cherish false hopes from you. Speak in a clear manner and remain in your house, and do not go about displaying your fineries as women used to do in the days of ignorance.
>
> (33:32–3)

> O Prophet, enjoin your wives amid daughters and the women of the Muslims to wear over their heads their covering. It is expected that they will be recognized, and not mistreated.
>
> (33:59)

Now let us consider these verses carefully. On the one hand, men have been instructed only to restrain their eyes and guard their morals against indecency. Women have been enjoined, like men, to observe these commands, but they have been given additional instructions also for

191

observance in social life. This clearly shows that some additional laws are required. Now we should see how the Holy Prophet (peace be upon him) and his Companions enforced their brief instructions in the Islamic Social System, and how their sayings and actions explain and illustrate the meaning of these instructions in actual, practical life.

Restraining the Eye

The first command that males and females have been given is to restrain their eyes. Generally people take it to mean a lowering of the eyes. But this does not clarify fully the meaning of the original. The divine commandment does not mean that people should always cast down their gaze and should never look up, but rather warns them of what has been called in hadith 'the adultery of the eyes'. Enjoying the beauty and decoration of other women by men and making other men the object of their eyes by women is liable to lead to evil results. Conflict [fasād] starts habitually and practically like this. Therefore, this door has been closed first of all, and this is what is meant by *ghadd-i-basar*.

Obviously, when humans live in this world, they use their eyes, and their gaze will fall upon everything. It is not possible that a man will never see a woman or that a woman will never see a man. That is why the supreme Lawgiver has absolved from blame the first, chance look. But what has been prohibited is that one should cast a second look and stare at the face which one finds attractive at first sight.

Hazrat Jarir says, 'I asked the Holy Prophet what I should do if I happen to cast a look by chance.' The Holy Prophet replied, 'Turn your eyes away' (Abu Da'ud).

According to Hazrat Buraidah, the Holy Prophet told Hazrat, 'Ali [is] not to cast a second look, for the first look was pardonable but the second was prohibited' (Abu Da'ud).

'On the Day of Judgment, molten lead will be poured into the eyes of the man who looks at the charms of a woman lustfully' (Takmilah, Fath-al Qadir).

But sometimes one has to have a look at the other woman, for example, a female patient who may be under the treatment of a doctor, or a woman who has to appear before a judge as a witness or as a party. Or one may have to help a woman who is left in a burning place, or a woman who is drowning in water, or a woman whose life or honour is in danger. In such cases, not just the face but even the most protected parts can be seen if required, and the body can also be touched. So much so that it is not only lawful but obligatory to rescue a drowning or a burning woman even by carrying her in one's lap. The Lawgiver commands that as far as possible one should keep one's intention pure on such an occasion. But if, in spite of that, one's emotions are a little excited naturally, it is not sinful. For one's looking at the other woman and having contact with her body was not intentional, but was necessitated by circumstances, and it is not possible for humans to suppress their natural urges completely.[1]

Likewise, it is not only lawful to look at a woman, but this has been enjoined by the sharia when one is considering marriage. The Holy Prophet himself practised this.

Mughirah bin Sh'abah says that he sent a message to a woman asking for her hand. The Holy Prophet said to him, 'You must meet her first, for that will enhance love and mutual regard between you' (Al Tirmizī).

According to Sahl bin S'ad, a woman came to the Holy Prophet and said that she intended to offer herself in marriage to him. Hearing this, the Holy Prophet raised his eyes and looked at her (Al Bukhari).

Abu Hurayrah says that he was sitting with the Holy Prophet when a man came and said that he intended to marry a woman from among the Ansar. The Holy Prophet asked him, 'Have you seen her?' He said he had not. The Holy Prophet told him to go and take a look at her, because the Ansar generally have some defect in their eyes (Muslim).

According to Jabir bin 'Abdullah, the Holy Prophet said that when a man sent a message to a woman asking for her hand, he should see her to confirm if there was anything that made him inclined to marry her (Abu Da'ud).

If one considers these exceptions carefully, one will find that the Supreme Lawgiver does not mean to prohibit looking at other women in all cases. Rather, the interest is in preventing the incidence of oppression and conflict. That is why he has prohibited only that casting of the eyes which is not necessary, which does not serve any social purpose, but is charged with desires instead.

This command applied both to males and to females. According to a hadith related by Hazrat Umm Salmah, one day she was sitting with the Holy Prophet, along with Hazrat Maimūnah, when Hazrat Ibn Umm

---

[1] For further details, please see the explanatory notes on v. 30 of Surah An-Nur (24) in the *Commentary* by Imam Razi; *Ahkam al Qur'an* by al Jassas and al Mabsut, *Kitab al Ihsan.*

Maktum, who was a blind man, called on the Holy Prophet. The Holy Prophet told her to observe pardah from him. Hazrat Umm Salmah said, 'Is he not a blind man? He will neither see us nor recognize us.' The Holy Prophet said, 'Are you also blind? Do you not see him?' (Al Tirmizi).

There is, however, a fine psychological distinction between a woman's looking at men and a man's looking at women. Man has by nature the propensity to take the initiative. If he is attracted by something, he attempts to acquire it. On the contrary, woman's nature is one of inhibition and escape. Unless her nature is totally corrupted, she can never become so bold and fearless as to make the first advances towards the male who has attracted her. In view of this distinction, the Lawgiver does not regard a woman's looking at other men to be as harmful as a man's looking at other women. In several hadith it has been reported that the Holy Prophet had himself shown Hazrat Aisha the performance given by a group from Abyssinia [Urdu *habshiyon*] on the occasion of an Eid.[2] This shows that there is no absolute injunction against women looking at men. Rather, what is not preferred [*makruh*] is to sit in the same gathering together with men and stare at them, and what is prohibited is to look at them in such a manner as may lead to evil results.

In another context involving his Companion Ibn Umm Maktum, the blind man, the Holy Prophet told Fatimah bint Qais to pass her period of *iddat* [the period following the death of or divorce from her husband that a woman must spend before remarrying] in the house of Ibn Umm Maktum. Qazi Abu Bakr Ibn 'Arabi has related in his *Ahkam al Quran* that Fatimah bint Qais wanted to pass her waiting term in the house of Umm Sharik. The Holy Prophet said that 'the house is visited by many people and instead you should stay in the house of Ibn Maktum, who is a blind man and you can stay there without observing pardah'. This shows that the real object before the Holy Prophet was to reduce the chances of

---

[2] This has been related in the *Collections* by Bukhari, Muslim, Nasa'i and Ahmad in different ways. Some people have tried to explain this by saying that the event took place when Hazrat Aisha was still a child and the commandments for veiling had not yet been handed down. But according to Ibn Hibban, this event took place in AH 7, when a deputation from Abyssinia visited Madinah. If that is correct, then Hazrat Aisha would have been fifteen or sixteen years of age at the time. Moreover, according to a report in Bukhari, the Holy Prophet also tried to cover Hazrat Aisha with a *chador* (loose cloth) at the same time. This shows that the injunctions for pardah had already been revealed.

mischief. The lady had to live with somebody, but the best course of action was to minimize sources of confusion and misconduct.

All this is based on sound wisdom. The person who is capable of penetrating to the core of the sharia can easily understand the wisdom of the commandment of *ghadd-i-basar* and the calibration of its rigidity and laxity in different circumstances. The only object of the Lawgiver is to stop people from relaying coded messages from our eyes, otherwise there is no enmity towards our eyes and seeing. In the beginning eyes are cast very innocently. The devil in ourselves gives very powerful reasons on the other side. He says that we need this to satisfy our aesthetic senses, endowed to us by nature. Just as we are allowed to enjoy other manifestations of the beauty of nature, why can we not enjoy human beauty and take spiritual pleasure from it? The problem is that the pleasure of looking often progresses to the pleasure of coupling. Who can dare deny that promiscuity in the past and today in this world has been spurred in the first instance by the fitnah of these eyes? Who can claim that their reaction on seeing a beautiful and young person of the opposite sex is the same as that caused by a beautiful flower? If there is a difference between the two reactions, as there surely is, and one of the two arouses desire, how can one justify the demand that the same freedom be accorded to gratifying one's aesthetic urge in both cases? The Lawgiver does not mean to erase our aesthetic urge. What He wants is that one should choose one's partner carefully according to one's taste and then make him or her the only object of all one's aesthetic craving. Then one may enjoy him or her as much as one may please. If one moves away from this centre, then one will involve oneself in indecency and obscenity. Even if one is able to restrict one's actions, one cannot save oneself from corruption of thought. One will waste most of one's energies through the eyes, and pollute one's heart by longing for sins not committed. One will fall in a false love again and again, and spend sleepless nights in vain. There will be a real loss of vitality in this throbbing and excitement of the heart. Is it not a great loss? And all this is the result of moving away from the person on which one's eyes should remain fixed. Therefore, keep your eyes under control. Looking at others without proper reason or with ill purpose is questionable. If, however, there is a genuine need or a social necessity, looking at the opposite sex is lawful, even if there is some likelihood of turmoil. For women it is permissible to look at men, but for men it is not permissible, unless, of course, inadvertently.

****

The Veil (*niqab*)

Any person who considers Quranic verses carefully, their well-known and generally accepted meaning and the practice during the time of the Holy Prophet, cannot dare deny the fact that the Islamic sharia enjoins women to keep their faces hidden from unknown people. This was the practice of Muslims during the time of the Holy Prophet himself. Though the term *niqab* has not been specified in the Quran, it is Quranic in spirit. Muslim women living at the time of the Holy Prophet to whom the Quran was revealed had made it a regular part of their dress outside the house, and even at that time it was called by the same name, *niqab*.

Yes! This is the same *niqab* or 'veil' [English word in text] that Europe loathes and detests. The very thought of this weighs heavily on the English conscience, and it is regarded as a mark of oppression, narrow-mindedness and barbarism. Yes, this is the same thing that is often mentioned first of all in pointing out the ignorance and backwardness of an Eastern nation. And when someone desires to describe the cultural and social advancement of an Eastern nation, the first thing that is mentioned with great satisfaction is that it has discarded the 'veil'. Now, we should be hanging our heads with shame. For this is not something that was devised and adopted later; it was indeed devised by the Quran itself and established by the Holy Prophet himself as a social custom. But the mere hanging of the head will be of no avail. If the ostrich buries its head in the sand, the hunter does not go away. Likewise, even if the Muslims hang their heads, they cannot cancel the Quranic verse, nor blot out the established facts of history. The more we try to cover it up with misinterpretations, this 'shameful blot' will become all the more glaring. Once you have admitted under Western influence that it is a shameful blot, then there is only one option left for you, which is to leave behind Islam itself because it enjoins *niqab*, modesty and other barbaric practices. You desire 'progress'. You want 'civilization'. How can you follow a religion that restricts women from becoming the light of social gatherings, advocates modesty, shyness and chastity, and forbids the queen of the house from becoming the 'delight of the eye'? How can such a religion allow 'progress' or 'civilization'? For 'progress' and 'civilization' cannot be achieved unless the woman, actually the *Lady sahiba*, spends at least a few hours exclusively on decoration of herself, perfuming her body, selecting attractive and appropriate clothing, enhancing the glamour of the face and arms, using lipstick and other beauty aids, and shaping her eyebrows and blackening her eyelids, so that when she goes out thus equipped she may bewitch all and sundry. And if this commitment to self-promotion is not satisfied, then some make-up and a mirror must be kept handy at all times to correct even minor disarray.

As we have repeatedly pointed out above, the objectives of Islam and Western civilization are poles apart. Therefore, the person who interprets the Islamic injunctions from the Western point of view commits a serious mistake. For the Western criterion of judging the value of things is radically opposed to that adopted by Islam. The things which are held as highly important and valuable in the West are indeed of little or no value in the eyes of Islam, and vice versa. Thus, the person who believes in the Western criterion will feel that every Islamic thing needs to be altered and modernized. That is why, when he begins to interpret the injunctions of Islam, he feels the need to modify them, leading to distortions. And even after their distortion he is not able to apply them properly to life, as he is obstructed time and again by the clear injunction of the Quran and Sunnah. Therefore, the proper thing for such a person to do would be that, before he considers practical measures, he should examine how far the objectives themselves, for the realization of which these measures have been devised, are acceptable. For if he does not agree with the objectives, then why should he take the trouble of discussing, and then distorting, the means of realizing them? Why should one not discard the religion itself whose objectives one does not believe in? Why not just leave the religion whose objectives one does not agree with? If, however, one believes in the objectives, then the only thing that remains to be decided is whether the practical measures devised to realize them are suitable or not, and this is a relatively easy debate to decide. But such an approach can be adopted only by honest, sincere people. As for hypocrites, they are the most wretched of all God's creation. It suits them to declare that they believe in one thing, whereas they actually believe in something quite different.

Indeed, all the disputes about the veil spring from this hypocrisy. People have tried their very best to prove that the present form of pardah was a custom of the pre-Islamic communities, and that the Muslims adopted this custom of ignorance long after the time of the Holy Prophet. The question is, why was it necessary to carry out this historical research in the presence of a clear verse of the Quran, the established practice of the time of the Holy Prophet, and the explanations given by his Companions and their pupils? Only to justify the objectives of life prevalent in the West. For without this, it was not possible to advocate for the concepts of 'progress' and 'civilization' copied from the West that have become deeply engrained in their minds. Since wearing the veil runs against these objectives and does not in any way fit in with Western concepts, they made efforts through historical research to blot out the tradition that is based on the clear laws of Islam. This open hypocrisy that had already been shown in the case of many other problems has again been shown in the matter of the veil as well. The true reason here is the same unprincipled behaviour, bankruptcy of reason and lack of moral courage that these people exhibit and which we have discussed above. Without this they would not have dared to refute the Quran with their so-called historical research, despite their profession of Islam. Had they been honest and sincere, they would either have discarded their concepts in favour of Islam (provided that they wanted to remain Muslims), or they would have openly discarded Islam, which prevents them from making 'progress'.

The person who understands the aims of Islamic laws and also has some common sense [English term in text] cannot fail to see that allowing women to move about with uncovered faces runs counter to the objectives held so dear by Islam. The face is the body part that is most likely to impress other humans. It is the index of natural human charms, the most attractive part and the greatest manifestation of human beauty. It pulls eyes and emotions towards itself. To understand this, one does not require any extensive knowledge of psychology. If one searches one's own heart, asks for the verdict of one's own eyes and analyses one's own psychic experiences, one will have to admit (provided that one is not hypocritical) that, of all decorations of the body, the natural charm placed by the Creator in the structure of the face has the greatest sex appeal [English term in text]. That is why if one has to marry a girl, one desires to see her face. If one is shown the whole body but not the face, one is not satisfied. This shows that the beauty of the face is by far the most important thing in the human body.

Now that this fact has been established, let us proceed further. If the intention is not to prevent sexual anarchy and emotional confusion in society, then the female should have the freedom to expose her breasts, arms, shins and thighs, besides her face, as in modern Western civilization. In this case, all those restrictions and limits that have been imposed by the Islamic pardah will be out of the question. But if, on the other hand, the object is to curb indecency and obscenity, then nothing can be more unreasonable than to close all the minor ways to indecency and instead fling the main gate wide open.

One may ask: why then has Islam allowed uncovering of the face in case of genuine need? The reply is that the law of Islam is not a one-sided, irrational law. On the one hand, it safeguards the morals of man; on the other, it takes into account his genuine needs also, and thus strikes a balance between the two sides of life. It intends to eradicate immorality, but at the same time it does not restrain a person from satisfying his genuine needs. That is why it has not given women an absolute command in respect of covering the face, as in respect of covering those parts that must be kept hidden [Urdu *satar*] and concealing the decoration, because this does not restrain her from attending to the needs of life. But, alternatively, if the hand and the face are kept permanently covered, she may find it extremely difficult to attend to her daily needs. Therefore, it was enjoined on women to cover the face with the veil, and this command has been relaxed with the proviso 'except what is unavoidable', so that she may uncover the face if required under necessity, provided that she does not mean to display her charms. Then, on the other side, men were enjoined to 'restrain their eyes', so that if a modest woman uncovered her face under necessity, they would cast their looks down and refrain from staring at her in an indecent way.

If one carefully considers these injunctions for pardah, one will find that the Islamic pardah is not a custom of ignorance, but a rational law. A custom of ignorance is something rigid: it does not permit of modification or change under any circumstances. If it covers a thing, it covers it for ever, and it cannot be uncovered whatever may happen. In contrast to this, a rational law is flexible. It permits of strictness and laxity according to the circumstances; it permits of exceptions to its rules according to the time and occasion. Such a law cannot be followed blindly: it demands discrimination. A sensible follower can decide for himself where he should obey the general rule and where under the law he is allowed to avail himself of the exceptions in view of 'genuine needs'. Then he himself can settle the question: how far in a particular situation can he make use of the exception, and how can he keep in view the object of the law? In all such matters, the conscience of an honest, sincere believer alone can be the true judge, as has been said by the Holy Prophet:

Ask for the judgment [*fatwa*] of your conscience and discard what pricks it.

That is why Islam cannot be properly followed without knowledge. It is a rational law, and to follow it rightly one needs to exercise reason and understanding at every step.

First Principles of Islamic Economics

Contents

The Principles and Objectives of Islam's Economic System

The chapter is intended to offer answers to the following crucial questions often raised regarding Islam's economic system:[1]

- Does Islam offer an economic system and, if so, what is the blueprint of that system? What is the position of land, labour, capital and organization in this blueprint?
- Can the funds of *zakāh* and *sadaqat* (mandatory and normal charity) be used for social welfare?
- Can we successfully introduce an interest-free economy?
- What is the interrelationship of the economic, political, social and religious systems in Islam?

Each of these questions merits a detailed discussion worthy of a book. The occasion, however, does not permit a lengthy discourse and, therefore, only brief answers are offered in the following paragraphs.

5.1 Basic Principles of Islam's Economic System

There are two parts to the first question. The first is whether Islam offers an economic system and, if so, what is its blueprint? Its second part is: what is the position of land, labour, capital and organization in that blueprint? The answer to the first part is that Islam has definitely provided an economic system. This, however, does not mean that it has prepared a blueprint with the minutest details for all times to come,

---

[1] Based on Sayyid Maududi's address at the seminar held in the Administration Department of the University of the Punjab, Lahore, 17 December 1965.

in which everything has been predetermined regarding the economic issues of mankind. What this actually means is that Islam has provided us the basic principles and determined the essential parameters according to which we can always prepare a system capable of satisfying our economic needs in all times and climes. The approach followed by Islam, as evident from a careful study of the Holy Quran and the Traditions of the Holy Prophet (peace be upon him), is that it establishes the four corners and then tells us that we can raise the edifice of a particular aspect of our life on the basis of those well-defined parameters. We are not permitted to transgress the predetermined limits, but are free therein to work out details as demanded by our circumstances, requirements and experience. From the sphere of personal life to each and every realm of human civilization and culture, this is how Islam has offered guidance to mankind. This is the course followed for our economic system as well. Islam has given us broad outlines and principles and set the four corners of the proposed structure to enable us to give concrete shape to an economic system of our own. One may very well see how our leading jurists had during their time formulated in detail statutes, by-laws, rules and regulations concerning the economic system of Islam. These are available in our books of jurisprudence and serve as an invaluable treasure house of knowledge on the subject. In fact, these detailed chapters on Islam's economic system occupy a unique position as the pioneering work of scholarship in the field of economics and a precursor to similar attempts that mankind was to subsequently witness in the world. Out of this treasury of knowledge we can borrow verbatim details that satisfy the needs of the time and evolve our own strategy for the new issues facing us today in light of the paradigms and parameters available to us. Whatever rules and regulations we frame are required, however, to be based essentially on the principles provided to us by the Quran and the Sunnah and to remain within their well-defined limits.

5.2 The Objectives of Islamic Economics

Having explained what we mean when we say that Islam has its own economic system, I now proceed to discuss at length the principles and rules that Islam has given us in the realm of economics. Before I start, let me first explain the most important objectives in this system, because we cannot otherwise properly understand those principles or apply them to our contemporary situation and needs, nor can we frame, using the deductive method, detailed laws, rules and regulations in their true spirit.

5.2.1 Personal Freedom

The prime factor for Islam in respect of the economy is safeguarding personal freedom and imposing only as much restriction as is necessary for the collective well-being of a society. Islam attaches great importance to human freedom. The reason for this is quite simple: every individual in Islam is accountable before the Lord for the deeds in his personal capacity. This is not a collective accountability. It is therefore essential to let each person have more and more avenues for the development and growth of his personality, according to his options and discretion, and to allow him the freedom of choice to do as he desires. This is why Islam attaches great importance to the individual's moral, political and economic freedom. One can imagine how free, if at all, a person can be to act according to his own views, if he is even free to hold them, who is dependent on someone else, an institution or a government, for his subsistence. Islam has therefore given us principles for an economic system that guarantee an individual's freedom to earn their daily bread. There are also restrictions, but only to the extent that they are necessary for a society's progress and prosperity. This is why Islam seeks to establish a political system that guarantees the active participation of the people and a government of their choice: a government answerable to the people, which they can change as and when they deem this is in the interests of the nation and the state; a government that is run in consultation with the people and representatives of their trust, where the people may enjoy complete freedom of criticism and expression; and a government whose powers should not be unlimited, but circumscribed by the parameters set by the Quran and the Sunnah as the supreme law of the land.

Furthermore, the basic human rights of the people are also guaranteed by Islam. These rights are not the gift of any state authority or world body, but have been decreed by Allah *subhanahu wa taala* [praise be to Allah] Himself, and nobody is authorized to violate or deny them to His subjects. All of these measures have been taken by Islam to ensure that an individual maintains his freedom, and they prevent the possibility of a repressive regime taking over the land and restraining the proper growth and development of someone's personality.

5.2.2 *Harmony in Moral and Material Progress*

The second objective of Islam's economic system is to guarantee the harmonious growth of human personality both morally and materially. Islam lays a special stress on the moral growth and development of man. For this, it is incumbent on a society to provide the individual with ample opportunities to help him choose to do good deeds. It seeks to create an environment that is conducive for the blossoming of noble human traits and moral virtues like magnanimity, co-operation, compassion, tolerance, etc. Because of this, Islam does not depend entirely on the strong arm of the law to establish social justice in the land. It assigns greater importance in this context to *imān* (faith), *ibadat* (prayers and other solemn acts of worship), education and moral upbringing in order to reform a person from within, to modify his taste and temperament, to change his way of thinking and to create within him a strong moral urge to stand upright and steadfast in all circumstances. If and when these measures fall short of producing the desired results, Muslim society should be morally strong enough to force the individual purely through social pressure to abide by its norms and values. In case social pressure also falls short of producing a change, Islam then uses the strong arm of the law as a last resort to establish justice. According to the Islamic standpoint, every social system is wrong that relies mainly on force to establish the rule of law and justice and that renders the individual incapable of doing good of his own free will.

5.2.3 *Promotion of Co-operation, Harmony and Justice*

The third important objective of the economic system of Islam is the promotion and sustainability of a society's unity and cohesion. Islam is the torchbearer of human unity and brotherhood, and is opposed to division and disharmony. Therefore, it does not encourage a society's division on the basis of class, clan and ethnic or linguistic considerations. The classes that naturally emerge under a particular social set-up are led to live in an environment of mutual co-operation, compassion and trust, rather than an atmosphere of hatred and conflict. When one examines the texture of human society analytically, one discovers that it is composed of two types of class. There is the category of classes that seek to promote a coercive political, social and economic system artificially, and then perpetuate their supremacy over other segments of society unlawfully. Racialist ideologies, such as Brahmanism and Zionism, or systems of landed aristocracy and financial imperialism, such as feudalism and the Western capitalist system, have been instrumental in producing and promoting this type of class. Islam itself does not create or patronize any such exploitative or anti-human system, nor would it ever allow such a system to sustain itself and prosper. In fact, Islam eliminates every anti-human social order through its reformatory and legal measures. The second category of classes consists of those which automatically develop owing to the diversity of human qualifications, capabilities and circumstances, and undergoes change naturally. Islam does not forcibly eliminate this category, nor does it permit the members of these classes to fight among themselves. On the contrary, it creates an atmosphere of amity and co-operation among them through its moral, political, social and economic structures. It makes people helpful and compassionate to one another and, by providing equality of opportunities to all, it creates an environment in which they freely intermix and gradually lose their separate identities to make a uniform whole naturally.

5.3 Basic Principles of the Islamic Economic System

Once you keep these three objectives in mind, you are in a better position to understand the fundamentals of the economic system of Islam in their true perspective. Let me now briefly explain some of the major principles of this system.

5.3.1 Parameters of Private Ownership

Islam reaffirms a person's right to own property, subject to certain conditions. It makes no distinction in this regard between the means of production and consumer goods, or between earned and unearned income. While granting people the right to own property, however, Islam circumscribes this right with certain limits. Islam does not approve of treating the means of production and consumer goods differently and excluding the former from the ambit of personal ownership. From the Islamic perspective, just as a person is authorized to have his own wardrobe, kitchenware and furniture, so he is entitled to own land, machines and factories. Similarly, as everybody can own the wealth he earns through his labour, he can also own the wealth left behind by his father, mother, wife or husband. He can also be a shareholder in an income earned on the principle of *Mudārabah* or *Mushārakah* through the capital he has invested, on which somebody may have laboured to produce dividends. Islam thus does not differentiate between one type of ownership and another, whether it is the ownership of the means of production or that of consumer goods, or whether it is earned or unearned income.

The difference that Islam makes between the various types of wealth is on whether they are earned or produced through fair means or foul, and whether it has been used in a right or wrong manner. The blueprint that Islam has prepared for the entire spectrum of mankind's economic life has been formed in such a manner that it leaves a person free, within certain limits, to earn his living. As explained earlier, human freedom is of prime importance to Islam, which builds the entire edifice of the community's growth and development on the cornerstone of this freedom. To grant a person the right of personal ownership of his economic means and resources is therefore essential for preserving this freedom. To deprive a person of this right and impose public ownership on all the resources of the land would naturally mean denying him his personal freedom, because under this kind of dispensation every individual automatically becomes a servant of the state machinery that controls its economic resources through its administration.

5.3.2 *Equitable Distribution of Wealth*

Another basic principle of Islam's economic system is that it aims at an equitable, but not necessarily equal, distribution of wealth. It does not seek an absolutely equal distribution of the means of living for every human being. Anybody studying the Quran will notice that such an equality does not exist anywhere in the whole of the universe. The very concept of parity is contrary to the dictates of nature. Has each one of us been granted the same level of health? Do all of us enjoy the same amount of intelligence? Do all of us have equally strong memories? Is every individual on a par with others in beauty, physical strength and intellectual prowess? Is everyone born under similar circumstances and in the same environment, and does each enjoy the same opportunities and avenues for progress and prosperity? If there is no equality anywhere in any of these matters, how logical is a claim for equality in the means of production or distribution of wealth? Practically speaking, such equality is not remotely feasible, and any attempt to enforce this through artificial means is bound to fail. Islam, therefore, does not seek an equal distribution of economic resources and economic gains. Instead, it places a stress on their equitable distribution and prescribes certain rules for this in order to achieve equity and justice. These rules may be summed up as follows.

The first rule in this context is that Islam has distinctly classified the means of the production of wealth into the two broad categories of lawful (*halal*) and forbidden (*haram*). On the one hand, it gives the individual the freedom to struggle for his economic well-being and to own what he earns; and on the other, this freedom is subject to the provisos of *halal* and *haram*. According to this rule, every person is free to earn his living through lawful means in a way that is convenient to him, and to earn as much as he can. He is also the lawful owner of all that he has earned. Nobody has the right to put a curb on his ownership or to deprive him either totally or partially of what he has earned. Of course, he is not authorized to secure even a farthing through unlawful or forbidden means. He is not simply unauthorized to make this kind of earning, but the law will forcibly stop him from any such attempt. He cannot be the owner of anything earned unlawfully and will also be liable for punishment according to the nature of the crime committed. This punishment may range from imprisonment to a fine, or even confiscation of his property. Steps will also be taken to prevent him from committing such crimes again.

The means of wealth production that are declared *haram* by the Islamic sharia are as follows: dishonesty in public accounts, bribery, distortion, misappropriation of public funds, theft and burglary, irregularity in weights and measures, trading in obscene and immoral items, prostitution and the sex trade, the production and sale of wine and other intoxicants, usury and all interest-based transactions, gambling, betting, speculation, all sale and purchase deals based on fraud or coercion and those causing bad blood or corruption, or which may be contrary to the demands of justice and the public interest. The sharia has banned all these means. Islam also prohibits hoarding, monopolies and cartels that deprive the common man of the opportunity to make use of his wealth and the means of its production against the dictates of reason and fair play.

Apart from these, anything that is earned through lawful means is the legal income of a man. He is entitled to make use of this wealth himself, or to transfer it to others by gift or donation. He may also use it to earn more wealth or leave it behind for his heirs. There is no restriction on this legal income that could prevent it from earning more wealth at any stage. If a person becomes a billionaire lawfully, Islam does not obstruct him. He is free to make as much headway economically as he can, so long as he does not cross the prescribed limits. Frankly speaking, it is not easy under an Islamic dispensation to make millions, if one strictly follows the lawful means. Except for God's grace, it needs extraordinary efforts and acumen to multiply one's wealth in a lawful manner. However, Islam does not tie anybody's hands to prevent him from seeking 'Allah's Blessings' through the means He approves, because unwarranted hurdles and checks leave no incentive for someone to put in more labour.

The wealth thus lawfully earned has been subject to certain restrictions on its use, which are summed up in the following paragraphs.

The first use of one's wealth is to spend it on oneself. Islam puts such restrictions on this use to prevent a person's conduct from becoming harmful for the individual and for society. He is forbidden to spend it on liquor, and so he cannot drink. He cannot indulge in fornication and illicit sexual relations. He cannot squander it in gambling. He can follow no immoral or ethically wrong course of personal conduct. He is not authorized to have gold or silverware for his own use, nor can he indulge in ostentatious living to show off his riches.

Another way to use one's personal wealth is to withhold a part of it from spending and keep it safe in one's coffers. Islam does not support this approach. It would like the flow of wealth to continue uninterrupted in a lawful manner. It therefore levies *zakāh* on the amount saved to allow a portion of this to reach the less privileged and be diverted to schemes of public welfare. The acts that are disapproved of by the Book of God include the hoarding of wealth, which has been forcefully condemned. We have been warned that those who amass gold and silver and do not spend it in the Way of Allah will face 'a painful chastisement on a Day when they shall be heated up in the Fire of Hell, and their foreheads and their sides and their backs shall be branded with it, (and they shall be told): "This is the treasure which you hoarded for yourselves. Taste, then, the punishment for what you have hoarded"' (Al Tawbah 9:34–5). The reason for this penalty is that Allah *subhanahu wa taala* has produced the treasures of the heavens and the earth for the benefit of mankind. Therefore, nobody is authorized to lock this in his golden chests. The message given to us is this: 'Earn as much as you can through lawful means; spend it on your personal needs; and then, whatever you save, bring it in circulation in whatever manner possible for you legally.'

Hoarding, for which Islamic economics uses the term *ihtikār*, is thus strictly prohibited in Islam. *Ihtikār* means to purposely hold back consumer goods to create a scarcity in their supply, thereby causing prices to soar. The principle that Islam has laid down for business and commerce sanctions no such unhealthy practice. If you have a commodity for sale and there is a demand for it in the market, you have no right to hold it back. Creating a scarcity of items for daily use simply to earn a little extra money turns a trader into a bandit, and Islam totally disapproves of this.

Monopolies and cartels are also disallowed by Islam for the same reason. In the Islamic scheme of things, the public good occupies the highest position, and monopolies and cartels prevent the general public from making use of the available economic resources. Islam has therefore made it unlawful for certain means and opportunities of earning a living to be declared the exclusive domain of a particular class of people, family or household, making it difficult for others to enter that sector. There is only room for that kind of monopoly which is inevitable for the collective good of a society. Otherwise, Islam seeks to keep the field of economic activities open to everyone who wants to try his luck and make use of an opportunity to his advantage.

If someone wants to invest his savings to earn more money, he can do so only through the channels permitted by Islam for earning a livelihood. No forbidden means can ever be used for this purpose, as mentioned earlier.

5.3.3 Social Obligations

Islam thus superimposes the right of society on private ownership and safeguards this right in various ways. The Holy Quran lays a special emphasis on the rights of kindred, which means that, in addition to an individual's own rights to his income, his relatives also have their right to his earnings. Each and every member of society who earns more than he actually needs is duty-bound to do his best to help those among his relations who have less than they need to satisfy their day-to-day requirements. When every family sincerely tries to fulfil its obligations towards those families in the community who are lacking, there is bound to be an overall economic improvement in society as a whole, leaving behind hardly any household in need of external support. The rights of one's mother, father and close relatives, therefore, occupy the highest position in the list that the Holy Quran has offered us in respect of *Huquq al Ibad* (Rights of Men or Human Rights).

Islam similarly acknowledges a neighbour's rights to one's income. This simply means that it seeks to establish a society that is self-sufficient and requires no outside help to sustain itself economically. Islam would like to see every street and locality peopled by God-fearing men who know that to live also means to let others live with honour and dignity, and that the needs of one person are the responsibility of everyone else around him.

After putting the onus on the two responsibilities above, Islam then makes every affluent person responsible for providing the best assistance he can to those who may approach him or may be in need of it:

> And in their wealth there was a rightful share for him who would ask
> and for the destitute.
>
> (al Dhariyat 51:19)

The needy who may ask for help do not include beggars, who may have taken up begging as a profession. Instead, it means a person whose need impels him to approach you with a request for help. Having satisfied yourself about his need, and whether you are in a position to extend the desired help, you have no option but to discharge your responsibility towards those who are actually asking you for their 'right'. As for those who for some reason are prevented from approaching you with their request, they also have the right to their share of your affluence, once you have confirmed their need.

In addition to the Rights of Men (*Huquq al ibad*) Islam has also enjoined Muslims to spend 'in the Way of Allah', thereby establishing the rights of society and the state to their wealth. The import of this injunction is that a Muslim is required to be generous, magnanimous, compassionate and considerate, and should spend his money open-heartedly on every good cause and in the service of his religion and society, not inspired by any selfish motive, but purely for the sake of Allah's pleasure. Islam injects a powerful moral passion in every individual through its education and training, and through the environment that it creates in a Muslim society, which motivates a person to volunteer his services for every good cause, not owing to any compulsion but of his own will.

5.3.4 Zakāh

Zakāh is the most outstanding feature of the economic system of Islam. In addition to *infaq fī sabīl Allāh* [voluntary spending in the Way of Allah], *zakāh* is levied on the prescribed amount of capital saved, on trade goods, business and commerce, agricultural produce and livestock, in order to lend support to those members of society who have lagged behind economically. The mandatory charity of *zakāh* and the voluntary spending in the Way of Allah (*Sadaqat*) are like regular and supererogatory prayers. There is no limit to the supererogatory prayer, and a man can offer as much as he likes for his spiritual advancement and nearness to the Lord. However, regular prayer is mandatory, and the supererogatory prayers, even if they are countless, cannot take its place. Similarly, *Sadaqat* cannot absolve one of the obligation to pay *zakāh*.

Zakāh should not be mistaken for a 'holy' tax. It is not a tax but *ibādah*, or an act of worship, and, like regular prayer, is one of the five Pillars of Faith. A tax is an amount that is levied by force on a person, which he may or may not like. A person who is taxed hardly feels honoured or gratified, nor does he regard it as an act of mercy and benevolence. In fact, even in developed economies, one can find plenty of people who try to seek a way to evade its application and avoid payment. Tax differs in principle from *zakāh*. Tax is levied to generate revenue to meet expenditure on services, the benefits of which eventually return to the taxpayer. The basic concept governing a taxation system is that you are required to contribute a certain amount from your income for the facilities you expect the government to provide you with. Your tax is, therefore, the contribution that you make for the services of which you are a beneficiary as a taxpayer.

On the contrary, *zakāh* is an act of worship, just like *ṣalāh*. It is imposed not by an act of parliament or a legislature, but has been made mandatory by Allah *subhanahu wa taala* and, as a believer, every Muslim is duty-bound to pay it willingly and never try to avoid its payment. Even in the absence of any official machinery to collect *zakāh*, the faithful man makes his own calculations to ascertain the amount payable by him on the due date. *Zakāh* is not meant to satisfy the social needs of the people. It is exclusively for the benefit of those who have somehow lagged behind or remained deprived of their due share of the national wealth and are in need of assistance, whether temporarily or permanently. Therefore, *zakāh* is absolutely different from tax in its essence, objectives, form and content. It is collected or paid not for the construction of roads, railways or canals, or to run the country's administration, but has been levied by the Lord to help the deserving get his due; the only dividend one should look for on its payment is Allah's pleasure and the reward of the Day of Reckoning.

There has been a misperception that there is no tax in Islam other than *zakāh* and *Kharaj* (land tax). The fact is that the Holy Prophet (peace be upon him) has himself declared: There is a right [of the state] to [Muslims'] property other than *zakāh*. There are taxes which Islam does not approve of. These include taxes such as those levied by the caesars, khosraus and despotic princes, which were deposited in royal coffers as their personal property and for which they were accountable to none but themselves. The sharia, however, puts no restriction on the taxation levied by an Islamic government that is run on the principles of popular participation or *shura*. The revenue thus gathered forms part of the public treasury and is spent with the people's consent in the national interest, and the government is held responsible for its proper utilization. In the case of an economic imbalance created in society prior to the establishment of an Islamic government, or wealth being amassed through illicit means by certain classes, the malaise cannot be remedied by the confiscation of property, but by levying direct taxes. The concentration of wealth in a few hands can also be effectively checked with the help of relevant Islamic laws. Allowing the rulers to confiscate property would naturally lead them to strengthening their hands with repressive laws, thereby giving them a licence to grow even more oppressive and commit more injustice and transgressions.

5.3.5 Law of Inheritance

Islam's law of inheritance has been framed with the sole objective of allowing the wealth, big or small, that is left behind by the deceased to pass on to a larger group of his heirs and next of kin in a well-defined manner. His mother, father, wife and children are among the prime beneficiaries, followed by his brothers and sisters and close relatives. If a person has no legal heir, the community as a whole becomes the heir, and the legacy goes to the public treasury.

These are the basic principles and parameters that are set by Islam for the economic well-being of a society. We are free to devise an economic system of our own within these parameters; it is for us to finalize the details, as demanded by the situation in our time. What we are strictly required to do is to follow neither the capitalist path of an unbridled economy nor the communist method of taking all the economic resources under state control. We have to adopt a system of a free economy that is restricted by certain limits, a system that leaves all avenues open to the individual for the moral growth and development of his personality; a system that will rarely need legislation to mobilize everyone to do their bit for the welfare of society; a system that leaves no room for the emergence of classes through unfair means and should promote co-operation among the legitimately existing natural classes, rather than conflict. Every means of livelihood that is declared *haram* by Islam will remain unlawful under this system, and only those means proclaimed *halal* will be legal. The rights that are guaranteed by Islam for acquiring and disposing of wealth earned through lawful means will remain secure. The state will have a proper mechanism for the compulsory collection of *zakāh* and its disbursement. Property that is left by the deceased will get distributed according to the law of inheritance, and every individual will be free to conduct his economic activities within the approved parameters, with no legislation to curtail this freedom. The law will not interfere in the unrestrained economic activities of individuals, so long as they continue to abide by the norms of justice and fair play. However, if they transgress the prescribed limits or try to establish monopolies and cartels, the law would then definitely take action, not to deny them their basic freedom, but to keep them firmly on the path of justice and to prevent any transgression and derailment.

I have discussed the first part of the question so far. Now let us move on to the second part concerning the position of land, labour, capital and organization in the blueprint of an Islamic economic system.

5.4 Position of Labour, Capital and Organization

To understand the exact position that labour, capital and organization occupy in the economic system of Islam, I would recommend studying the laws concerning *Muzāra'ah* and '*Mudārabah*' that are explained and elaborated in the books of Islamic jurisprudence. The way that modern-day books on economics define land, labour, capital and organization as economic factors is quite different from the way these are treated in works of scholarship by pioneer Muslim jurists and scholars. They did not write books dealing exclusively with economics but contributed detailed chapters on principal issues concerning the subject. The wording used was very different from the jargon-laden language of today's books on economics as a discipline. Except for those who are held captive by these high-sounding terms and phraseologies, anybody who is interested in economics and issues of economic relevance can easily understand the significance and import of the various themes discussed in juristic language and the concepts underlying them. The Islamic law of *Muzāra'ah* and *Mudārabah* that the books of jurisprudence discuss in detail provides the necessary guidance about the Islamic approach to land, labour, capital and organization.

Muzāra'ah is a method of farming where the land belongs to one person but is cultivated by another and both share the profits on its produce. *Mudārabah* is a form of investment wherein the capital belongs to one person and is used by another for business and trade and both share the profits. The way that the rights of both the landowner and the investor, as well as those who 'labour' in these transactions, have been reaffirmed and safeguarded by Islam clearly shows that, according to Islam, land, human labour, enterprise and capital are all economic factors that are jointly eligible to a share in the profit. Initially, Islam leaves the onus for determining the share ratio of the different production factors to common sense, in order to let people settle their matters amicably among themselves without the law having to intervene. But this is true only so long as people handle their affairs judiciously according to the dictates of conscience and good sense. In the case of any injustice, however, the law definitely takes action. For example, if I as the owner give my farmland to someone else for cultivation, employ somebody on wages to till it or give it on a contract basis to someone for farming and settle the terms with the other party in a proper manner, the court will have no reason to intervene. But if I commit an injustice and violate the terms of the contract, the court will then intervene to ensure justice for the aggrieved party. The law can determine the rules and regulations by which such disputes should be settled so that neither the owner of the land nor the labourer engaged in farming suffers on any count. Similarly, when an investor, the labourers and the organization manage their affairs amicably by mutual consent, the law has no cause to intervene. But when any one of these is high-handed and violates the other side's rights, the law will be required to settle the matter justly and provide rules and regulations guaranteeing the equitable distribution of dividends among all stakeholders.

The Question of Interest

8.1 Islamic Injunctions concerning Interest

Let us try first to understand what *ribā*, or 'interest', is, according to the Quran and the Sunnah. What are its parameters? What are the specific cases on which the injunctions regarding its prohibition apply? What are the alternatives that Islam offers for the economic well-being of man, and how would it like to resolve economic problems?

8.1.1 Meaning of *Ribā*

The Holy Quran uses the word ribā for 'interest'/'usury'. The root of this word consists of the letters ر+ب+و, which mean 'addition', 'growth' and 'increase'. Hence it is said: [Arabic terms:] 'someone climbed up the mound'; 'he grew up under someone's patronage'; and 'he made the thing grow'. In Arabic, *rabwah* means 'raised ground', or 'hillock'. The word and its derivatives have been used in the Holy Quran to mean 'increase', 'growth' and 'swelling', as well as interest. Here are a few examples:

> and no sooner than We send down water upon it, it begins to quiver and swell.
>
> (*al Hajj* 22:5)

> Allah deprives interest of all blessing, whereas He blesses charity with growth.
>
> (*al Baqarah* 2:276)

> so that one people might take greater advantage than another.
>
> (*al Nahl* 16:92)

[A]nd We gave them refuge on a lofty ground.

(*al Mu'minun* 23:50)

and give up all outstanding interest . . . If you repent even now, you have the right of the return of your capital.

(*al Baqarah* 2:278–9)

Whatever you pay as interest so that it may increase the wealth of people does not increase in the sight of Allah.

(*al Rum* 30:39)

It is evident from the above *ayat* [Quranic verses] that any addition to the principal amount comes under the category of ribā. However, the Book of God does not prohibit every addition and increase on the principal amount. It has banned only a particular kind of addition, and this is why it is called *al ribā* (with the definite article 'al'), which is the Quranic term for all forms of interest and usury. Usury was a normal form of transaction in pre-Islamic days. The *Jahili* Arabs (of the Days of Ignorance) equated it with business and trade. Islam told them that an increase on the principal amount caused by al ribā is different from an increase gained through business and trade (al bay'):

Seized in this slate they say: 'Buying and selling is but a kind of interest', even though Allah has made buying and selling lawful, and interest unlawful.

(*al Baqarah* 2:275)

As the exact nature of al ribā and its negative impact on *Jahili* society was well known, the Quran made no further elaboration on this and simply commanded believers to give up this abominable form of economic dealing.

8.1.2 Ribā of the Days of Ignorance

In pre-Islamic Arabia, various forms of al ribā were practised. According to Abu Qatadah, a merchant often sold a commodity to a person in return for an amount that would be paid after a certain period. When the deadline expired, the payment time was extended to a new date and the amount raised for the commodity sold. Another form of usury in practice during *jahiliyyah*, as narrated by Mujahid, was that the debtor seeking a loan used to assure the lender that he would pay them so much extra in addition to the principal amount of the loan (Ibn Jarir, vol. III, 62). Abu Bakr al Jassas has also cited similar kinds of ribā in his *Ahkam al Quran* (vol. I). According to Imam Razi, the most common *Jahili* practice was to lend somebody a loan on condition that he paid a predetermined amount of interest for a certain period on a monthly basis and, on the expiry of that period, would return the principal amount. If the debtor failed to repay the loan on the agreed date, he was offered a fresh deadline at an enhanced rate of monthly interest (*Tafsīr al Kabīr*, vol. II, 351).

These were the popular forms of interest-based transactions, which the pre-Islamic Arabs called al ribā; it was this practice, in all its various forms, that the Holy Quran declared unlawful and strictly forbidden.

8.1.3 Basic Difference between Ribā and Bay'

Now let us examine the following: (i) What is the difference in principle between the normal way of trade and business (bay') and al ribā (interest-based transactions)? (ii) What are the basic features of al ribā that make it different from bay'? (iii) Why has Islam prohibited al ribā while allowing bay'?

In normal trade and business deals (bay'), the seller offers a certain commodity for sale at a price fixed by him and the buyer negotiates, and thus a deal is agreed by mutual consent. This transaction is inevitably marked by either of the following two conditions: the seller producing the commodity himself through his own personal labour and capital; or the seller acquiring it by purchasing it from a third source. In both cases, he adds to his capital, which he invested in producing or acquiring the commodity, an amount of his labour which entitles him to his profit. Ribā, on the other hand, is a form of transaction where a person lends his capital to somebody on condition he charges an added payment during a certain period over and above the principal amount of the loan. This is a deal of capital versus capital, with an additional sum that is determined beforehand for the grace period. It is this additional sum which is ribā, or interest, and which is not charged in return for any goods or services, but just in lieu of the grace period. In the case of bay' or a trade deal, if the seller imposes an additional amount on the buyer over and above the actual price of the commodity, should the latter fail to settle payment after the mutually agreed date, any addition to the actual price would fall under the category of ribā.

Ribā or 'interest' can, therefore, be defined as the amount added to the principal sum in return for the grace period and determined beforehand as a precondition. There are thus three constituent parts of ribā: (i) an addition to the principal sum; (ii) determination of this addition according to a fixed term; and (iii) the deal being conditional on the payment of an additional amount. A loan deal that consists of these three ingredients would be an interest-based transaction, irrespective of the nature of the loan – whether it is taken to satisfy one's personal needs or as an investment in a production venture, and whether the borrower is a rich or poor person.

The difference in principle between bay' and ribā may be further elucidated as follows:

- In bay', the profit is exchanged between buyer and seller on an equal footing because the buyer gets a benefit from the goods purchased from the seller and the seller gets the benefit of the labour, enterprise and time he contributed in making the goods available to the buyer. Conversely, there is no such exchange of profits in an interest-based transaction. The person receiving interest does secure a fixed amount of money, which is definitely beneficial to him; but the one who pays interest only gets in return a grace period which he is never sure will benefit him or not. If the borrower has obtained a loan for his personal needs, the grace period offered to him is definitely harmful and not beneficial. But if the loan has been taken to improve his business, trade, agriculture, industry or any other commercial venture, there is an equal chance of profit or loss for the borrower. The lender, on the other hand, has nothing to worry him and is always assured of getting a fixed amount of interest on his principal sum. He is completely unconcerned whether the borrower is suffering losses or enjoying gains. Hence, interest-based deals are either made for the gain of one party and the loss of the other, or for the definite and predetermined gains of one and the uncertain and undefined gains of the other.
- In business and trade deals, the seller receives the amount of profit he determines for his commodity only once from his client. In the case of ribā, however, the capitalist extending a loan continues to draw interest on his principal sum, and the amount of interest continues multiplying with the passage of time. Whatever the quantum of benefit that is earned by the borrower, it cannot exceed a certain limit. However, the advantages drawn in return by the lender are unlimited. It may happen that the benefit accrued to the lender through interest may exceed his entire resources of wealth, and even then continue multiplying endlessly.

- In trade, the matter ends once the buyer and seller have concluded a deal. After making payment, the buyer owes nothing more to the seller. In an interest-based transaction, however, the borrower has not only to return the principal sum after making use of the loan, but also the amount of interest accrued thereon.

- In an agricultural, industrial and commercial venture, the entrepreneur invests his labour, capital and time and reaps the harvest of dividends. In an interest-based venture, however, the lender invests his capital, which comes from the excess of his needs, and becomes the controlling partner in the earnings of other stakeholders without putting in his own personal labour or money. His position is not that of the customary shareholder, who shares both loss and gain in proportion to his investment. The lender is a partner who enjoys the dubious benefit of a claim to a fixed and predetermined amount of interest, regardless of whether the venture runs a loss or profit, and irrespective of the actual proportion of the profit earned.

8.1.4 Rationale for Prohibition

These are the factors behind why the All-Merciful has declared *bay'* *halal* and *ribā haram*. In addition to the reasons mentioned above, there are other factors to the illegality of interest. On ethical grounds, one cannot justify interest in any form. It is a system that gives rise to the traits of stinginess, selfishness, apathy and capital-worship, as well as the materialistic trend in society. It sows the seeds of discord among nations and communities, and weakens the bonds of compassion and co-operation among fellow humans. It sets the trend of amassing wealth and promoting only self-interest. It prevents the free flow of capital in society and actually reverses the direction of its flow from the have-nots towards the haves. Because of this, resources get concentrated into the hands of the moneyed class, which eventually leads to a total collapse of the social structure. Those with an insight into the realms of economics and the social sciences are aware of this fact all too well.

One also cannot deny the fact that an interest-based system of economy is in total disharmony with the blessed blueprint, according to which Islam wants to rebuild human civilization and culture, reorganize society economically and rejuvenate individuals morally. Even some apparently inconsequential types of interest-based transaction are too damaging for this blueprint. This is why the Lord has sternly commanded believers to give up all transactions involving usury or modern-day interest:

Believers! Have fear of Allah and give up all outstanding interest if you do truly believe. But if you fail to do so, then be warned of war from Allah and His Messenger.

(*al Baqarah* 2:278–9)

8.1.5 Strict Nature of Ban

There are many other sinful acts about which believers have been warned by the Holy Quran of punishment in the Hereafter. No crime has, however, been dealt with in such harsh terms as usury and interest. The Holy Prophet (peace be upon him) therefore tried his best to eliminate all forms of interest within the Islamic Caliphate. The treaty he signed with the Christians of Najran contained a particular clause making it binding on them not to indulge in any interest-based activities or the treaty would be deemed to be cancelled, and they would be liable to attack by the defenders of the Islamic social order. The usury dealers of the *Bani Mughirah* [a tribe] were notorious for their practice throughout Arabia. After the conquest of Mecca, the Holy Prophet (peace be upon him) cancelled all of their interest deals. He wrote to the governor of Mecca, declaring he would wage war against them if they dared challenge the law and restart their age-old practice. Hazrat Abbas, the well-revered uncle of the Prophet of Islam, was himself an established moneylender in Mecca. During his Farewell Pilgrimage (*Hajjat al Wada*), *Sayyidina* Rasul Allah declared that he had annulled all deals according to which the borrower had to pay interest on his loan, and all of the interest accumulated on loans extended earlier by his uncle Abbas was also no longer valid. The Holy Prophet (peace be upon him) added, 'He who takes interest, or offers interest, or writes deeds of interest-based deals, or stands witness to such deals, are all accursed by the Lord.'

The purpose of these injunctions was not just to prohibit a particular form of interest or usury that was in practice in those days and keep the doors open for all other forms of financial exploitation. Instead, the objective was to ban forever every form of interest and thereby do away with the capitalist mindset and exploitative economic systems and social behaviour. These injunctions also aim at establishing a new socio-economic order that is marked by compassion and co-operation instead of selfishness, magnanimity instead of miserliness, *zakāh* instead of interest and the *Bayt al Māl* instead of banking. The Quranic injunctions seek to check the consequences of the capitalist system, which compel a community to set up co-operatives, insurance companies, the system of provident funds and also the unnatural system of communism.

8.2 Need for Interest: A Rational Reassessment

So far we have discussed the question of usury and interest in light of the teachings of the Holy Quran and the Sunnah (Tradition of the Holy Prophet). Let us now look at this from the standpoint of reason and common sense.

To begin with, let us ask whether interest is really plausible. Is it reasonable for a person to ask for an extra amount in addition to the sum extended on loan? Does it conform to the dictates of justice to ask for an additional amount over and above one's principal sum? These are a few of the most pertinent questions on the basis of which a major part of the debate on the subject gets settled automatically and a majority of the issue is resolved. If interest is something that is plausible, the question of its prohibition obviously loses significance. But if it cannot be justified from the standpoints of reason and justice, then the question naturally arises as to why people insist on retaining such an anti-social and irrational practice.

Let us examine the plausibility of the arguments that are generally advanced by advocates of an interest-based system of economy.

8.2.1 Compensation for Elements of Risk and Sacrifice

The most favourite plea in support of interest is that a person giving a loan to somebody out of his hard-earned and carefully saved money is actually taking a risk of the borrower defaulting. He lends money which he could have used himself, and there is thus also an element of sacrifice in his gesture. If the borrower takes a loan to satisfy some of his personal needs, he ought to pay rent on the money obtained through the loan in the way he does for the house he hires, or the furniture and means of conveyance that he borrows. The interest that the borrower thus pays covers this element of risk that the lender has taken by offering him a loan, while at the same time being compensation for the sacrifice of extending on loan an amount he could have utilized for his personal needs. If the borrower uses the loan in a profitable venture, the lender is then even more justified in demanding interest on his principal sum. If the borrower is getting a benefit from the lender's money, why should the lender forgo his dividend?

As for the first part of this plea, it is absolutely correct that the lender risks the default of the money, and that there is also an element of sacrifice in offering a loan to someone rather than making use of the amount himself. The question, however, arises: How does this justify the lender's right to demand that the borrower should pay him on a monthly, half-yearly or annual basis 5 or 10 per cent extra in compensation for the risk he may have taken or the sacrifice he made? The best he could do to counter the element of risk is: (i) retain as a mortgage (*Rahn*) something of equal value from the borrower; (ii) extend a loan on the basis of some surety (*Kafalah*); (iii) ask the borrower to furnish a guarantor (*Damin*); or (iv) refuse a loan if he is not satisfied, rather than take the risk. The element of risk is not a commercial commodity that has its cost, nor is it a house or a means of conveyance to justify rent.

As for the aspect of sacrifice, it remains a sacrifice as long as it does not degenerate into a commercial deal. If somebody is willing to sacrifice for someone in need, he should do it in a true spirit of sacrifice and then rest content with the moral dividends of a moral act. But if he seeks a financial return for his sacrifice, he would then simply be a merchant and would have to justify why he should be paid an extra amount on a monthly, half-yearly or yearly basis over and above the actual sum extended to somebody in need of a loan. We may further ask: Wasn't the amount of money the lender offered as a loan in excess of his own needs? If not, how could he have afforded to advance it as a loan? It is therefore evident that the lender, by extending a loan on interest, is not performing an act of charity or benevolence; nor is it an act of sacrifice by him.

Let us now examine the claim of equating interest with rent. Is it justifiable to take the additional amount that a lender imposes on the principal sum of a loan as rent? Rent is an amount of money which is charged on the use of items that their owner spends his time, labour and capital maintaining and that are devalued and subject to wear and tear during their use by those who hire them. The above definition of rent is applicable to things that are commonly used, such as residential accommodation, means of transport, items of furniture, etc. It cannot, however, be applied either to consumer goods, like wheat, rice, fruit, vegetables, etc., or currency, which is just a medium of exchange for goods and services.

What a lender can claim from the borrower is that, because he is offering the opportunity to benefit from his personal money, he therefore deserves to share in the benefits. This seems to sound logical. But the question arises: Do you think that the poor man who has to borrow a paltry sum of money from you to feed himself and his family is reaping so large a benefit that it entitles you to seek an extra amount from him each month as a dividend for the sum advanced to him on loan? He has certainly benefited, and it is you who have provided him with the opportunity for this benefit by lending him money. But on what grounds, be they reason, justice, social service or commercial ethics, does this authorize you to determine a certain value of the benefit accrued to the poor borrower and to add to his worries by demanding that he pay you an additional sum of money? How can you justify your action, which results in the rate of your dividends continuing to rise with the increase in the borrower's sufferings? If you don't have the heart to feel for the hard-pressed and give money to the needy that is in excess of your personal needs, the least you can do is lend them the required amount after satisfying yourself of its return. If you don't feel like offering them the loan, nobody will force you to do this and you can rest content with your riches. But how on earth can you justify your cruel act of taking advantage of someone else's worries? Is this a plausible kind of business, turning the hardship and suffering of a person into an opportunity for making money, and reducing the hungry and the dying to investment avenues? How is it that the more humanity suffers, the better the prospects are for lenders to reap a bumper harvest of the money they have advanced on interest?

The financial worth of an opportunity given to someone to benefit from a loan that is extended to him can only really be of value if it has been advanced for a business or commercial enterprise. In this case, the lender has a reason to demand a share in the benefit the borrower has got from the loan. It is obvious, however, that capital in itself has no capacity to generate dividends. It is only through human labour and enterprise that it can become an instrument of benefit. In addition, this benefit does not start flowing at once; instead, it takes time for the labour and enterprise to produce results. Moreover, one never knows how much time the labour, capital and enterprise will take to bear fruit. He similarly does not know if the return he is expecting will be as planned, or whether he will suffer losses and even go bankrupt. If this is the position of every enterprise and entrepreneur in reality, how rational is it on the part of the lender to demand dividends on his loan from a time before the principal sum has even been put to use? How can he expect the entrepreneur to determine beforehand the rate and quantity of his profits? How can the borrower be sure of the amount he may gain in return or the loss he may suffer despite his best efforts?

The only plausible option for the capitalist extending a loan is to become a partner with the borrower and share the profit or the loss of the joint venture. The lender may become a shareholder with the entrepreneur, participating with him in the profit and loss of the enterprise at a predetermined rate. However, he has no right to demand that the borrower pay him a fixed amount of interest on a month-to-month or year-to-year basis on the loan he extends without taking into consideration the gestation period of the loan before it bears fruit, as well as the chances of profit and loss. Is it rationally acceptable to allow the lender to press the borrower to pay a predetermined amount of interest, even if the borrower may have suffered a loss, earned less or only made enough profit to pay the interest? Is it justifiable that a person who invests his entire physical and intellectual capabilities, his time and his resources, to see a venture grow should be forced to let a major portion of his gains pass on to a lender whose only contribution is a certain amount of money in a loan? Even the bull toiling in an oil-expeller is entitled to fodder at the end of his hard day's labour. Unfortunately, however, the capitalist would not like an entrepreneur to get the dividends of his labour that rightly belong to him.

Let us presume that the profit earned by an entrepreneur is more than the amount of interest fixed by the capitalist on his loan. Even in this case, how can one justify the capitalist's right to predetermine and impose interest over the loan extended from his excess finances, while traders, craftsmen, industrialists, farmers and all those who are the actual producers and who contribute their time, physical energy, intellectual faculties and the entire resources of their bodies and minds to produce and provide society with its essential requirements have no security at all of a profit or guarantee against any possible loss? Is it right to let the entrepreneur face the risk of fluctuating rates of profit and the vagaries of an unpredictable market, while the moneylender may sit back comfortable and smug, assured of receiving a guaranteed amount on a monthly or yearly basis over and above the principal sum he invested as a loan?[1]

8.2.2 Compensation for Opportunity and Grace Period

The preceding discussion makes it abundantly clear that the plea for the permissibility of interest, which initially sounded reasonable, becomes untenable once it is viewed logically. There is definitely no justification for any amount of interest on a loan that is taken to meet one's own pressing personal needs. Even the advocates of interest-based deals are now reluctant to justify this kind of interest. As for a loan obtained for commercial purposes, the questions that defy an answer remain: 'What is the nature of the commodity, the cost of which one is made to pay a certain amount of interest to cover?' 'What is the substantial object that the lender is giving to the borrower in addition to the principal sum of the loan, and what is its value, in lieu of which he is entitled to demand a fixed amount of interest not only once, but on a month-by-month or year-by-year basis?' These are questions that have boggled the minds of even the champions of an interest-based system. According to some, it is the opportunity to benefit that entitles the lender to claim a certain amount of interest from the borrower. But, as noted earlier, this opportunity cannot entitle him to demand as a cost a predetermined, definite amount on a multiplying basis.

There are also those who try to justify the system of interest on the basis that it is in lieu of the grace period allowed to a borrower for use of the principal sum. This period of time, they claim, has its own value, and that value goes on increasing with each passing day. From the moment that the entrepreneur invests the amount of the loan in his enterprise until the time he brings his product to market, each and every moment is

---

[1] On the analogy of interest, one may very well object to a fixed amount of land revenue because the farmer can also never be sure of his produce until it is harvested. I endorse this point and have a different view about the permissibility of a predetermined amount of land revenue per acre, as this would be identical to a fixed rate of interest. My viewpoint in this respect is that the right kind of farmland management, according to the sharia, is *Muzāra'ah*, that is, the landlord and the farmer distributing the produce equitably among themselves. This is a deal similar to sharing the profit in a commercial venture (*Mushārakah*). For details, one may refer to my book *Masala-i-Milkiyyat-i-Zamin* (The Question of Landholdings).

precious. If he is allowed no grace period and the capital is immediately taken back from him, he cannot run his enterprise, and the commercial venture will go to waste. The lender, therefore, has every right to demand his share of the benefit that is earned by the borrower utilizing this period of grace that has enabled him to bring his finished product to market. The lender is thus justified in determining the cost of this period on the basis of its length and duration.

The following most pertinent questions still remain unanswered, however:

(i) How can the person lending money foresee that the borrower will definitely earn a profit from that money and that there are no chances of him incurring a loss?

(ii) How can he determine in advance the rate of that profit, on the basis of which he is justified in demanding a definite amount as his share?

(iii) On what basis can he precisely calculate the monthly or yearly rate of profit that the borrower will earn during the grace period in advance so that he can justify a claim to a predetermined sum of interest on a monthly or annual basis? The advocates of the system have no convincing answers to satisfy these questions. This naturally leads us to one conclusion: that the only plausible option for the capitalist is to participate with the borrower in his commercial venture as a shareholder on a profit-and-loss-sharing basis.

8.2.3 Sharing of Profit

A group supporting interest believes that profitability is intrinsic to capital, and the mere fact of someone using another's money to his advantage is therefore in itself a cogent reason entitling the lender to demand interest from the borrower. According to them, it is thus incumbent upon the latter to pay the former the desired amount. Capital has the power to support production and supply goods for public use. It helps in boosting production, which is not possible without the support of capital. A greater amount of capital leads to better quality and more value-addition, and consequently better access to the market. Conversely, less capital means poorer quality, less value-addition and even less production, limiting access to markets and lowering the price for a poorer-quality product. They would say that this proves the real worth of capital and its intrinsic quality of profitability, and hence the fact that mere use of capital by the borrower for his commercial venture makes it incumbent upon him to pay his lender an additional amount of interest on the principal sum.

To begin answering this, the very premise of profitability as intrinsic to capital is self-evidently wrong, and the claim that is based on this is, to say the least, fallacious. The quality of profitability is generated in capital only when it is invested by an entrepreneur in a productive venture. It is only at this point that one can argue that the lender should also have a share in the profit of the enterprise. In the case of a loan being used by the borrower for the payment of medical bills, to meet the expenses of funeral charges or to support pressing domestic needs or other similar contingencies, how can one justify its being profitable, and force the borrower to pay interest over and above the principal sum of the loan that he was compelled to obtain to meet a dire need?

Secondly, capital invested in profitable ventures does not necessarily add more value to justify the premise that it is profitable in itself. Sometimes the investment of more capital in an enterprise proves counterproductive and, instead of bringing greater dividends, actually causes a loss. The root cause of the crisis through which the world of trade and commerce is passing today is the fact that capitalists have too much money and go on investing fervently in profitable ventures. The rapid increase in the volume of production, however, automatically leads to a decline in the prices of the goods produced, and the increased supply to markets eventually causes an erosion of their value and a loss of profitability. The result is that the entrepreneur is ultimately compelled to beg for anti-dumping measures. This shows that capital's innate profitability faces a big question mark, and the entrepreneur loses all hope of reaping a good return for his investment.

Moreover, whatever potential quality the capital may have depends entirely for its fruition on so many other factors. These include hard work, the physical and intellectual potential and experience of its users, the congeniality of the economic and socio-political atmosphere at the time of use, and safety from natural calamities and disasters. These are among the essential preconditions for capital to bear fruit. In the absence of any one of these, not only is the profitability of capital lost, but the principal amount also often suffers loss. A capitalist who invests in interest-based ventures, however, neither shares the responsibility for the fulfilment of these preconditions nor is he ready to forgo his interest in the event of any mishap. His plea remains that the use of his capital alone entitles him to the extra amount of the interest, regardless of whether the borrower makes any gains or even suffers a loss.

Hypothetically speaking, even if we accept the claim about capital's profitability, how can this rate of profitability be calculated in advance in order to determine the rate of interest? We fail to understand how a capitalist who advances a loan in 1949 to a commercial concern for a ten-year term and to another for twenty years can be sure of the rate of his capital's future profitability, especially when the market interest rate in 1959 is likely to be different from that in 1949, with further change by 1969. How can he justify his premature calculation of the rate of interest, regardless of the future realities and the interplay of market forces ten and twenty years ahead?

8.2.4 Compensation for Time

The last plea in this context has been more intelligently devised. This seeks to press the following points: one is naturally keen to get an immediate return on an investment, preferring today's cash over tomorrow's credit. A longer-term investment decreases the value of any benefits promised. The gains that accrue today are much more attractive and precious than those expected later on. The satisfaction of an immediate need is better than future promises of even greater gains.

On the basis of this hypothesis, the certain gains of today naturally have precedence over the dubious benefits of tomorrow. The value of a loan that a person takes today is therefore much greater than the amount he would pay back to the lender tomorrow. The interest is thus the additional value that compensates for the loss a lender incurs in the intervening period on his principal sum. The argument can be illustrated further by the following example. Someone comes to a moneylender with a request for a loan of 100 rupees. The terms that moneylender offers in order to agree the deal is that the borrower will pay him 103 rupees in return a year later. The deal in fact envisages an exchange of 103 rupees for 100 rupees, and the additional sum of 3 rupees is intended to balance the psychological rather than the economic difference between its value today and a year later. If this additional amount is not included, the principal amount will not be equal to the future value that the lender has determined for it at the time of lending.

The argument seems to sound logical. However, the way that the psychological difference between the present and future value of the principal sum has been determined is, in fact, fallacious.

Is it factually correct that human nature tends to value the present much more than the future, and that the future is of lesser worth than the present? If this is the case, why is it that the majority of people prefer to save as much as they can afford for the future, rather than spending all their earnings today? Perhaps you may not have come across even 1 per cent of those carefree people who have no interest in their future and the future of their families, and who are willing to sacrifice their tomorrows for the luxuries and comforts of today. At least 99 per cent of men and women are by their very nature always aware of the need to strive for a better future, for which they are ready even to forgo their present-day comforts. They are impelled by this instinct to save from their income for the future. Islam has therefore established the institutions of *zakāh* and *sadaqat* to check the haves, on the one hand, from becoming too money-minded and to ensure, on the other, a better living and secure future for the have-nots.

Even if we accept for a while the hypothesis that one can forgo tomorrow's loss for today's gain, the overall argument remains untenable as far as the question of interest is concerned. At the time of the loan deal, the value of the lender's 100 rupees was assessed to be 103 rupees a year later. However, did the actual value remain as was predetermined when the borrower went to pay his loan after one year? If he fails to pay this amount on the due date, will the borrower have to pay the lender 106 rupees another year later? Can anybody predict the money's future value with certainty? Who can guarantee its upward trend? Is the exchange rate of the rupee higher today than it was in the past? Can you claim that the actual worth of the principal sum of a loan will go on multiplying with each passing day? Can you rule out the possibility of a recessionary trend in the market and an inflationary trend in the cost of goods and services that would continue eroding the worth of your money? Can you justify, in light of the answers to these queries, your demand for an extra amount over and above what you have extended to the borrower as a loan?

8.2.5 Reasonableness of an Interest Rate

This is the total sum of arguments advanced by protagonists of an interest-based system of economy. The above analysis has exposed the hollowness of their ideas. There is little weight in their arguments to justify why interest should be offered or claimed. It is really quite intriguing how intellectuals and scholars in the West have willingly accepted a phenomenon that is so irrational and untenable as an economic system and become an established fact! It is equally surprising how they could feel so inspired by this that they focus so greatly on the rate of interest as though the whole concept was something completely 'reasonable'! It is difficult to find any discussion on interest itself in modern Western literature, and whether interest-based deals are justified at all. Instead, their arguments have remained focused on the rate of interest and whether a certain rate is a bit on the high side, and hence objectionable, or whether it is 'reasonable' and, therefore, acceptable.

Leaving aside the question about the reasonableness of a certain rate of interest, which in itself is hardly justifiable or rationally acceptable, let us examine the grounds for describing a particular rate of interest as reasonable, and the basis on which one can approve or disapprove of it. Let us look into the criteria on the basis of which the world has been determining rates of interest for interest-based transactions, and whether any rationale has been followed in this.

As we examine the question critically, the fact that immediately grabs our attention is that the world has so far known no rate of interest that can be claimed to be reasonable. Different rates that have been declared reasonable on different occasions were eventually rejected as unrealistic and unreasonable. The same rate of interest has often been found acceptable in one place and unrealistic in another. The Aryan intellectual Kautilya regarded a rate of interest between 15 and 60 per cent as quite reasonable, which could then go even higher if the level of risk rose. During the period from the mid eighteenth to the early nineteenth centuries, the financial deals of India's Princely States with the local moneylenders and the East India Company were generally franchised at an annual interest rate of 48 per cent. During the First World War, the British Indian government obtained war loans at a 6½ per cent annual interest rate.

From 1920 to 1930, the rate of interest for co-operative societies remained between 12 and 15 per cent, while local courts designated a 9 per cent annual interest rate as reasonable from 1930 to 1940. During the time leading up to the Second World War, the 'discount rate' of the Reserve Bank of India was fixed at 3 per cent per annum, and this continued even during the war.

This was the situation in our own subcontinent. You will notice a very similar situation in Europe as well. During the sixteenth century, a

10 per cent rate of interest was viewed as reasonable in England. In the 1920s, the central banks of some European countries charged 8 to 9 per cent interest. The League of Nations endorsed the same rate. Today, both the United States and the West as a whole reject the old rates as too hard and exploitative. They have now settled on new rates ranging from 2½ to a maximum of 4 per cent. This rate goes down even further to ½ or ¼ per cent in certain situations. In sharp contrast to this, the rate of interest allowed by Britain under its 'Money Lenders Act' of 1927 for loans extended to poor people is to 48 per cent per annum, while US courts have permitted the American money-mafia to charge interest at a rate ranging from 30 to 60 per cent per annum. Now which of these varying rates of interest can be declared 'reasonable' and 'rational', and which others 'atrocious' and 'criminal'?

Let us now move on to the question of whether a particular rate of interest can be logically natural and reasonable. The moment that you begin to ponder this question, your common sense comes to the conclusion that, if anyone is in a position to determine in advance the exact value of any benefit the borrower is likely to get from a loan he is offered, it may then be considered 'natural' if a particular rate of interest is imposed on him. So, for example, if anybody could foresee with certainty that the use of 100 rupees for one year will definitely fetch dividends worth 25 rupees, it would then be possible to determine the lender's share in the value of dividends at a rate of 5, 2½ or 1¼ per cent. However, it is obviously not possible to predetermine the amount of profit the capital will fetch. On the other hand, the money-mafia that determines the market rate of interest never takes into consideration the aspect of profitability or otherwise of the money loaned to the borrower. Actually, the normal practice of moneylenders is to fix the rate of interest in terms of the borrower's constraints and needs, while rates of commercial interest are fixed by market manipulators on considerations that have hardly any relevance to reason or the dictates of justice and fair play.

8.2.6 Rationale for Varying Rates of Interest

In the money business, the basic factor encouraging moneylenders to determine an interest rate is the gravity of the borrower's need. The more helpless he is, the better the prospects are for the money barons to squeeze more out of him. If the borrower is not very hard-pressed or is seeking a larger amount to borrow, the rate of interest will naturally go down. However, the rate will continue to swell with a rise in the gravity of the borrower's need. The heartlessness of the interest-based system is such that, in the case of a loan being sought by a poverty-stricken father for the treatment of his desperately ill son, the interest rate of a money-lender could rise as high as 400 to 500 per cent. The criterion for a 'rational' rate of interest in this situation would be the same as that practised by, for example, the Sikh vendor at Amritsar railway station in 1947 who demanded 300 rupees for a glass of water from a Muslim refugee migrating to Pakistan, who desperately needed the 'aqua vitae' for his child who was dying of thirst.

As for the second category of interest, the commercial interest that the market manipulators determine, the economists generally hold one of the following two opinions.

- One group of economists is of the view that the law of supply and demand is the basis for the rise and fall in the rate of commercial interest. When investors are few in number and investment-worthy capital is growing, the rate of interest continues to decline until a time comes when it reaches its lowest ebb and borrowers rush to use the opportunity to obtain more loans to invest in their businesses and trade. When demand for money surges and loan-worthy capital records a downward trend, the rate of interest then registers a sharp rise until it reaches a point where demand for loans comes to a halt.

Let us peep through the smokescreen created by this phenomenon. We see that the capitalist is not willing to participate in a proper and judicious manner with the entrepreneur, sharing the profit as well as any loss in a venture. Instead, he speculates about the likely benefit accruing to the entrepreneur on the sum of the loan being advanced, and accordingly determines in advance the rate of interest. On the other hand, the entrepreneur also speculates about the dividends he is likely to earn, and on this basis tries not to let the interest on a loan exceed his profit. Both parties thus resort to speculation. The capitalist naturally ensures a rosy picture for himself, and his expected profit is always on the higher side; while the entrepreneur is more cautious and keeps in view the prospects of both gain and loss. A 'tug of war' is therefore inevitable between the two, because of the conflicting nature of their interests, rather than a congenial relationship of co-operation and consideration. When an entrepreneur seeks to invest in a venture with the hope of better dividends, the money baron starts raising the value of his capital until it finally becomes barely possible for the entrepreneur to avail himself of a loan, owing to the unreasonably high rate of interest. This prevents further investment, and the whole process of an economic upswing comes to a grinding halt. When a recession takes over, the economic realm and the capitalist realize that their own doom is around the corner. The rate of interest is then lowered to a level that inspires those in commerce and business to take loans at cheaper rates, with the expectation of earning a higher rate of profit, and capital starts pouring in to aid the market's buoyancy. It is thus quite obvious that, due to the absence of a reasonable and healthy relationship of participatory co-operation between the capitalist and the entrepreneur, the global economy suffers tremendously and faces alternative highs and lows that adversely affect the world's economic health. The capitalist's stranglehold has helped to boost the spirit of speculation and minting of money through interest. This has naturally poisoned the bilateral relationship between capital and enterprise, and the raising and lowering of interest rates are now done in such a way as to keep the entire world's economic health always at risk.

- According to the second viewpoint, fluctuations in the rate of interest are justified on the grounds that a capitalist raises the interest rate only when he thinks that he needs capital for his own use, but when he has no such urge, he lowers its rate. As for why the capitalist prefers to retain his money in cash, it is said that he does this mainly because he is keen to save money for his personal or commercial needs, and also to meet other contingencies. Furthermore, the capitalist prefers to have enough cash in reserve to help him maximize his profit in the event of a decline in the currency's value or a rise in the interest rate. As the capitalist's desire to retain his wealth for better gains in the future may vary owing to various personal, social, political or economic factors, he is therefore justified in raising the interest rate as this desire grows and to lower it when he feels he has less need to retain his capital.

When viewed dispassionately, this apparently plausible justification for the capitalist's desire to make use of his money as he likes is shown to be as fallacious as the first one. So far as his personal needs are concerned, the capitalist's desire to keep his capital intact to meet various contingencies should affect no more than 5 per cent of his wealth, and hence this is not a cogent reason to justify his manipulation of the capital market. The actual reason for withholding 95 per cent of his money at some times, and letting it flow through the market's loan channels at others, is entirely different. It is in fact the capitalist's extremely selfish mindset and the narrow outlook through which he perceives the world situation and the scenario at home that are responsible for the rise and fall in interest rates. He views everything in a lopsided manner and is always eager to keep the weapon in his control that he may use when society faces hardships, calamities and problems in order to exploit these for his own interest and thereby add to his riches. He therefore withholds his capital for the sake of speculation, raises the rate of interest, abruptly stops the flow of capital to local trade and industry, and opens up the floodgates of economic recession. When he subsequently realizes that he has reaped the best harvest of his gains through these unhealthy means and can earn no more, or rather faces the risk of a loss, his actions take a new turn, and he tries to entice and attract entrepreneurs with the lure of loans offered at lower rates of interest. He announces that he has plenty of money which they can use at reduced rates of interest in trade and industry.

These are the two factors that, according to today's economic experts, play a major role in determining rates of interest. However, there remain questions that have continued to defy answers: how can anyone justify as rational and logical the capitalist's desire to earn an extra amount over and above his principal sum as interest? How can he be indemnified and allowed to manipulate the money market for his narrow personal gain at the cost of the vast majority who suffer? We thus arrive at the inevitable conclusion that the interest-based system of economy is actually the most exploitative and injurious for humanity's economic health.

Islamic Law and Constitution

Chapter 9 The Problem of the Electorate

Chapter 10 Some Constitutional Proposals

Appendices
1 Basic Principles of the Islamic State by the Ulama of Pakistan
2 Ulama Amendments to the BPC Report
3 Comments on the Draft Constitution (1956)
4 Comments on 1956 Constitution
5 White Paper on the Problem of the Electorate
6 Abul A'la Maududi: A Biographical Sketch – *By the Editor*

Islamic Law

It is an irony of fate that, nowadays, the demand for the enforcement of Islamic law has become surrounded by such a thick mist of misgivings that a mere reference to it, even in a Muslim country like Pakistan, raises a storm of criticism. Thus, for instance, the questions are asked: can a centuries-old legal system be adequate to fulfil the requirements of our modern state and society? Is it not absurd to think that a law which had been framed under certain particular circumstances in bygone days can hold good in every age and every clime? Do you seriously propose to start chopping off the hands of thieves and flogging human beings in this modern, enlightened age? Will our markets again abound in slaves and deal in the sale and purchase of human beings as chattels and playthings? Which particular sect's legal system is going to be introduced here? What about non-Muslim minorities, who will never tolerate the dominance of Muslim religious law and will resist it with all the force at their command? One has to face a volley of such questions while discussing the problem, and, strangely enough, not from non-Muslims but from the Muslim educated elite!

To be sure, these questions are not the outcome of any antagonism towards Islam but mostly of sheer ignorance, which must quite naturally breed suspicion. And to our utter misfortune, ignorance abounds in our ranks. We have people who are otherwise educated but who know practically nothing about their great ideology and their glorious heritage. No wonder, then, that they labour under strong prejudices.

This state of degradation, however, has not come as a bolt from the blue; it is, rather, the culmination of a gradual process of decay spread over many centuries. Commencing with stagnation in the domains of knowledge and learning, research and discovery, and thought and culture, it finally culminated in our political breakdown, making many a Muslim country the slave of non-Muslim imperialist powers. Political slavery gave birth to an inferiority complex, and the resultant intellectual serfdom eventually swept the entire Muslim world off its feet, so much so that even those Muslim countries that were able to retain their political freedom could not escape its evil influence. The ultimate consequence of this evil situation was that when Muslims woke up again to the call of progress, they were incapable of looking at things except through the coloured glasses of Western Thought. Nothing that was not Western could inspire confidence in them. Indeed, the adoption of Western Culture and Civilization and aping the West even in the most personal things became their craze. Eventually, they succumbed totally to the slavery of the West.

This trend towards Westernism was also the result of the disappointment that came to the nation on account of Muslim religious leaders. Being themselves the victims of the widespread degeneration that had engulfed the entire Muslim world, they were incapable of initiating any constructive movement or taking any revolutionary step that could combat the evils afflicting Muslim society. Quite naturally, this disappointment turned discontented Muslims towards that system of life which had the glamour of being successful in the modern world. Thus they succumbed to the onslaughts of modern thought, adopted the new culture of the West and began to ape blindly Western modes and manners. Gradually, the religious leaders were pushed into the background and were replaced, as regards power and control over the people, by men bereft of all knowledge of their religion and imbued only with the spirit of modern thought and Western ideals. This is why we find that many a Muslim country has, in the recent past, either completely abrogated the Islamic law or confined its operations to the domain of purely personal matters only – that is, a position conferred on non-Muslims in a truly Islamic state.[1]

---

[1] The first country where the abrogation of Islamic law started was India, although the sharia continued in force long after the British had come to power – so much so that the penalty of severing the hand of a habitually hardened thief was awarded as late as AD 1791. Thereafter the process of suppression began till at last, by the middle of the nineteenth century, the whole of the sharia had been abrogated, excepting of course injunctions regarding purely personal matters such as marriage, divorce, etc. Other states where Muslims themselves were in power took their cue from the Muslims of India, and

In all those Muslim countries that suffered from foreign domination the leadership of political and cultural movements fell into the hands of those who were shorn of all Islamic background. They adopted the creed of nationalism, directed their efforts towards the cause of national independence and prosperity along secular lines, and tried to copy, step by step, the advanced nations of this age. Consequently, if these gentlemen feel vexed by the demand for an Islamic constitution and Islamic laws, it is quite natural for them. It is also natural for them to sidetrack or suppress the issue, as they are ignorant of even the ABC of the Islamic sharia. Their education and intellectual development has alienated them so completely from the spirit and the structure of Islamic ideology that it is, at least for the moment, very difficult for them to understand such demands.

As regards the Muslim religious leadership, it has in no way fared better, because our religious institutions are tied to the intellectual atmosphere of the fifth century AH, as a consequence of which they have not been able to produce such leaders of Islamic thought and action as might be capable of administering the affairs of a modern state in the light of Islamic principles. This is the situation prevailing throughout the Muslim world and is, indeed, a very real obstacle facing Islamic countries in their march towards the goal of an Islamic renaissance.

Notwithstanding certain similarities, the case of Pakistan is not, however, the same as that of other Muslim countries. This is so because it has been achieved exclusively with the object of becoming the homeland of Islam. For the last ten[2] years, we have been ceaselessly fighting for the recognition of the fact that we are a separate nation by virtue of our adherence to Islam. We have been proclaiming from the rooftops that we

---

the leading part in this transition was taken by the Muslim Native States of India. In 1884, Egypt changed her own laws to the Code Napoléon, leaving only the matters of divorce, marriage and inheritance to the jurisdiction of the Qadis. In the twentieth century Turkey and Albania took a further lead over their fellow Muslim states and proclaimed themselves to be completely secular states in the pattern of those of Italy, France, Switzerland and Germany, making inroads into Muslim personal law itself that no non-Muslim state would dare to do. Albania led the way by penalizing polygamy, and Turkey followed her by changing the mandatory provisions of the Holy Quran in respect of divorce and inheritance. There now remain only Afghanistan and Saudi Arabia where the sharia is accepted as state law, though even there the spirit of the sharia has long since disappeared, and the whole of sharia too is not being enforced.

[2] This speech was delivered in 1948.

have a distinct culture of our own, and that we possess a worldview, an outlook on life and a code of living fundamentally different from those of non-Muslims. We have all along been demanding a separate homeland for the purpose of translating into practice the ideals envisaged by Islam, and at last, after a long and arduous struggle, in which we sustained a heavy loss of life and property and suffered deep humiliation in respect of the honour and chastity of a large number of our womenfolk, we have succeeded in attaining our cherished goal – this country of Pakistan. If, now, after all these precious sacrifices, we fail to achieve the real and ultimate objective of making Islam a practical, social, political and constitutional reality, a living force to fashion all the facets of our life, our entire struggle and all our sacrifices become futile and meaningless.

Indeed, if, instead of an Islamic, a secular and godless constitution was to be introduced, and if, instead of the Islamic sharia, the British Civil and Criminal Procedure Codes had to be enforced, what would have been the sense in all this struggle for a separate Muslim homeland? We could have had them without that. Similarly, if we simply intended to implement any socialistic programme, we could have done so in collaboration with the communist and the socialist parties of India without plunging the nation into this great bloodbath and mighty ordeal.

The fact is that we are already committed before God, man and history to the promulgation of an Islamic constitution and the introduction of an Islamic way of life in this country, and no going back on our words is possible. Whatever the hurdles, and howsoever great they may be, we have to continue our march towards our goal of a full-fledged Islamic state in Pakistan.

No doubt, there do exist many hardships and difficulties in the way of achieving this goal. But what great goal can be, or has ever been, achieved without facing difficulties boldly and intelligently? And I must emphatically say that the difficulties that impede our way are in no way insurmountable. Indeed, none of them is real, except the difficulty that many among those who hold the reins of power are devoid of faith in the efficacy of Islamic ideology, which, in its turn, is not due to any defect in Islam but is purely a product of their own gross ignorance of Islamic teachings.

The first task, therefore, is to explain to our educated people the meaning and the implications of Islamic law – its objectives, its spirit, its structure, and its categorical and unchangeable injunctions, along with the reasons for their permanence. They should also be informed of the dynamic element of Islamic law, and how it guarantees the fulfilment of the ever-increasing needs of progressive human society in every age. Then, they should be enlightened in regard to the rational foundations of the sharia. Finally it is also necessary to expose the hollowness of the vituperative criticisms against Islam and to remove thereby the fog of misunderstanding that shrouds the issue. If we succeed in accomplishing this task and consequently gaining the support of the Muslim intelligentsia, we will pave the way for the establishment of an Islamic state and the creation of an Islamic society in Pakistan. It is with this intention that I am making this speech before the students of the Law College [Lahore].

Law and Life

The term 'law' bears reference to the query, 'What should be the conduct of man in his individual and collective life?'

The query presents itself to us in connection with innumerable matters. Hence its reply covers a very wide range of topics, wider than what the term 'law' technically signifies. It includes our system of education and training in the light of which we strive to mould the character of individuals; it comprehends our social system which regulates our social relationships; it encompasses our economic order, according to which we formulate the principles of production, distribution and the exchange of wealth. Thus we possess a vast system of rules that determine our conduct in various walks of life. Technically speaking, all these acts of rules are not 'law'.

The term 'law' is technically applied only to such of the rules as are enforceable by the coercive power of the state. But, obviously, no one who wants to understand them can afford to confine his attention to them alone. He must take into consideration the entire scheme of moral and social guidance prescribed by a particular ideology, because it is only then that he will be able to appreciate the spirit and objectives of the 'law' and to form a critical opinion about its merits and demerits.

It should not be difficult to understand that the principles we recommend relating to a particular system of life are basically derived from and are deeply influenced by our conceptions about the ends of human life and by our notions of right and wrong, good and evil, and justice and injustice. Consequently, the nature of a legal system depends entirely upon the source or sources from which it is derived. Thus, the differences discernible in the legal and social systems of different societies are mainly due to the differences of their sources of guidance and inspiration.

This means that unless we are prepared to take into consideration the origins and the background of the whole system of life and of the society that it brings into existence, and to appreciate the complete process of the development of that system and the evolution of that society, we will not be able to understand, much less criticize on any rational basis, the mandatory legal provisions of the system – especially when our knowledge of those provisions consists, in the main, of hearsay and conjecture.

I do feel that a comparative critical study of the Islamic and Western system of life would be the best way to explain and elucidate my viewpoint. If the differences between the original sources and the basic postulates of both systems are kept in mind, the radically different schemes of life that both envisage can be easily understood. But the paucity of time at my disposal does not permit such a digression, and consequently I shall confine myself, at present, to the exposition of the Islamic sharia only.

Sources of the Islamic System of Life

The first source of the Islamic system of life is a book or, to be more exact, 'the Book'. The world received several editions of it under the titles of the Old Testament, the New Testament, the Psalms, etc., the last and final edition being the one presented to mankind under the name of the Quran.

The second source of this system is the persons to whom the different editions of the Book were revealed and who, by their preachings and their conduct, interpreted them to the people. As different personalities, they bore the names of Noah, Abraham, Moses, Jesus and Muhammad (peace be on them all), but, as the bearers and upholders of the same mission of life, all stand under the general title of 'the Messenger'.

The Islamic Concept of Life

The view of life that Islam has presented is that this universe of ours, which follows a set course of laws and functions according to an intelligent and well-laid-out plan, is in reality the Kingdom of the One God – Allah. It is He Who created it. It is He Who owns it. It is He Who governs it. The earth on which we live is just a small part – a province –

of this huge universe, and, like all other parts thereof, it also functions completely under the control of God. And as regards ourselves – that is, we human beings – we are nothing more than His 'born subjects'. It is He Who created us, sustains us and causes us to live. Hence, every notion of our absolute independence is nothing but a sheer deception and misjudgment. God controls every fibre of our being, and none can escape His grip.

Every thinking mind is aware of the fact that a very large sector of our life is governed and directly controlled by a Higher Power and with such absoluteness that we are practically helpless in respect of it. From the time we are conceived in the wombs of our mothers till the moment we breathe our last, we are subject to God's inexorable laws of nature to such an extent that we cannot claim to be free from their control even for a single moment.

Of course there is another sphere of our life in which we possess a certain amount of freedom. This is the moral and social sphere of life, in which we are bestowed with a free will and independence of choice in respect of individual as well as collective affairs and behaviour. But this independence can hardly justify our rejection of the guidance of our Creator and His laws. It is only to give us a choice in leading our lives as the obedient subjects of God – an attitude consistent with the real order of things – or in being disregardful of His commandments, and thus rebelling against Him and our true nature.

Obviously, to the faithful, the guidance and law of God are the truest and most consistent attitude for mankind. They set the standard for the orderly behaviour of man both individually and collectively and in respect of the biggest as well as the smallest task he may have to face. Having once accepted the philosophy of life enunciated by 'the Book' and 'the Messenger' as the embodiment of reality, one has no justification for not obeying God's revealed guidance in the sphere of one's choices also. Indeed, it is but rational that we should admit God's sovereignty in this sphere, just as we do, perforce, in the domain of our physical life. And this for several reasons:

Firstly, the power and the organs through which our free will functions are gifts from God and not the result of our own efforts.

Secondly, the independence of choice itself has been delegated to us by God and not by our personal endeavour.

Thirdly, all those things in which our free will operates are not only the property but also the creation of God.

Fourthly, the territory in which we exercise our independence and freedom is also the territory of God.

Fifthly, the harmonization of human life with the universe dictates the necessity of there being one Sovereign and a common Source of law for both spheres of human activity – the voluntary and the involuntary, or, in other words, the moral and the physical. The separation of these two spheres into watertight compartments led to the creation of an irreconcilable conflict that finally lands not only individuals but even the biggest nations in endless trouble and disaster.

The Final Book of God and the Final Messenger stand today as the repositories of this truth, and they invite the whole of humanity to accept it freely and without compulsion. God Almighty has endowed man with free will in the moral domain, and it is to this free will that this acceptance bears reference. Consequently, it is always an act of volition and not of compulsion. Whosoever agrees that the concept of reality stated by the Holy Prophet and the Holy Book is true, it is for him to step forward and surrender his will to the will of God. It is this submission which is called *Islam*, and those who do so, that is, those who of their own free will accept God as their sovereign and surrender to His divine will and undertake to regulate their lives in accordance with His commandments, they are called *Muslim*.

All those persons who thus surrender themselves to the will of God are welded into a community, and that is how 'Muslim society' comes into being. Thus, this is an ideological society – a society radically different from those that spring from the accidents of race, colour or country. This society is the result of a deliberate choice and effort; it is the outcome of a 'contract' which takes place between human beings and their Creator. Those who enter into this contract undertake to recognize God as their sovereign, His guidance as supreme and His injunctions as absolute law. They also undertake to accept, without question or doubt, His classification of good and evil, right and wrong, and the permissible and the prohibited. In short, Islamic society agrees to limit its volition to the extent prescribed by the All-Knowing God. In other words, it is God and not man whose will is the source of law in a Muslim society.

When such a society comes into existence, the Book and the Messenger prescribe for it a code of life called sharia, and this society is bound to conform to it by virtue of the contract into which it has entered. It is, therefore, inconceivable that any Muslim society worth the name can deliberately adopt a system of life other than the sharia. If it does so, its contract is automatically broken, and the whole society becomes 'un-Islamic'.

But we must clearly distinguish between the everyday sins of individuals and a deliberate revolt against the sharia. The former may not imply breaking the contract, while the latter would mean nothing less. The point that should be clearly understood here is that if an Islamic society consciously resolves not to accept the sharia and decides to enact its own constitution and laws, or borrow them from any other source in disregard of the sharia, such a society breaks its contract with God and forfeits its right to be called 'Islamic'.

The Objectives and Characteristics of the Sharia

Let us now proceed to understand the scheme of life envisaged by the sharia. To understand that, it is essential that we should start with a clear conception of the objectives and fundamentals of the sharia.

The main objective of the sharia is to construct human life on the basis of *Ma'rufat* (virtues) and to cleanse it of *Munkarat* (voices). The term Ma'rufat denotes all the virtues and good qualities that have always been accepted as 'good' by the human conscience. Conversely, the Munkarat denote all the sins and evils that have always been condemned by human nature as 'evil'. In short, the Ma'rufat are in harmony with human nature and its requirements in general, and the Munkarat are just the opposite. The sharia gives a clear view of these Ma'rufat and Mankarat, and states them as the norms to which individual and social behaviour should conform.

The sharia does not, however, limit its function to providing us with an inventory of virtues and vices: it lays out the entire scheme of life in such a manner that virtues may flourish and vices may not contaminate human life.

To achieve this end, sharia has embraced in its scheme all the factors that encourage the growth of the good and has recommended steps for the removal of impediments that might prevent its growth and development. This process gives rise to a subsidiary series of Ma'rufat consisting of the causes and means initiating and nurturing the good and, further, of Ma'rufat consisting of prohibitions of preventives to good. Similarly, there is a subsidiary list of Munkarat that might initiate or allow growth of evil.

The sharia shapes Islamic society in a way conducive to the unfettered growth of the good, of virtue and of truth in every sphere of human activity, and gives full play to the forces of the good in all directions. And at the same time it removes all impediments in the path of virtue. Alongside this, it attempts to eradicate evil from its social scheme by prohibiting vice, by obviating the causes of its appearance and growth, by closing the inlets through which it creeps into society, and by adopting different measures to check its occurrence.

Ma'rufat

The sharia classifies Ma'rufat into three categories:

the mandatory (*Fard* and *Wajib*)
the recommendatory (*Matlub*), and
the permissible (*Mubah*).

The observance of the mandatory (Ma'rufat) is obligatory for a Muslim society, and the sharia has given clear and binding directions about them. The recommendatory (Ma'rufat) are those which the sharia wants a Muslim society to observe and practise. Some of them have been clearly demanded of us, while others have been recommended by implication and deduction from the Sayings of the Holy Prophet (peace be upon him). Besides this, special arrangements have been made for the growth and encouragement of some of them in the scheme of life enunciated by the sharia. Others still have simply been recommended by the sharia, leaving it to society or to its more virtuous elements to look to their promotion.

This leaves us with the permissible Ma'rufat. Strictly speaking, according to the sharia everything that has not been expressly prohibited by it is permissible. It is not at all necessary that an express permission should exist about it, or that it should have been expressly left to our choice. Consequently the sphere of permissible Ma'rufat is very wide, so much so that, except for a few things specifically prohibited by the sharia, everything is permissible for a Muslim. And this is exactly the sphere where we have been given freedom and where we can legislate according to our discretion, to suit the requirements of our age and conditions.

Munkarat

The Munkarat (or the things prohibited in Islam) have been grouped into two categories: *haram* (i.e., those things which have been prohibited absolutely) and Makruh (i.e., those things which have been simply disliked). It has been enjoined on Muslims by clear and mandatory injunctions to refrain totally from everything that has been declared *haram*. As for the Makruhat, the sharia signifies its dislike in one way or another, that is, either expressly or by implication, also as to the degree of such dislike. For example, there are some Makruhat bordering on *haram*, while others bear affinity with the acts that are permissible. Of course, their number is very large, ranging between the two extremes of prohibitory and permissible actions. Moreover, in some cases explicit measures have been prescribed by the sharia for the prevention of Makruhat, while in others such arrangements have been left to the discretion of society or to the individual.

The Characteristic of the Sharia

The sharia thus prescribes directives for the regulation of our individual as well as collective life. These directives touch such varied subjects as religious rituals, personal character, morals, habits, family relationships, social and economic affairs, administration, rights, the duties of citizens, the judicial system, the laws of war and peace, and international relations. In short, it embraces all the various departments of human life. These directives reveal what is good and bad, what is beneficial and useful, and what is injurious and harmful, what the virtues are that we have to cultivate and encourage, and what the evils are that we have to suppress and guard against, what the sphere of our voluntary, untrammelled, personal and social action is, and what its limits are, and, finally, what ways and means we can adopt in establishing such a dynamic order of society, and what methods we should spurn. The sharia is a complete scheme of life and an all-embracing social order where nothing is superfluous and nothing is lacking.

Another remarkable fact about the sharia is that it is an organic whole. The entire scheme of life propounded by Islam is animated by the same spirit, and hence any arbitrary division of the scheme is bound to harm the spirit as well as the structure of the sharia. In this respect it might be compared to the human body, which is an organic whole.

A leg pulled from off the body cannot be called one-eighth or one-sixth of a man, because after its separation from the living human body the leg can no more perform its human function. Nor can it be placed in the body of some other animal with any hope of making it human by virtue of the limb. Likewise, we cannot form a correct opinion about the utility, efficiency and beauty of the hand, the eye or the nose of a human being separately without judging the place and function within a living body.

The same can be said in regard to the scheme of life envisaged by the sharia. Islam signifies the entire scheme of life and not just any isolated part or parts thereof. Consequently, it cannot be appropriate to view the different parts of the sharia in isolation from one another and without regard to the whole; nor will it be of any use to take any particular part and bracket it with any other 'ism'. The sharia can function smoothly and can demonstrate its efficacy only if the entire system of life is practised in accordance with it and not otherwise.

Many of the present-day misunderstandings about the sharia are themselves due to this faulty attitude in judging its worth, namely, forming opinions about its different aspects separately. Some of its injunctions are isolated from the main body of Islamic laws, and then they are considered from the perspective of modern civilization, or they are viewed as if they were something completely self-contained. Thus, people take just one injunction of the sharia at random, which becomes maimed after its removal from context, view it in the context of some modern legal system, and criticize it on account of its incongruity with present-day conceptions. But they fail to realize that it was never meant to be isolated, for it forms an organic part of a distinct and self-contained system of life.

There are some people who take a few provisions of the Islamic penal code out of context and jeer at them. But they do not realize that those provisions are to be viewed against the background of the whole Islamic system of life covering the economic, social, political and educational spheres of activity. If all these departments are not working, then those isolated provisions of our penal code can certainly work no miracles.

For example, we all know that Islam imposes the penalty of amputating the hand for committing theft. But this injunction is meant to be promulgated within a full-fledged Islamic society, where the wealthy pay Zakat to the state and the state provides for the basic necessities of the needy and the destitute; where every township is enjoined to play host to visitors at its own expense for a minimum period of three days; where all citizens are provided with equal privileges and opportunities to seek an economic livelihood; where monopolistic tendencies are discouraged; wherein people are God-fearing and seek His pleasure with devotion; wherein the virtues of generosity, helping the poor, treating the sick and providing for the needy prevail to the extent that even a small boy is made to realize that he is not a true Muslim if he allows his neighbour to sleep hungry while he has taken his meal. In other words, it is not meant for present-day society, where you cannot get a single penny without having to pay interest; where, in place of *Bayt al Māl*, there are implacable moneylenders and banks that, instead of providing relief and succour to the poor and needy, treat them with callous disregard, heartless refusal and brutal contempt; where the guiding motto is 'Everybody for himself and the devil take the hindmost'; where there are great privileges for the privileged ones while others are deprived even of their legitimate rights; where the economic system, propelled by greed and piloted by exploitation, only leads to the enrichment of the few at the cost of crushing poverty and intolerable misery of the many; and where the political system serves only to prop up injustice, class privileges and distressing economic disparities. Under such conditions, it is doubtful whether theft should be penalized at all, never mind cutting off a thief's hands, because to do so would, as a matter of fact, amount to protecting the ill-gotten wealth of a few bloodsuckers rather than awarding adequate punishment to the guilty.[1]

On the other hand, Islam aims at establishing a society in which no one is compelled by force of circumstance to steal. For, in the Islamic social order, apart from the voluntary help provided by individuals, the state guarantees the basic necessities of life to all. But, after providing all

---

[1] Here it must not be misunderstood that I am defending theft or any other form of lawlessness. Not in the least! My intention is only to show the vast and radical differences that reign between the context in which the punishment was and is applicable and the state of affairs we are today enveloped in. The only logical conclusion that follows is the need for a change in the entire system of life. When the entire structure of society is changed and a new way of life is established, the incongruity between the injunction and the present context of affairs would be obliterated and the avenue for its application would be opened.

that, Islam enjoins a severe and exemplary punishment for those who commit theft, as their action shows that they are unfit to live in such a just, generous and healthy society and would cause a greater harm to it if left unchecked.

Similar is the case of the punishment for adultery and fornication. Islam prescribes a hundred stripes for the unmarried and stoning to death for the married partners in the crime. But, of course, it applies to a society where every trace of suggestiveness has been destroyed, where mixed gatherings of men and women have been prohibited, where the public appearance of painted and pampered women is completely non-existent, where marriage has been made easy, where virtue, piety and charity are current coins, and where the remembrance of God and the Hereafter is kept ever fresh in men's minds and hearts. These punishments are not meant for that filthy society wherein sexual excitement is rampant, where nude pictures, obscene books and vulgar songs have become common recreations, wherein sexual perversions have taken hold of the cinema and all other places of amusement, wherein mixed, semi-nude parties are considered the acme of social progress, and wherein economic conditions and social custom have made marriage extremely difficult.

Legal Aspects of the Sharia

From this discussion, I think it has become fairly clear that what we, at present, technically call 'Islamic law' is only part of a complete scheme of life and does not have any independent existence in isolation from that scheme. It can neither be understood nor enforced separately. To enforce it separately would, in fact, be against the intention of the Lawgiver. What is required of us is to translate into practice the entire Islamic programme of life and not merely a fragment of it. Then, and then alone, can the legal aspects be properly implemented.

This scheme of the sharia is, however, divided into many parts. There are aspects of it which do not need any external force for their enforcement; they are and can be enforced only by the ever-awake conscience kindled in a Muslim by his faith. There are other parts that are enforced by Islam's programme of education, training of a man's character and the purification of his heart and his morals. To enforce certain other parts, Islam resorts to the use of the force of public opinion: the general will and pressure of society. There are still other parts that have been sanctified by the traditions and the conventions of Muslim society. A very large part of the Islamic system of law, however, needs for its enforcement in all its details the coercive powers and authority of the state. Political power is essential for protecting the Islamic system of life from deterioration and perversion, for the eradication of vice and the establishment of virtue and, finally, for the enforcement of all these laws that require the sanction of the state and the judiciary for their operation.

Speaking from a purely juridical viewpoint, it is this last part, out of the whole Islamic scheme of life, to which the term 'law' can be appropriately applied. For it is only those injunctions and regulations which are backed by political authority that are, in modern parlance, termed 'law'. But as far as the Islamic conception is concerned, the entire sharia stands as synonymous with 'law', because the whole code of life has been decreed by the All-Powerful Sovereign of the universe. However, to avoid confusion, we shall apply the term 'Islamic law' to those portions only of the sharia that demand the sanction of state power for their enforcement.

Major Branches of Islamic Law

The establishment of a political authority that can enforce Islamic law requires a constitutional law, and the sharia has clearly laid down its fundamentals. The sharia has provided answers to the basic questions of constitutional law and has solved its fundamental problems, namely, what is the basic theory of the state? What is the source of the authority of its legislation? What are the guiding principles of state policy? What are the qualifications of the rules of an Islamic state? What are the objectives of an Islamic state? In whom does sovereignty reside, and what are the different organs of the state? What is the mode of the distribution of power between the different organs of the state, namely, the legislature, the executive and the judiciary? What are the conditions for citizenship? What are the rights and duties of Muslim citizens? And what are the rights of non–Muslim citizens (zimmis)? The guidance that the sharia has provided in respect to these questions constitutes the constitutional law of Islam.

Besides laying down the fundamentals of constitutional law, the sharia has also enunciated the basic principles of administrative law.

Besides that, there are *precedents* in administrative practice established by the Holy Prophet himself (peace be upon him) and the first four rightly guided caliphs of Islam. For instance, the sharia enumerates the sources of income permissible for an Islamic state and those that are prohibited. It also prescribes the avenues of expenditure. It lays down rules of conduct for the police, the judiciary and the administrative machinery. It defines the responsibilities of the rulers regarding the moral and material well-being of the citizens, laying particular emphasis on their obligations as regards the suppression of vice and the establishment of virtue. It also specifically states to what extent the state can interfere in the affairs of its citizens. In this connection, we find not only directive principles, but also many categorical injunctions. The sharia has given us the broad framework of administrative law – exactly in the same way as it has given the fundamentals of constitutional law and has left it to the discretion of Muslims to build up the details in accordance with the demands of the age or country in which they live – subject, of course, to the limits prescribed by the sharia.

Proceeding further, we find the sharia guiding us in connection with public as well as personal law – which are essential for the administration of justice. This guidance covers such an extensive field that we can never feel a need to go beyond the sharia for meeting our legislative requirements. Its detailed injunctions are such that they can always fulfil the needs of human society in every age and in every country – provided, of course, that the entire Islamic scheme of life is in operation. They are so comprehensive that we can frame detailed laws on their basis for every emergency and every fresh problem for which the legislature has been given the right to legislate. All laws thus framed are to be considered an integral part of the Islamic law. That is why the laws framed by our jurists in the early days of Islam for the sake of the 'public good' form part and parcel of the Islamic law.

Lastly, we have that part of the law that deals with the relations of the Islamic state with other states, that is, international law. In this connection, too, the sharia gives us comprehensive regulation relating to war and peace, neutrality and alliance, etc. Where, however, no specific injunctions are to be found, the laws can be framed in the light of the general directives as laid down on their behalf.

Permanence and Change in Islamic Law

This brief classification and elucidation shows that the guidance of the sharia extends to all branches of the law that have been evolved by the ingenuity and needs of the human mind so far. This is a standing testimony to the independence of the Islamic law and its inherent potentialities. Anybody who takes the trouble of making a detailed study of the subject will be able to distinguish between that part of the sharia which has a permanent and unalterable character and is, as such, extremely beneficial for mankind, and that part which is flexible and has thus the potential to meet the ever-increasing requirements of every time and age.

The unalterable elements of Islamic law may be classified under the following heads:

1 Those laws that have been laid down in explicit and unambiguous terms in the Quran or the authentic Traditions of the Prophet, such as the prohibition on alcoholic drinks, interest and gambling, the punishment prescribed for adultery and theft, and the rules for inheritance etc.

2 The directive principles laid down in the Holy Quran and authentic Traditions, for example, the prohibition on the use of intoxicants in general, or the nullification of all exchange transactions that are not the outcome of the free will of both the parties, or the principle that men are protectors and in charge of women.

3 The limitations imposed on human activity by the Quran and the Traditions of the Prophet, which can never be transgressed, for example, the limitation in connection with the plurality of wives where the maximum number has been fixed at four, or the limitation that the number of divorces, to a wife cannot exceed three, or the limitation imposed on a will, the amount of which cannot exceed one-third of the total inheritance etc.

It is these unalterable mandatory provisions of Islamic law that give a permanent complexion to the Islamic social order and the characteristic features of its culture. In fact, one cannot find a single culture in the entire history of mankind that can retain its separate entity and its distinct character without possessing an unalterable and permanent element.

If there are no permanent elements in a culture and every part of it is subject to change, amendment and modification, it is not an independent culture at all. It is just like a fluid, which can take any and every shape and can always suffer transfiguration and metamorphosis.

Moreover, a thorough study of these directives, injunctions and limitations will lead every reasonable man to the conclusion that they have been given to us by the sharia only for those matters where the human mind is likely to commit errors and go astray. On all such occasions, the sharia has, so to speak, set the signposts by issuing directives on making categorical prohibitions so that we may proceed along the right path. And these signposts, far from impeding the march of human progress, are meant to keep us on the road and save us from skidding off it. In this connection, it might not be out of place here to refer to the laws of the sharia governing marriage, divorce and inheritance, which were the target of very bitter criticism in the recent past. It is these very laws, however, to which the world is now turning for guidance, though after innumerable bitter experiences.

The second part of Islamic law is that which is subject to modification according to the needs and requirements of the changing times, and it is this part of Islamic law that endows it with wide possibilities of growth and advancement and makes it fully capable of fulfilling all the needs of an expanding human society in every age.

This part consists of the following:

a *Taweel* (interpretation): This consists in probing into the meanings of the injunctions found in the Quran and the Sunnah. As such, it has always occupied, and still occupies, a place of immense importance in Islamic jurisprudence. When those endowed with penetrating insight and legal acumen ponder over the injunctions of the Quran and the Sunnah, they find that many of them are open to different fruitful and valid interpretations. Consequently, every one of them accepts some particular interpretation according to his lights on the merits of the case. In this way, the doors of difference of opinion have always been open in the past, are open even today and will continue to remain so in the future.

b *Qiyas* (deduction by analogy): This consists in applying to a matter, with respect to which there is no clear guidance, a role or injunction available for some similar matter.

c *Ijtihad* (disciplined judgment of jurists): This consists in legislating on matters for which neither any explicit injunctions nor even precedents exist, subject of course, to the general principles and precepts of the sharia.

d *Istihsan* (juristic preference): This means framing rules, if necessary, in non-prohibited matters in conformity with the spirit of the Islamic legal system.

Anyone who considers the possibilities inherent in the abovementioned four ways of legislation can never reasonably entertain any misgivings as to the dynamism, adaptability, progressive nature and power of evolutionary growth of the legal system of Islam. But it should be remembered that not every Tom, Dick or Harry is entitled to exercise the right of *Taweel*, *Qiyas*, *Ijtihad* and *Istihsan*. Nobody has ever recognized the right of every passerby to give a verdict on problems of national importance. Undoubtedly, it requires profound legal knowledge and a trained mind to enable one to speak with authority on any legal matter.

Similar is the case with Islamic law. Obviously, to achieve the status of a jurist one should be fully conversant with the Arabic language and literature. He should also have a complete grasp of the real, historical background of the injunctions of Islam. He should have special insight into the Quranic style of expression. He should have a thorough knowledge of the vast literature of the Traditions of the Holy Prophet, as well as of the Traditions themselves.

In the special field of analogous deduction, a Muslim jurist is required to possess a keen sense of legal judgment and the requisite capacity for the interpretation of facts on the basis of analogy; otherwise it would not be possible for him to save himself from falling into errors. As regards *Ijtihad*, or original legislation, it requires the jurist to have not only a deep knowledge of Islamic law but also a developed sense of interpreting matters in the true Islamic spirit. Similarly as regards *Istihsan* or the consideration of public good and legislation for that purpose, it calls for a complete understanding of the entire Islamic scheme of life, as also a complete grasp of the spirit of Islam, so that he may adopt only those things that can be appropriately assimilated into the Islamic scheme and that do not amount to driving square pegs into round holes.

And, over and above all these intellectual accomplishments, there is another thing that is vitally essential, and that is unstinted devotion and loyalty to Islam and a deep sense of accountability before

God. As regards those who care little for God and of the final accountability, whose watchword in life is sheer expediency, and who prefer the non-Islamic values of culture and civilization to those given by Islam, they must be regarded as the last persons to whom the work of Islamic legislation can be entrusted. For, in their hands, Islamic law will only suffer perversion and corruption. It will not grow, evolve and prosper.

Tafhīm ul Quran

Surah al Fatihah

This surah is named al Fatihah because of its subject matter. Fatihah is that which opens a subject or a book or any other thing. In other words, al Fatihah is the same as a preface or beginning of a work.

Period of Revelation

It is one of the very earliest revelations to the Holy Prophet. In fact, we learn from authentic traditions that it was the first complete surah that was revealed to Muhammad (peace be upon him). Before this, only a few miscellaneous verses had been revealed, which form parts of Surah 'Alaq, Surah Muzzammil and Surah Muddaththir, etc.

Theme

This surah is in fact a prayer that Allah has taught to all those who want to make a study of His book. It has been placed at the very beginning of the book to teach this lesson to the reader: if you sincerely want to benefit from the Quran, you should offer this prayer to the Lord of the Universe.

Compelled by nature, humans pray for that which they desire in their heart and only in that case, when there is a clear sense that the One prayed to has the power to grant this wish. Thus, this preface reminds humans to seek guidance for the right path of life, to study the Quran with the mental attitude of one seeking truth and in acknowledgment of the fact that the Lord of the Universe is the source of all knowledge. One should, therefore, begin the study of the Quran with a prayer for guidance.

From this theme, it becomes clear that the real relation between al Fatihah and the Quran is not that of an introduction to a book but that of a prayer and its answer. Al Fatihah is the prayer from the human, and the Quran is the answer from God [*khuda*] to his prayer. The servant prays to Allah to ask for guidance, and the Master places the whole of the Quran before him in answer to his prayer, to say this is the guidance you begged from Me.

(1:1) In the name of Allah, the Merciful, the Compassionate![1]
(1:2) Praise[2] be to Allah, the Lord[3] of the entire universe.

---

[1] The civilization that Islam teaches its followers includes this important rule, that they should begin their activities in the name of God. If this principle is followed consciously and with sincerity, it will necessarily yield three beneficial results. First, such a person will be able to avoid many misdeeds. The habit of pronouncing the name of God will provide a pause when such a person is about to commit some wrongdoing, because they will stop to think whether the task they are about to undertake is really worthy of the name of God. Second, pronouncing the name of God before starting good and legitimate tasks ensures the correct mental orientation, and that in turn helps with choosing a good starting point. Third, and this is the most important benefit, a task started in the name of God will enjoy God's support, and God will bless the effort, protecting it from the machinations of Satan. For whenever man turns to God, God turns to him as well.

[2] As we explained in the introduction, the character of this surah is that of a prayer. The prayer begins with praise of the Being to whom our prayer is addressed. This indicates that there is a civilized and dignified way of praying. It does not become a cultivated person to blurt out his petition. Refinement demands that our requests should be preceded by a wholehearted acknowledgment of the unique position, infinite benevolence and unmatched excellence of the One to Whom we pray.

Whenever we praise someone, we do so for two reasons. First, because excellence calls for praise, irrespective of whether that excellence has any direct influence on us or not. Second, we praise one whom we consider to be our benefactor and towards whom we experience a deep feeling of gratitude. God is worthy of praise on both counts. It is incumbent on us to praise Him not only in recognition of His infinite excellence but also because of our feeling of gratitude towards Him, arising from our awareness of the blessings He has lavished upon us. It is important to note here that it is not merely that praise is owed to God, but that all praise is owed to God alone. By saying this, a very important reality has been revealed that cuts off the possibility of worshipping other creatures at the root. Wherever there is any beauty, any excellence, any perfection, in whatever thing or in whatever shape it may manifest itself, its ultimate source is none other than God Himself. No human beings, angels, demigods, heavenly bodies, in short, no created beings, are possessed of an innate excellence. Excellence is a gift from God. Thus, if there is anyone at all to whom we owe adoration and worship, debt and gratitude, humility and obedience, it is the creator of excellence, rather than its possessor.

[3] In Arabic the word *rabb* has three meanings: (i) Lord and Master; (ii) Sustainer, Provider, Supporter, Nourisher and Guardian; and (iii) Sovereign, Ruler, who controls and directs. God is the *Rabb* of the universe in all three meanings of the term.

(1:3) The Merciful, the Compassionate!⁴
(1:4) Master of the Day of Recompense.⁵
(1:5) You alone do we worship,⁶ and to You alone do we turn for help.⁷
(1:6) Direct us to the straight path.⁸

---

4. It is part of the essence of being human that when we are deeply impressed by the greatness of something, we try to express our feelings by using superlatives. If the use of one superlative does not do full justice to our feelings, we tend to re-emphasize the extraordinary excellence of the object of our admiration by adding a second superlative of nearly equivalent meaning. This would seem to explain the use of the word *Rahim* following *Rahman*. The form of the word *Rahman* connotes intensity. Yet God's mercy and beneficence towards His creatures is so great, so extensive and of such an infinite nature that no one word, however strong its connotation, can do it full justice. The epithet *Rahim* was therefore added to that of *Rahman*.

5. This means that God will be the Lord of the Day when all generations of mankind gather together in order to render an account of their conduct, and when each person will be finally rewarded or punished for his deeds. The description of God as Lord of the Day of Judgment following the mention of his benevolence and compassion indicates that we ought to remember another aspect of God as well, namely, that He will judge us all, that He is so absolutely powerful that on the Day of Judgment no one will have the power either to resist the enforcement of the punishments that He decrees or to prevent anyone from receiving the rewards that He decides to confer. Hence, we ought not only to love Him for nourishing and sustaining us and for His compassion and mercy towards us, but should also hold Him in awe because of His justice, and should not forget that our ultimate happiness or misery rests completely with Him.

6. The term *ibadah* is used in Arabic in three senses: (i) worship and adoration; (ii) obedience and submission; and (iii) service and subjection. In this particular context the term carries all these meanings simultaneously. In other words, we say to God that we worship and adore Him, that we are obedient to Him and follow His will, and also that we are His servants. Moreover, man is so bound to God that none but He may be the subject of man's worship and total devotion, of man's unreserved obedience, of man's absolute subjection and servitude.

7. Not only do we worship God, but our relationship with Him is such that we turn to Him alone for help and succour. We know that He is the Lord of the whole universe and that He alone is the Master of all blessings and benefactions. Hence, in seeking the fulfilment of our needs we turn to Him alone. It is towards Him alone that we stretch forth our hands when we pray and supplicate. It is in Him that we repose our trust. It is therefore to Him alone that we address our request for true guidance.

8. We beseech God to guide us in all walks of life towards a way that is absolutely true, that provides us with a proper outlook and sound principles of behaviour, a way that will prevent our succumbing to false doctrines and adopting unsound principles of conduct, a way that will lead us to our true salvation and happiness. This is man's prayer to God as he begins the study of the Quran. It is, in short, to illuminate the truth, which he often tends to lose in a labyrinth of philosophical speculation; to enlighten him as to which of the numerous ethical doctrines ensures a sound course of conduct; to show which of the myriad ways and byways is the clear, straight, open road of sound belief and right behaviour.

(1:7) The way of those whom You have favoured,[9] who did not incur Your wrath, who are not astray.[10]

---

[9] This defines the 'straight way' which we ask God to open to us. It is the way that has always been followed by those who have enjoyed God's favours and blessings. This is the way that has been trodden from the beginning of time by all those individuals and communities that have unfailingly enjoyed God's favours and blessings.

[10] This makes it clear that the recipients of God's favour are not those who appear, briefly, to enjoy worldly prosperity and success. All too often, these people are among those whom God has condemned because they have lost sight of the true path of salvation and happiness. This negative explanation makes it quite clear that *in 'am* [favour] denotes all those real and abiding favours and blessings that one receives as a reward for righteous conduct through God's approval and pleasure, rather than those apparent and fleeting favours that those such as the pharaohs, nimrods and korahs used to receive in the past, and that are enjoyed even today by people notorious for oppression, evil and corruption.

Index

CAMBRIDGE TEXTS IN THE HISTORY OF POLITICAL THOUGHT

Titles published in the series thus far

Dante *Monarchy* (edited and translated by Prue Shaw)

Albert Venn Dicey *Writings on Democracy and the Referendum* (edited by Gregory Conti)

Diderot *Political Writings* (edited and translated by John Hope Mason and Robert Wokler)

The Dutch Revolt (edited and translated by Martin van Gelderen)

Early Greek Political Thought from Homer to the Sophists (edited and translated by Michael Gagarin and Paul Woodruff)

The Early Political Writings of the German Romantics (edited and translated by Frederick C. Beiser)

Emerson *Political Writings* (edited by Kenneth S. Sacks)

The English Levellers (edited by Andrew Sharp)

Erasmus *The Education of a Christian Prince with the Panegyric for Archduke Philip of Austria* (edited and translated by Lisa Jardine; translated by Neil M. Cheshire and Michael J. Heath)

Fénelon *Telemachus* (edited and translated by Patrick Riley)

Ferguson *An Essay on the History of Civil Society* (edited by Fania Oz-Salzberger)

Fichte *Addresses to the German Nation* (edited by Gregory Moore)

Filmer *Patriarcha and Other Writings* (edited by Johann P. Sommerville)

Fletcher *Political Works* (edited by John Robertson)

Sir John Fortescue *On the Laws and Governance of England* (edited by Shelley Lockwood)

Fourier *The Theory of the Four Movements* (edited by Gareth Stedman Jones; edited and translated by Ian Patterson)

Franklin *The Autobiography and Other Writings on Politics, Economics, and Virtue* (edited by Alan Houston)

Gramsci *Pre-Prison Writings* (edited by Richard Bellamy; translated by Virginia Cox)

Guicciardini *Dialogue on the Government of Florence* (edited and translated by Alison Brown)

Hamilton, Madison and Jay (writing as 'Publius') *The Federalist with Letters of 'Brutus'* (edited by Terence Ball)

Harrington *The Commonwealth of Oceana and A System of Politics* (edited by J. G. A. Pocock)

Hegel *Elements of the Philosophy of Right* (edited by Allen W. Wood; translated by H. B. Nisbet)

Hegel *Political Writings* (edited by Laurence Dickey and H. B. Nisbet)

Hess *The Holy History of Mankind and Other Writings* (edited and translated by Shlomo Avineri)

Hobbes *On the Citizen* (edited and translated by Michael Silverthorne and Richard Tuck)

Hobbes *Leviathan* (edited by Richard Tuck)

Hobhouse *Liberalism and Other Writings* (edited by James Meadowcroft)

Hooker *Of the Laws of Ecclesiastical Polity* (edited by A. S. McGrade)

Nicholas of Cusa *The Catholic Concordance* (edited and translated by Paul E. Sigmund)

Nietzsche *On the Genealogy of Morality* (edited by Keith Ansell-Pearson; translated by Carol Diethe)

Paine *Political Writings* (edited by Bruce Kuklick)

William Penn *Political Writings* (edited by Andrew R. Murphy)

Plato *Gorgias, Menexenus, Protagoras* (edited by Malcolm Schofield; translated by Tom Griffith)

Plato *Laws* (edited by Malcolm Schofield; translated by Tom Griffith)

Plato *The Republic* (edited by G. R. F. Ferrari; translated by Tom Griffith)

Plato *Statesman* (edited by Julia Annas; edited and translated by Robin Waterfield)

Political Thought in Portugal and Its Empire, c.1500–1800 (edited by Pedro Cardim and Nuno Gonçalo Monteiro)

The Political Thought of the Irish Revolution (edited by Richard Bourke and Niamh Gallagher)

Price *Political Writings* (edited by D. O. Thomas)

Priestley *Political Writings* (edited by Peter Miller)

Proudhon *What Is Property?* (edited and translated by Donald R. Kelley and Bonnie G. Smith)

Pufendorf *On the Duty of Man and Citizen according to Natural Law* (edited by James Tully; translated by Michael Silverthorne)

The Radical Reformation (edited and translated by Michael G. Baylor)

Rousseau *The Discourses and Other Early Political Writings* (edited and translated by Victor Gourevitch)

Rousseau *The Social Contract and Other Later Political Writings* (edited and translated by Victor Gourevitch)

Seneca *Moral and Political Essays* (edited and translated by John M. Cooper; edited by J. F. Procopé)

Shundai *Writings on Political Economy* (edited and translated by Peter Flueckiger)

Sidney *Court Maxims* (edited by Hans W. Blom, Eco Haitsma Mulier and Ronald Janse)

Sorel *Reflections on Violence* (edited by Jeremy Jennings)

Spencer *Political Writings* (edited by John Offer)

Stirner *The Ego and Its Own* (edited by David Leopold)

Emperor Taizong and ministers *The Essentials of Governance* (compiled by Wu Jing; edited and translated by Hilde De Weerdt, Glen Dudbridge and Gabe van Beijeren)

Thoreau *Political Writings* (edited by Nancy L. Rosenblum)

Tönnies *Community and Civil Society* (edited and translated by Jose Harris; translated by Margaret Hollis)

Utopias of the British Enlightenment (edited by Gregory Claeys)

Vico *The First New Science* (edited and translated by Leon Pompa)

Vitoria *Political Writings* (edited by Anthony Pagden and Jeremy Lawrance)